Taps for a Jim Crow Army

Taps for a Jim Crow Army

LETTERS FROM BLACK SOLDIERS IN WORLD WAR II

Phillip McGuire, Editor

WITH FOREWORDS BY
Benjamin Quarles
AND
Bernard Nalty

THE UNIVERSITY PRESS OF KENTUCKY

Copyright © 1983 by Phillip McGuire
Reprint copyright © 1993 by The University Press of Kentucky

Scholarly publisher for the Commonwealth,
serving Bellarmine College, Berea College, Centre
College of Kentucky, Eastern Kentucky University,
The Filson Club, Georgetown College, Kentucky
Historical Society, Kentucky State University,
Morehead State University, Murray State University,
Northern Kentucky University, Transylvania University,
University of Kentucky, University of Louisville,
and Western Kentucky University.

Editorial and Sales Offices: Lexington, Kentucky 40508-4008

Library of Congress Cataloging-in-Publication Data

Taps for a Jim Crow army : letters from black soldiers in World War II
/ [compiled and edited by] Phillip McGuire ; with forewords by
Benjamin Quarles and Bernard Nalty.
    p.   cm.
    Originally published: Santa Barbara, Calif. : ABC-Clio, 1983.
    Includes bibliographical references and index.
    ISBN 0-8131-1851-4. — ISBN 0-8131-0822-5 (pbk.)
    1. World War, 1939-1945—Participation, Afro-American—History—
Sources.   2. United States.   Army—Afro-American troops—History—
Sources.   3. Racism—United States—History—20th century—Sources.
4. Afro-American soldiers—Correspondence.   I. McGuire, Phillip,
1944-   .
   D810.N4T3   1993
   940.54'03—dc20   93-1718

To my late father, Reverend George McGuire, and Mrs. Eloise J. Taylor, both of whom helped me to bear the cruelties of poverty and society.

Contents

Foreword

IN THE DECADE since its publication, Phillip McGuire's *Taps for a Jim Crow Army: Letters from Black Soldiers in World War II* has established itself as an indispensable source for the study of race relations in recent American history. Dr. McGuire focuses on the United States Army in World War II, deftly summarizing the official policy of granting African Americans better, though not equal, treatment and opportunity within the confines of racial segregation. The blacks whose letters he has collected testify to the cruel contradiction inherent in accepting racism beneath the American flag while at the same time fighting an Axis coalition dedicated to racist ideology.

Before the United States entered World War II, Charles Houston, an attorney and civil rights activist, warned that African Americans would no longer tolerate the indignities and mistreatment they had endured during the previous conflict. Despite the views of Houston and other spokesmen for the nation's blacks, President Franklin D. Roosevelt remained wary of challenging institutionalized racism. He hoped to include African Americans in the defense effort without offending those whites, including a number of powerful senators and representatives, who believed in separating the races. The President proposed to incorporate blacks into the armed forces without integrating the races. In working toward this objective, the Roosevelt administration affected a number of changes intended more as symbols than as genuine reforms. For example, William H. Hastie, a federal judge and former dean of the Howard University School of Law and an outspoken advocate of racial integration, became an assistant to the secretary of war for matters involving black troops. Colonel Benjamin O. Davis, Sr., received promotion to brigadier general and became the first African American to attain that rank.

As the letters collected by Dr. McGuire clearly demonstrate, the administration failed to gain the support of African Americans by making concessions short of genuinely equal treatment; a cross section of blacks in uniform, ranging from the college educated to the barely literate, raised their voices in protest. This clamor, reinforced by Hastie's resignation and echoed by the black press and the civil rights organizations, influenced various members of the Roosevelt administration who nudged the services down the long road toward racial integration. Military necessity, moreover, exerted further pressure that helped compel the reluctant armed forces to assign African Americans to combat units or warships, to send them off to fight, and in some instances to assign blacks to serve alongside whites. The Navy sought to boost the morale of both races by integrating the crews of a few fleet auxiliaries and thus expand the number of men eligible for duty at sea. The Army, desperate for infantrymen after suffering unexpected losses in the Battle of the Bulge, integrated the battlefields of Europe by assigning platoons of volunteers from black service units to previously all-white rifle companies. The Army Air Forces trained blacks to fly and sent them into battle, but they learned, flew, and fought in racially segregated organizations. The Marine Corps, though thoroughly dedicated to separating the races, accepted an unavoidable mingling of black service and white combat units on the beachheads of the Pacific.

Dr. McGuire captures the mood of the African American soldier in World War II as brilliantly as Wallace Terry, in his *Bloods: An Oral History of the Vietnam War by Black Veterans*, presents the hopes and fears, triumphs and disappointments, of the generation of blacks who fought their battles in Vietnam. The techniques differ, McGuire relying on letters and Terry using interviews; in both books, however, the emotions ring true, and the impact is equally powerful.

The fact that Terry could write as he has about manifestations of racism twenty years after World War II raises the question of whether that conflict, despite the progress toward integration, actually sounded taps for Jim Crow, the embodiment of American racism. After the fighting ended in the summer of 1945, the services—except the Air Force, which separated from the Army in September 1947—tried to reverse the trend toward equal treatment, claiming that Jim Crow still lived. They insisted that the segregated armed forces reflected the racial attitudes of the segregated society they defended, but those attitudes had begun to change. Indeed, just three years after the war, President Harry S. Truman dared to take a stand against racism in the military and naval services.

Outraged by the brutality of white racists and hopeful of gaining the support of those African Americans, mostly in the large cities of the North, who could exercise the right to vote, Truman in July 1948 issued an executive order that, in effect, racially integrated the armed forces. Despite the order—which helped Truman put together the coalition of blacks, farmers, and union members that won him the 1948 election—the Army, Navy, and Marine Corps remained racially segregated when they went to war in Korea in the summer of 1950. Once the fighting began, the need to make efficient use of manpower in a time of limited mobilization forced these services to do what Truman had ordered and the Air Force had already done. The armed forces could no longer squander human resources by maintaining separate personnel systems for blacks and whites. The genuine requirements of the armed forces, rather than the accident of race, had to determine the standards for recruiting, training, and assignment. In short, some five years elapsed between the sounding of taps for Jim Crow and the actual burial.

Since the Korean War, as Dr. McGuire points out in his conclusion, the ghost of Jim Crow has returned from time to time to haunt the armed forces and compel them to deal anew with racial prejudice. Perhaps the most successful response to revived racism proved to be a mandatory program of education in race relations, undertaken in 1971 during a period of bitter animosity between blacks and whites. Over the years, the armed services have tended to deal piecemeal with the recurring manifestations of racism, taking action when military efficiency suffers, monitoring progress, and, when racial harmony improves, moving on to some other issue. Racial prejudice, however, has such deep roots in American society that it resists intermittent treatment and requires the kind of unceasing attention that it has yet to receive.

Bernard C. Nalty
Hyattsville, Maryland

Foreword
to First Edition

"HERE I AM again and gripes are foremost as usual," ran the opening sentence of a letter written by James Pritchett on January 12, 1944, from Camp Livingston in Louisiana, and addressed to James C. Evans, Assistant Civilian Aide to the Secretary of War. Reproduced in full in this revealing work, Private Pritchett's observations re-echo the note of grievance, the protest refrain, so pervasive in letters written by black soldiers in World War II. The recipient of Pritchett's thoughts was himself a symbol of the settled climate of complaint in Negro soldier circles, for Evans was a black functionary in an office, Civilian Aide to the Secretary of War, specifically created to handle charges of color prejudice in the military and recommend remedies for any unfairnesses in its racial policies and practices.

Fault-finding was a normal reaction of the rank and file, especially of those not making a career in army service, and black soldiers were no exception. Differing from their white counterparts, however, black soldiers attributed approximately half of their grievances to prejudice against their group. In wartime, as in peacetime, one would expect to meet those who treated every problem as though it derived from the racial problem; hence undoubtedly there would be instances in which a problem common to all soldiers would be viewed by some blacks as racially rooted. In defining their more serious complaints as uniformly stemming from race, however, black soldiers were not wide of the mark. "More often than not," as Professor McGuire points out, "their protest was overwhelmingly legitimate."

It was not without reason that blacks distrusted the military. In many respects army culture differed from civilian culture, but the two have behaved alike in their treatment of blacks. Army policy as regards blacks, a bittersweet relationship since colonial times, had been shaped not only by military manpower needs but also by white attitudes toward blacks as

armsbearers and toward having black troops stationed in their communities. In response to civilian pressures, and not out of line with their own
racial beliefs, army policymakers had followed a pattern of segregating
black soldiers and of assigning them to service-type manual labor units
rather than to combat arms branches.

Although encountering multiple discriminations, black soldiers historically have viewed their military service in terms of the opportunities it
presented. From colonial times the army, despite its race-related short-
comings, had something to offer to black enlistees, and they in turn had
eagerly responded. Moreover, a time of war was a time of transition,
inducing people to accept change, and making it possible to mount a
more forceful attack on traditional patterns of prejudice. Blacks viewed a
war as a catalyst for a better day, with racial stereotypes and taboos on
the run. In a time of war, black leaders were emboldened to speak out
more forthrightly. In myriad ways a war deepened the consciousness of
color among blacks—and revived their dreams.

Like blacks during former wars, those of World War II believed that
their contribution as armsbearers and homefront workers, along with the
spirit of the times, would ameliorate their lot and that changes favorable
to their group would result from the war. Former wars had indeed resulted
in some gains for blacks, but these had fallen far short of black goals.
Despite the fact that in the aftermath of every previous war black Americans felt they had been let down, the blacks of World War II were hopeful that this time the sequel would be different, the promised land no
mirage.

Such hopes were not groundless, black Americans having developed a
better feeling about themselves and about their possibilities during the
some two decades since World War I. In this between-wars period, for
instance, a new pride in race had been stimulated by the charismatic
Marcus Garvey, who unabashedly proclaimed that black was beautiful.
The spirit of racial self-worth had been strengthened by a cadre of black
scholars who had proceeded to document the significant role of blacks in
American history, thus responding to the challenge of bibliophile A. A.
Schomburg that the Negro "must remake his past in order to make his
future." This sense of self-esteem was reenforced by a host of "new

Negro" musicians, artists and creative writers, their themes race-centered but their spirit shareable by all. Another voice of self-expression was to be found in the Negro press and periodicals, their drumbeat against injustice and inequity taking on a more insistent tone following World War I.

Between wars, black spirits similarly had been buoyed by political and economic gains, however modest. Having wholeheartedly supported Franklin D. Roosevelt in his election to the presidency in 1932 and thereafter, blacks could count on a friend in the White House and one whose wife, Eleanor, had far outdistanced all preceding first ladies in their esteem and affection. In matters economic the black worker had made some gains, the American Federation in 1936 granting a charter of fullfledged membership to the Brotherhood of Sleeping Car Porters, a hardwon and notable victory. Five years later and on the eve of America's entry into World War II, the Brotherhood's leader, A. Philip Randolph, deeply disturbed because black workers were not sharing equally in the mushrooming jobs in defense and military equipment, called for a March on Washington, a direct action to be taken by 100,000 protestors. Not caring to run such a risk, President Roosevelt issued Executive Order 8802, establishing a Fair Employment Practices Committee (FEPC), thus for the first time officially affirming a federal government policy of nondiscrimination in employment.

Such developments as the FEPC, combined with the growing sense of self-awareness among blacks, had its effect on those who joined the army following Pearl Harbor. Their faith that race relations were improving led these recruits to believe that their military services would result in better conditions for them and for other blacks both during and after the war. Black soldiers were well aware that the top brass were loath to challenge racial discrimination head-on, since military policymakers were always quick to point out that the army was not a social laboratory.

Nonetheless these soldiers would remain expectant, retaining their open-minded attitude toward the war and their participation therein. Hence while sharing the traditional soldier motivations—love of adventure, patriotism, the seeking of fame and glory, among others—the black armsbearers were also prompted by a status drive, an upward mobility

spur. Moreover, some black soldiers harbored greater-than-normal enemy
hostility to the German leader, Adolph Hitler, whose "master race" theories branded Negroes as genetically inferior.

If black soldiers felt that they had a stake in the war, how do we
account for this flood of complaining letters that Professor McGuire sets
before us? Somewhat paradoxically, these expressions of soldier unhappi-
ness with army conditions stemmed from the stepped-up expectations of
their writers. It was hope, not despair, that bred black soldier dissatisfaction. These letters, however angry in tone and content, reflected a basically forward-looking temperament, conveying a sense of puzzlement as
to why the new day was so tardy in its timing. Hence, these soldiers
viewed their letters as constructive, not in any way subversive. Not sur-
prisingly, therefore, a letter critical of army policy concerning blacks
might bear the signature "A Loyal Negro Soldier." Viewed from this
perspective and as a collective whole, these letters might be construed as
a literature of liberation.

Direct and explicit, the letters are not hard to follow despite some
lapses in writing style. The educational level of these World War II black
soldiers, although considerably below that of the whites in the service, was
markedly higher than that of the black enlistees of World War I. Their
writing reflects the increased level of black literacy and, concomitantly,
the increased black awareness that words were weapons.

A more readily discernible characteristic of these letters is their blunt-
ness. Mincing no words, they are outspoken rather than muted, frank
rather than guarded. Not written to family or friends, the letters are
devoid of small talk, personal reminiscence, light banter or freewheeling
fancy. Letters with a purpose, they were addressed to people in high
places, including the president of the country.

A number of these letters were sent to the black press to foster awareness. Thus a letter to the publisher of *The Afro-American Newspapers*
besought him "to kindly expose this statement in any issue of your paper
and reveal same to the *NAACP*." The sender of a letter to the *Pittsburgh
Courier* said that he "would appreciate it in the highest if you would
make this a headline article in your next edition." The influential *Courier*
was a favorite of black soldier letter-writers, the paper having launched

the "Double-V" campaign: victory on the homefront and victory over the Axis. A letter to William H. Hastie from the "Men of Fort Leonard Wood" bore the complimentary close, "Yours for a Double Victory."

It is this public, "hear ye, hear ye," cry that gives these letters their special force and flavor. They urge their recipients to come and see for themselves whether or not their charges against the army are just. Such an open and standing invitation to check on their allegations marks these letters with the stamp of credibility. Sent to persons or agencies with powers of investigation, these letters were not likely to flirt with the truth, at least not consciously.

These letters unveil a wide range of black soldier experiences and attitudes, McGuire making an effort to include a diversity of military units and theatres of operations, overseas not excepted. Without such broad and inclusive coverage, the full scope, prevalence and subtlety of Jim Crowism in the army would have remained a matter of hearsay and doubt. These soldiers speak for themselves, their own words an assurance that we are correctly ascertaining their viewpoints.

Enriched and illuminated by these documents assembled by Professor McGuire, military history takes on its full meaning in all its varied aspects—economic, social, and psychological. In World War II the interaction between army policies and civilian policies with reference to blacks was close and continuous, resulting in changes in both. As with no previous black soldier generation, this one dared to describe racial conditions in all their stark reality. Thus in these letters we meet a historically oppressed group of longtime Americans who had become emboldened to take a stand for full racial equality, and by so doing had initiated a redefinition of their status.

The hopes of these black letter-writers would fall far short of realization, color prejudice being so deeply rooted in American life. As succeeding generations of blacks would well learn, the battle for racial equality was still far from won. Nonetheless these blacks of World War II would leave their mark upon the country for which they had borne arms. They had succeeded in establishing an unlodgeable beachhead on the still resistant shores of racial equality. It was in their spirit that the black American would face the postwar world, finding inspiration in their example.

And viewed more broadly, these black soldiers had sustained and perpetu-
ated the black protest tradition, a heritage antedating the birth of the
nation.

In passing, the reader of these letters is reminded that, like archival
sources in general, they are repetitive. As a consequence, a given letter
might well carry some information that logically belongs elsewhere in the
book, in some other chapter. Time permitting, therefore, readers would
do well to inspect this volume as widely as possible, however circum-
scribed the type and range of the data they seek. Moreover, this collec-
tion of letters, intrinsically interesting and hitherto not readily available,
will abundantly repay a random reading as well as a search for specifics.
In addition to its thematic importance this study well illustrates the great
potential of archival records in reconstructing the Afro-American past.

BENJAMIN QUARLES
Professor of History Emeritus
Morgan State University

Acknowledgments

GRATEFUL ACKNOWLEDGMENT is offered to the staff of the Modern Military
Branch of the National Archives for providing invaluable assistance in the
location and reproduction of these letters. They are deeply thanked.

I owe a debt of appreciation to Professor Arnold H. Taylor of the
Department of History and Vice President for Academic Affairs Lorraine
A. Williams of Howard University, to Professor and retired Chairman of
the Department of History of Morgan State University Roland C. Mc-
Connell, and to Professor and retired Chief of the Legislative and Natural
Resources Branch of the National Archives Harold T. Pinkett for their
warm support and encouragement during the years I have known them.

I am particularly indebted to Professor Emeritus Benjamin Quarles of
Morgan State University, Professor A. Russell Buchanan of the University of California at Santa Barbara, and M. Joyce Baker, Ph.D., Educational Services Director for ABC-Clio. These historians extended
themselves and provided detailed criticism of the manuscript. Their scru-
tiny and wise counsel helped me immeasurably to improve the entire
work.

Gratitude is also due Bonnie M. Simrell, editor-in-chief of Clio Books,
my editor, Barbara H. Pope, and the entire Clio Books staff for aiding me
from the inception of this project to its finish.

A special note of appreciation is extended to my colleagues at the
University of North Carolina at Wilmington. Professor and Chairman of
the Department of History Melton A. McLaurin, History Professors
Robert B. Toplin and John H. Haley, and Professor Sandy D. Martin of
the Department of Philosophy and Religion supported me with encouragement.

The comments of close friends and Professor Samuel Barber of the
Department of Music at North Carolina A & T State University helped
me considerably to maintain my enthusiasm. In addition, I am deeply

thankful for the suggestion that the late Bell T. Wiley of Emory University made at the inception of this study.

Finally, Mrs. Evelyn R. Ferguson, Mrs. Dorothy V. Roth and Mrs. Fernande S. Brideau, secretaries for the History Department, deserve my special thanks for a fine job of typing. Their skill and intelligence contributed to this work.

As usual, I am responsible for any mistakes or weakness found in this book.

Introduction

THE INTEGRATION and usage of black Americans in the armed forces became grave questions for both the military and the black community during World War II. While segments of black America demanded integration and full opportunity for its black soldiers, War Department officials and politicians insisted that the military would not be used as a "sociological laboratory" for effecting social change.[1]Although this attitude reflected the overall policies of the War Department, the Army, however reluctantly and belatedly, did undergo some noteworthy shifts during the war.

But just as black Americans in the larger society found the American "dream" an illusion, black soldiers in particular experienced racial discrimination in the armed forces. Most of them were never accepted as military equals to white soldiers. Blacks were relegated to segregated and distinct combat units, to separate training schools, and to segregated camp facilities. More often than not they made up the service and supply units and, even within these, black troops faced what they considered to be unwarranted degrees of discrimination. The soldiers claimed they did their duty and fought proudly to make the world "safe for democracy." Yet, for them, the vestiges of racism were inescapable. In their letters, the soldiers told of these debilitating experiences from the day they entered the Army to the day of their discharge.

Collectively these letters contain a remarkable history of black soldiers' experiences during the Second World War. They tell the story of the agonies of segregation and discrimination from the perspective of the soldiers themselves. To them serving in the armed forces meant having to endure the anguish of an American institution unwilling to make the democratic rhetoric of World War II a reality for its black members. And yet numerous letters revealed that in their written complaints black soldiers expressed loyalty to the United States and to the ideals for which it stood.

In 1941, when the United States entered the war, black soldiers joined an army in which the parameters of their world already had been established. It was in 1937 that the War Department's personnel division concluded an extensive study on black participation in the armed forces. The plan indicated that the military wanted to avoid the grave mistakes made in the use of black troops in World War I.[2] A ban prohibiting the induction of black volunteers was lifted, and the training of 50 percent more white officers was authorized to handle the projected increase in black personnel. Other features of the new policy included plans to raise the number of black personnel in the army to equal the proportion of blacks in the total population, to mobilize more black troops before an actual national emergency existed, to reserve portions of warrant officers, chaplains, and reserve officers in black units for blacks, to confine black officers in the National Guard to positions authorized for blacks, to restrict black officer candidates to the number required to fill authorized positions in black units, and to limit blacks assigned to reception, placement, and training centers to the general corps area from whence they came.[3]

Except for one major addition in 1940, the 1937 plan provided the guidelines for the Army's treatment of black personnel throughout World War II. Although not classified, the contents of the 1937 plan were known only to high-level officials in the War Department. Details were not disclosed because Commandant of the Army War College Major General H. E. Ely convinced Secretary of War Harry H. Woodring and the military chiefs of staff that the plan should remain secret. As a rationale, the Commandant explained that he doubted "the wisdom of the War Department announcing this policy at large. Its early announcement will give time for its careful study by those seeking political capital, for points on which the War Department may be attacked, or embarrassed."[4]

Events in the black community suggested that Commandant Ely understood the potentially explosive nature of the Army's plan. Charles H. Houston, veteran of World War I and special counsel to the National Association for the Advancement of Colored People (NAACP), was one of the first black leaders in the late 1930s to address the issue of fair treatment for blacks in the military. On October 8, 1937, he appealed to President Roosevelt to issue an executive order that would ban all racial discrimination in the armed forces. Houston respectfully asked the President "to give Negro citizens the same right to serve their country as any other citizen, and on the same basis."[5]

On the same day Houston reminded Secretary Woodring that the United States could not hope to win a major war without the support of black manpower. He spoke for blacks, and wanted Woodring to be aware that the black community was loyal but "the Negro population will not silently suffer the discrimination and abuse which were heaped upon Negro soldiers and officers in World War I." "We urge you," stated Houston, "to remove all racial barriers to service in all branches of the Army."[6]

Houston's declaration signaled the beginning of an intense campaign by the black press. Its leading exponent was *The Pittsburgh Courier*. Under Robert L. Vann, editor and publisher, the *Courier* pressed for at least 10 percent black personnel in the Army on a nonsegregated basis.[7] The *Courier* also requested that the President appoint two blacks annually to West Point, and proposed that the War Department create an all-black army division commanded by black officers. Vann cited black loyalty, black achievements in battle, and the long-term elimination of prejudices as the major reasons for the *Courier*'s crusade. Vann's campaign for total integration was short-lived, however, and by late 1938 he had accepted the idea that segregation was a means by which blacks at least could increase their total numbers in the military. Vann's new position was based on the results of a nationwide *Courier* survey, which he concluded indicated a consensus of the black community that to attempt full military integration at this time would fail. His analysis was supported by leaders in the black community such as Charles H. Houston, Dr. Rayford Logan, historian and chairman of the Committee for the Participation of Negroes in the National Defense Program, and Roy Wilkins, assistant secretary of the NAACP, as well as most of the black press.

Vann asked New York Congressman Hamilton Fish, who had been a company commander of black troops in the 369th Infantry in World War I, to introduce to the House what Vann called the *Courier*'s Army bills. Representative Fish complied and in 1940 the bill to end discrimination passed Congress and was made a part of the 1940 Selective Service Act. However, the provisions for an all-black army division and the annual presidential appointment of two blacks to West Point failed.[8]

In the meantime, Vann's acceptance of quotas and the policy of segregation created a rift between him and the NAACP. The executive secretary of the NAACP cautioned that "segregation in public institutions always works to the disadvantage of the segregated group and must be resisted with all the united strength we can command." Walter White felt "to do otherwise is to take the road towards being permanently labelled as a pariah group which in turn will mean spiritual defeatism and death."9

Roy Wilkins agreed with White's position. As editor of the *Crisis*, the official news organ of the NAACP, Wilkins published a statement that left no doubt as to his stance: "the *Crisis* wants Negroes all through the Army, and the Navy, and other defense services. There is no reason why we should not have Negro aviators, or generals or admirals." Thus, in contrast to Vann's acceptance of segregation, the idea of fully integrating every branch of the armed forces became the single most important campaign for the *Crisis*, and the NAACP used it continually to rally support from the black community.10

In September 1939, for example, White addressed a lengthy letter to President Franklin D. Roosevelt. In it he reviewed the crisis in Europe and expressed fears that the United States would be drawn into the war. He then asked Roosevelt to take steps to correct the evils of prejudice that permeated every aspect of the military; in particular, he emphasized the creation of an interracial commission to investigate alleged discriminatory practices in the military.11

The president, through his aide General Edwin Watson, rejected White's idea of an interracial commission, denying that discrimination existed in the armed services. Watson referred to the four black regiments in the regular army as proof of black participation in the defense of their country and ended his letter with the assurance to White that Roosevelt was committed to including blacks in the country's future mobilization plans.12

White responded to the president after first rallying support in the black community from such notables as Thurgood Marshall, counsel for the NAACP, William H. Hastie, dean of Howard University Law School, Roy Wilkins, and Charles H. Houston. Houston, however, supported Vann and the *Courier*'s position, and did not respond to White. Wilkins and Marshall suggested that White stress the point that the NAACP was diametrically opposed to the separate black units in the regular army, and Hastie prepared a list of discriminatory practices and complaints from black soldiers that he thought White should emphasize. Both suggestions were included in White's next message to the president.[13]

Momentum for an integrated military gathered force during 1940. A resolution of the National Negro Congress, entered in the Congressional Record in April, actively urged young blacks to refuse to fight for democracy abroad when they continued to suffer from the effects of discrimination and segregation in the United States.[14] Although the War Department still kept confidential its plan for mobilizing black manpower, a form letter to answer inquiries on the matter had been written. To charges of segregation and discrimination against black soldiers, the department responded that "the War Department has given serious thought to questions involving the induction of Negroes into the military services. However, the War Department is not an agency which can solve national questions relating to the social and economic position of the various racial groups composing the nation." The department then reminded the dissidents that it "administers the laws affecting the military establishment; it cannot act outside the law, nor contrary to the will of the majority of the citizens of the nation."[15]

As the year wore on, black leaders became increasingly cynical and more militant in their demands for equal opportunity and the integration of the armed forces. Some wondered if the War Department would allow the same World War I prejudices against black soldiers to impede their full participation in the defense of the country in the Second World War. The black press posed questions such as: In the event of war, what proportion of blacks would serve in the armed forces? Would blacks be used in combat or be restricted to labor and supply units? Were blacks going to be admitted to officer candidate schools? Would blacks serve in segregated or mixed units? Until these questions were answered, black leaders expressed a lack of enthusiasm for military preparedness. Even the *Pittsburgh Courier* revised its position after the death of its publisher, Robert L. Vann, on November 1, 1940. The new editor, Percival L. Prattis, joined White, Wilkins, and other integrationists, editorializing the day following Vann's death: "We must stop asking for more segregation even if there is a prospect of having complete Negro units in every branch of the service; we must start fighting segregation sincerely."[16]

Stafford King, Minnesota state auditor and civilian aide to the secretary of war, warned Secretary of War Woodring that unless blacks were accorded the same privileges as white enlistees, they might become victims of Axis propaganda.[17] King's warning generated some concern in the War Department. Speaking for the black cause, Adjutant General Emory S. Adams told Woodring that form letters would not satisfy black leaders, and further insisted that "the colored race is entitled to greater and better representation in our Army for obvious reasons, many of which are set forth in Mr. King's letter, and this whole subject should have careful and immediate study to determine the future policy of the War Department in the premises. It is recommended that this study be initiated without delay." The department's general staff made the study that Adams suggested but the final recommendation consisted only of more of the same, that is, that more black units be added to the regular army.[18]

When the Selective Service and Training Act became law on September 16, 1940, black leaders considered it a milestone for black soldiers because of two antidiscrimination clauses. The first provided that all men between the ages of 18 and 36 were eligible to volunteer for service in the land and naval forces of the United States. The second clause prohibited discrimination (based on race and color) in the selection and training of men. However, a third position gave the War Department final authority in deciding who would or would not be accepted in the military, prompting leaders in the black community to voice their concern about the intention of the legislation. Sensitive to racist implications, they argued that the provision could be implemented so as to leave blacks desiring to enlist no redress if they were rejected, possibly rendering the antidiscrimination clauses in the Selective Service Act virtually ineffective.[19]

Evidence suggests that such concern was appropriate. As blacks were given the opportunity to serve in the army, they volunteered for induction in record numbers. Many were turned away, however, and as the black community had feared, the law provided no method or means to redress the grievance of any black American on rejection.

The reasons for rejection ranged from overt Army actions to more subtle excuses. The First Army Headquarters (one of nine geographical service commands that included Maine, Connecticut, Massachusetts, New Hampshire, Rhode Island, and Vermont) sent secret orders to its draft boards requesting that no blacks be inducted in the first draft. Although the order to Connecticut was rescinded when Governor Raymond Baldwin threatened to expose it to the public and to President Roosevelt, the antiblack request did not fade away. Late in 1940 the War Department itself ordered Connecticut's draft boards to fill their quotas with white men only, and it fell to Governor Robert Hurley, Baldwin's successor, to instruct the draft boards to ignore the War Department's order.[20] A survey by Roy Wilkins showed that twenty-five cities in seventeen states had no blacks on the draft boards. Moreover, white recruiting officers often failed to serve induction notices to black I-A registrants, despite the War Department's promise to create more black ground units to absorb the new inductees. When pressed, the War Department claimed that separate facilities were inadequate to house the new inductees.

Another factor may have been the absence of black advisors in the office of the director of the Selective Service and in the War Department. One who addressed this issue was Mary McLeod Bethune, founder and president of the National Council of Negro Women and director of the Division of Negro Affairs of the National Youth Administration in Roosevelt's administration. Mrs. Bethune asked Mrs. Roosevelt, whom Secretary of War Henry L. Stimson regarded as an agitator, to urge the president to appoint black advisors to the office of the director of the Selective Service and to the War Department. She stressed that the request was a result of long consultation with other black leaders, all of whom agreed that these appointments were necessary to ensure that the policies of the War Department were effectively carried out. Mrs. Bethune also assured Mrs. Roosevelt that she and the other leaders were prepared to offer the names of the best qualified men for these positions.[21]

Illiteracy was another major factor that prevented the inclusion of blacks. Over 75 percent of the black inductees who failed the Army Classification Test came from the South and border states, which accounted for only 25 percent of the white inductees. According to a study conducted by Professors Eli Ginzberg and Douglas Bray of Columbia University, 90 percent of the blacks who failed the test had been deprived of adequate educational and cultural opportunities. Their conclusions were anticipated by Major

Campbell C. Johnson, who later became special assistant to the director of the Selective Service. As early as 1944, Johnson blamed the South for the high rate of illiteracy among black inductees.[22]

Furthermore, the War Department apparently seized the opportunity to use illiteracy as a tactic to discriminate against blacks while accepting illiterate whites without question. According to his diary, Secretary of War Henry L. Stimson had sanctioned this policy. He admitted that "the Army had adopted rigid requirements for literacy mainly to keep down the number of colored troops and this is reacting badly in preventing us from getting in some very good but illiterate [white] recruits from the southern mountain states." To solve the manpower shortage, at least from the southern region of the country, Stimson recommended that the Army embark upon a voluntary recruitment program aimed at bringing more whites into the service. Thus the War Department was willing to actively recruit illiterate whites but unwilling to do the same for illiterate blacks.[23]

On October 9, 1940, the War Department finally announced the confidential guidelines established in 1937 for the treatment of black personnel in the army. The policy itself might have received a favorable response from black leaders had it not been accompanied by a general statement that "the policy of the War Department is not to intermingle colored and white enlisted personnel in the same regimental organization. This policy has proven satisfactory over a long period of years and to make changes would produce situations destructive to morale and detrimental to the preparation for National defense." The statement continued "for similar reasons the department does not contemplate assigning colored Reserve Officers other than of the Medical Corps and Chaplains to existing Negro combat units of the Regular Army. These regular units are going concerns, accustomed through many years to the present system. Their morale is splendid, their rate of reenlistment is exceptionally high and their field training is well advanced." The final sentence was probably the most devastating to the hopes of black leaders. The department refused to accept the idea of experimenting with mixed units and used as its rationale the war as a time too critical for such experimentation.[24]

Because the War Department had rejected the idea of integration, blacks renewed their challenges to President Roosevelt and to the War Department for failure to end segregation. Black leaders based their protest on three basic principles: (1) segregation was morally wrong since it embodied an undemocratic doctrine of racial inferiority; (2) segregation denied full military opportunities to black soldiers, relegated them to an inferior status, and destroyed their *esprit de corps*; and (3) segregation was an unnecessary luxury. These leaders also believed that had the War Department been aware of the considerably greater expense involved in maintaining a segregated army, official zeal for a black and white military would have wavered.[25]

Eugene K. Jones, successor to George E. Haynes as executive secretary of the National Urban League, sent a letter to President Roosevelt in protest of the October 9 announcement. He declared: "We deny that the segregationist policy of the War Department, though it has been pursued over a long period of years, has been satisfactory to thoughtful Negro citizens. We deny also that to make changes in this policy would produce situations destructive to morale." Jones also called the President's attention to a unanimous resolution adopted at the League's 30th annual conference. In summary, the resolution stated: "The National Urban League is unalterably opposed to the policy and practice of racial discrimination and segregation in the Army, Navy, Air Force, and Marine Corps of the United States."[26]

More adamant in its tone than the Urban League, the Citizens' Nonpartisan Committee for Equal Rights in National Defense demanded that the War Department's policy be revised. In telegrams to President Roosevelt and to the War Department the Committee stated: "We want no discrimination or segregation in the Army, Navy, Air Corps, or Industrial Defense. This is our just desert in a democratic Government, and the need for national unity demands immediate revision of the stated policy."[27]

In an effort to quiet or delude the black community, Roosevelt's press secretary, Stephen Early, released a statement to the press implying that military segregation had been sanctioned by A. Philip Randolph, president of the Brotherhood of Sleeping Car Porters, Walter White, and T. Arnold Hill, director of the National Urban League's Department of Industrial Relations, at their White House meeting on September 27. Randolph, White and Hill, however, denounced Early's statement as a gross fabrication of the truth and demanded that Roosevelt make a public statement exculpating them of any participation in such an agreement.

In a letter to White, Early made it clear that the White House could not be held responsible for inferences drawn from press releases.[28] White was not satisfied, insisting that Early's words, "as a result of that conference," conveyed to the public that he, Randolph, and Hill supported segregation in the armed forces when in fact they were diametrically opposed to it. The moral implications of the statement worried these leaders, who feared that if Roosevelt did not exonerate them publicly the black community would think the struggle for integration had come to a halt. Therefore, they reiterated to President Roosevelt that whatever Early's intentions, Americans, black and white, would acept the erroneous inferences as truth. Roosevelt finally capitulated and wrote a letter to each of the men, which was reprinted in the official news organ of their respective organizations. The President assured them that he regretted that Early's remarks had been misunderstood, and expressed sorrow that their positions, the White House, and the position of the War Department had not been made clear to the public. Roosevelt ended his letter remarking that "these measures [components of the October 9 policy statement] represents a very substantial advance over what has been the practice in past years. You may rest assured that Negroes are given fair treatment on a nondiscriminatory basis."[29] Roosevelt's letter notwithstanding, Walter White and Roy Wilkins subsequently went on a nationwide speaking tour. They spoke in every major city in an effort to solidify black support, which had fluctuated because of Early's statement.[30]

Meanwhile, shortly before the 1940 presidential election, two damaging incidents occurred that proved politically advantageous for the black community. First, the *New York Age* editorialized rumors that Colonel Benjamin O. Davis, Sr., was resigning his commission because President Roosevelt had ignored him in appointing thirty-four white colonels to brigadier general. The second incident was a political embarrassment. Following a speech Roosevelt had delivered in Madison Square Garden, Stephen Early kicked James Sloan, a black policeman, in the groin for unknowingly blocking Early's entrance to a presidential train bound for Washington, D.C. This incident made news headlines in major newspapers across the country. Although Early had publicly apologized to Sloan and to the New York Police Commissioner, black leaders were outraged.[31]

President Roosevelt also apologized publicly for Early's conduct. But black leaders were not satisfied. Hastie, White, Weaver (special advisor to Secretary of Interior Harold Ickes), Hill, Jones, Marshall, Randolph, Houston, Will W. Alexander (presidential advisor on black affairs), and Wilkins formulated strategy to quell the crisis, but they used the incident and the threat of the black vote to gain some military concessions from the government. Secretary of War Stimson apparently felt pressure from the leaders as he noted in his diary that "there is a tremendous drive going on by the Negroes, taking advantage of the last weeks of the campaign in order to force the Army and Navy into doing things for their race which would not otherwise be done and which are certainly not in the interest of sound national defense." Finally, Stimson wrote, "but they are making such progress in their drive that the friends of Mr. Roosevelt are very much troubled and are asking us to do anything we can."[32]

In the meantime, Roosevelt and his aides were discussing and mapping strategy at the White House. Because they felt the black vote was important to the outcome of the 1940 presidential election, Harry Hopkins, chief aide, called in Will Alexander to help resolve the President's dilemma. Black leaders had already met with and instructed Alexander to state four basic demands in return for the black vote. Thus he informed Hopkins that the black community wanted segregation abolished in the armed forces, Colonel Benjamin O. Davis, Sr., promoted to brigadier general, Major Campbell C. Johnson appointed assistant to the selective service director, and Judge William H. Hastie appointed assistant secretary in the War Department.[33]

Except for the abolition of segregation, the government yielded to black demands, and shortly after the political crisis three significant appointments were made: National Director General Lewis B. Hershey announced the appointment of Major Johnson as executive assistant to the office of the selective service; President Roosevelt promoted Colonel Davis to brigadier general; and the War Department announced the appointment of Hastie as civilian aide to the Secretary of War. Johnson and Davis accepted their positions without hesitation. Their appointments were praiseworthy mainly because they were firsts for black Americans. However, Secretary Stimson considered Davis' promotion political appeasement and having no substantive value. He remarked sarcastically

that "I had a good deal of fun with Knox over the necessity that he was
facing of appointing a colored Admiral and a battle fleet full of colored
sailors according a Resolution passed by the Colored Federal Employees
Association and I told him that when I called next time at the Navy
Department with my colored Brigadier General I expected to be met with
the colored Admiral."[34]

Unlike the appointments of Davis and Johnson, Hastie's appointment
became a controversial issue, and he delayed acceptance of the post.
Hastie's attitude toward the newly created position was based largely on
his conviction that the office of the civilian aide was just another bu-
reaucratic office established to appease the black community and capture
its vote in the 1940 presidential election. Then, too, his knowledge of
Emmett J. Scott's role as the black special assistant to Secretary of War
Newton Baker during World War I worried him. He viewed Scott as an
adjuster of racial ills and black complaints rather than a leading voice for
justice and social change within the military establishment. Hastie was
particularly concerned that the black community might view him as an
appeaser on racial matters. Consequently, Hastie refused to accept the
post until the War Department announced publicly that he had been
persuaded to represent the interest of blacks in the War Department
although he strongly opposed a segregated military.[35]

Hastie eventually accepted the post, and in a letter to Hastie, Secretary
Stimson spelled out his duties in detail. They included aid to the department in developing plans that would ensure the most effective use of
black manpower, recommending ways to improve the department's plans
to organize black units in all branches of the services, assisting in the
employment of civilian blacks at military installations, investigating discriminatory complaints of black soldiers as well as those of black civilians, and cooperating with blacks on the Selective Service Committee and
other agencies concerned with blacks in the armed forces.[36]

Hastie was not exactly sure what Stimson's letter meant. He noted,
however, that it did not include a specific statement that the War Department was committed to the elimination of segregation and the other discriminatory policies that were major sources of frustration in the black
community. He and other black leaders were anxious to have such a
commitment in writing. But Stimson refused to provide one, either in

writing or verbally. In fact, the War Department's official position regarding black and white relations remained the same: "The Army would not be used as a sociological laboratory for effecting social change within the military establishment." In light of the department's stance, Hastie publicly responded to his appointment in such a way as to ensure that his opposition to segregation and discrimination was well known. He declared: "I have always been constantly opposed to any policy of discrimination and segregation in the Armed Forces of this country. I am assuming this post in the hope that I will be able to work effectively toward the integration of the Negro into the Army and to facilitate his placement, training, and promotion."[37]

Shortly after Hastie's appointment, Secretary Stimson remarked that "he seems like a rather decent negro who is now Dean of Law in the Law School of Howard University in this city." By October 1942, Stimson would accuse Hastie of having an unrealistic attitude toward solving the race problem in the armed forces, but at the time of Hastie's appointment, Stimson was probably aware that black leaders, the black press, and the black community expected Hastie to be "more than a rubber stamp official" who would work toward integration and the elimination of the inequalities blacks experienced in the armed services. Stimson probably was also aware that Hastie's determination to do an effective job stemmed from his sources of power and his previous career as a public servant and lawyer for the NAACP. Drawing on his capacity to articulate the facts and the immorality of racism and segregation, Hastie was always supported by a majority of the black press and black leaders. All the black national pressure organizations, many white liberals and, to some degree, white national organizations also supported Hastie. As nongovernmental opponents of racism and segregation, these elements were instrumental in exposing the discriminatory policies and practices of the armed forces.[38]

Since Hastie and the other black leaders expected little sympathy from the War Department, they felt it was equally important for them to constantly stress to black soldiers that while they fought for the elimination of discrimination within and outside the government, it was necessary to maintain good discipline and the highest possible rate of military efficiency. Hastie summed up the leaders' aspirations as he prepared to lead the campaign for integration within the War Department. He said: "The man in uniform must grit his teeth, square his soldiers and do his best as a soldier, confident that there are millions of Americans outside the armed forces, and more persons than he knows in high places within the military establishment, who will never cease fighting to remove all social barriers and every humiliating practice which now confronts him. But only by being, at all times, a first-rate soldier can the man in uniform help in this battle which shall be fought and won."[39]

Thus Hastie and the black leaders all agreed that the time was right for them to put pressure on the federal government to take the initiative in promoting equal opportunity and the integration of the armed forces. To this end, Hastie suggested to Walter White and A. Philip Randolph that in their upcoming meeting with President Roosevelt they should emphasize three major points: (1) that blacks vigorously opposed segregated army units; (2) that many whites supported this opposition; and (3) that the Army was not, as Congress had mandated, training blacks for the Army Air Corps. He also wanted them to inquire whether all black units would be officered by blacks; whether blacks would be included in medical training programs; and whether the War Department would make sincere efforts to prevent discrimination against civilian blacks in awarding defense contracts. In all these matters, Hastie urged White and Randolph to convey to the President as strongly as they could the idea that the black community was diametrically opposed to segregation and the attitude of the federal government toward its black soldiers. Hastie then noted, "If such inquiries are made, I will undoubtedly be asked what the situation is with reference to particular matters. I think between us we will be able to give a more comprehensive picture of the seriousness and diversity of the problems than the persons in authority now have."[40]

Although Hastie and the other black leaders demonstrated solidarity on the issue of army integration, the NAACP and the National Urban League, sensing some confusion and antipathy in the black community, called a black leadership conference in New York City shortly after the Japanese attack on Pearl Harbor. Sixty prominent blacks met to consider the black community's part in the war effort. Judge William H. Hastie, now civilian aide to the Secretary of War, introduced a resolution, with only five dissenting votes, which stated that "colored people are not wholeheartedly and unreservedly all out in support of the present war effort." Walter White summed up the sentiments of the group and attributed the apathy among blacks to discrimination and segregation in the armed services and war industries.[41]

A faction, however, had developed in the black community. A small group of black accommodationists opposed integration while the war was in progress. For example, Eddie W. Reevers, editor of the *Messenger*, voiced the sentiments of conservative blacks who felt that such men as Hastie, White, and Randolph, as well as the leading black press such as the *Pittsburgh Courier*, had incited racial hatred among the black masses. As early as August 1941, Reevers had written to Secretary of War Stimson claiming that millions of loyal blacks supported the policies of the War Department. In the same spirit, Charles M. Thomas, editor of the *Washington Tribune*, sent a letter to Stephen Early, stating that there was general dissatisfaction with Hastie's performance as civilian aide. Dr. William Pickens, former director of branches for the NAACP, echoed the same feelings. In May 1942, he was quoted in the *Richmond Times Dispatch*, a southern white newspaper, as having said that the black community was loyal as a group but suffered from the traitorous influences of some foolish leaders in its midst. Pickens further stated: "It [the Army] is planning to win a war in spite of segregation or those who oppose segregation. Blacks could demand their full citizenship rights after Hitler and the Axis Powers had been defeated. Everything must be sacrificed in winning this war. Such sacrifices are not sacrifices at all."[42]

While Pickens, Thomas, and Reevers, and the conservative black press supported segregation during the war, their position did not arouse much enthusiasm among the black masses. Instead, integrationists such as Hastie, White, and Randolph, major civil rights organizations, and an overwhelming majority of the black press wielded the most influence. Thus, in spite of the black conservatives, the integrationists continued to spearhead the black community's thrust toward desegregating the armed forces.[43]

In March 1942, however, the black press startled its white colleagues by assuming a more determined stance, one that was made visible by the adoption of the "Double V" symbol for victory *at home* as well as abroad. Despite admonitions from Director of the Office of War Information, Archibald MacLeish and criticisms from members of their own community, black editors insisted that they would not cease the "Double V" campaign until blacks in the military and in the larger community were accorded their full constitutional rights as citizens and soldiers. Besides, said the editors, 91.2 percent of the black community approved of their efforts to force the government to integrate the military.[44]

The case of Winfred W. Lynn furnished an example of blacks' dedication to eliminating segregation and racial discrimination in the military. Lynn was notified in June 1942 by Local Board 261 of Jamaica, New York that he had been classified I-A. He replied: "Gentlemen: I am in receipt of my draft-reclassification notice. Please be informed that I am ready to serve in any unit of the armed forces of my country which is not segregated by race. Unless I am assured that I can serve in a mixed regiment and that I will not be compelled to serve in a unit undemocratically selected as a Negro group, I will refuse to report for induction."[45]

Not receiving the assurances he wanted, Lynn refused to report for duty, claiming that his induction into segregated units violated Section 4(A) of the 1940 Draft Act, which states: "In the selection and training of men under this act, and in the interpretation and execution of the provisions of this act, there shall be no discrimination against any person on account of race or color." The Act also states " . . . in classifying a registrant there shall be no discrimination for or against him because of his race, creed, or color." Subsequently, Lynn was arrested and indicted for draft evasion. Thus with his case began a two-year saga of the only legal challenge to the jim crow practice of the military in the Second World War.[46]

A lower court judge informed Lynn that to have his case heard he had to submit to induction and then file suit against his superior officer. He did so, and the Federal District Court in New York ruled against him by refusing to hear the case. Thereupon the case was appealed to the U.S. Circuit Court of Appeals. There, the lower court's decision was upheld. Finally, his case reached the U.S. Supreme court in 1944. The justices refused to hear the case on the grounds that Lynn was on active duty overseas and therefore outside the jurisdiction of the court, and that the military officer against whom he had originally brought the suit had retired from active service. The Supreme Court also declared that ". . . if Congress had intended to prohibit separate white and Negro quotas and calls we believe it would have expressed such intention more definitely than by the general prohibition against discrimination appearing in Section 4."[47]

Although Lynn's case generated almost no press coverage, Selective Service Director General Lewis B. Hershey reacted to his charge that discriminatory segregation and racial quotas violated the Draft Act by commenting publicly that he regretted the case, "but unfortunately the army gets the final say." Hershey went on to say, "what we are doing, of course, is simply transferring discrimination from everyday life into the army. Men who make up the army staff have the same ideas [about blacks] as they had before they went into the army."[48]

In view of Lynn's case, black leaders had raised questions in 1940 about the Draft Act clause that made the army the final arbiter in determining the circumstances under which it could draft men. Lynn's case confirmed their earlier fears—that the Army could strip virtually all force from the antidiscrimination clause of the Draft Act.[49]

Unfortunately for blacks, the Supreme Court had come down on the side of the Army and adopted discriminatory segregation and racial quotas as official military policy. The Lynn case nevertheless dramatized the extent to which blacks were willing to go to redress their grievances.

So the battle went on between the black advocates of integration and those military and political voices who maintained that military efficiency demanded segregation. Throughout the war, changes were being made in the way black soldiers were traditionally treated, but segregation and patterns of racial discrimination continued to manifest themselves on and off the military posts. According to their letters, black soldiers were humiliated, despised, denied regular army privileges, insulted by post commanders, subjected to military and civilian police brutality, accused of crimes they did not commit, constrained by traditional mores, unfairly discharged from military service, denied adequate medical services, court martialled excessively, and denied adequate entertainment. Their treatment often suggested that they were viewed not as American soldiers but as wards of the armed forces.

As a result of these practices the *esprit de corps* of black soldiers remained low throughout the war. But their burdens became easier to bear because of men like Hastie, other black leaders, and the nongovernmental forces who were their spokesmen within and outside of the government. These men, women, national organizations, and the black press represented to black soldiers a bond of brotherhood to which they appealed for help and relief from the agonies of racism.

The soldiers' letters presented in this volume were sent to black and white national leaders, to the civilian aides to the secretaries of the war, to the black national self-help organizations, and to the black press. The letters represent various black army units and reveal the diverse experiences and attitudes of the soldiers. In an attempt to capture and preserve the authenticity, character, spirit, content, and flavor of the correspondence, the letters were typed exactly as they were written and typed by the soldiers themselves. This accounts for inaccuracies in grammar, spelling, punctuation, capitalization, style, and structure.

Although the letters were eventually housed in the files of the assistant secretary of war, they were first received by individuals within and outside the war department, the African-American press, and the National Association for the Advancement of Colored People (NAACP), as they were the prime movers in the campaign against the vestiges of racial discrimination and segregation in the armed forces.

When, for example, the soldiers complained of their treatment in letters to Judge William H. Hastie, Truman K. Gibson, Jr., Colonel Marcus H. Ray, and James C. Evans (all former civilian aides to the secretaries of war), these letters were later placed in the section designated as the office of the civilian aide files within the records of the assistant secretary of war.

The editors of the African-American press, the press itself, and members of the NAACP who received correspondence normally used the contents of the soldiers' letters to augment their "Double V" campaign before sending the letters on to the office of the civilian aide in the war department.

As other national leaders such as Congressman William L. Dawson, Walter White, and Eleanor Roosevelt received soldiers' letters, they, too, forwarded them to the office of the civilian aide or to the office of the secretary of war. Subsequently, all of the letters contained in this book ended up in the files of the civilian aide to the secretary of war, which were housed within the records of the assistant secretary of war at the National Archives in Washington, D.C.

NOTES

1. "Colonel Eugene Householder's Remarks at the Conference of Negro Newspaper Representatives," Washington, D.C., December 8–9, 1941, Civilian Aide to the Secretary of War Subject File, 1940–1947, National Archives Record Group (hereafter cited as NARG) 107; Judge William H. Hastie, private interview with author, United States Court of Appeals, Washington, D.C., March 6, 1974.

2. Because the War Department had not adequately planned for the drafting, training, and assignments of black soldiers as combatant and noncombatant troops in World War I, much of their performance record was marred during and after the war with official reports and racist inuendo as ineffective soldiers. For more detail see Arthur E. Barbeau and Florette Henri, *The Unknown Soldiers; Black American Troops in World War I* (Philadelphia: Temple University Press, 1974).

3. Ulysses Lee, *United States Army in World War II: Special Studies: The Employment of Negro Troops* (Washington, D.C.: United States Government Printing Office, 1966), 37–41.

4. Quoted in Lee, *The Employment of Negro Troops*, 39; Lee Finkle, "Forum For Protest: The Black Press and World War II," (unpublished Ph.D. dissertation, New York University, 1971), 73.

5. Letter, Charles H. Houston to President Franklin D. Roosevelt, October 8, 1937, Box C-376, National Association for the Advancement of Colored People Papers, Manuscript Division, Library of Congress, Washington, D.C. (hereafter cited as NAACP Papers).

6. Letter, Houston to Harry H. Woodring, October 8, 1937, Box C-376, NAACP Papers; Finkle, "Forum For Protest: The Black Press and World War II," 170–171.

7. The 10 percent figure was based upon the black proportion of the total population.

8. Andrew Buni, "Robert L. Vann of the *Pittsburgh Courier*." Paper intended for the annual meeting of the Association for the Study of Afro-American Life and History, October 25, 1974, 4–7; *The Pittsburgh Courier*, February 16, 1938; Finkle, "Forum For Protest: The Black Press and World War II," 171–177; 182.

9. Letter, Walter White to the Editor of *The Pittsburgh Courier*, June 11, 1938, Box C-377, NAACP Papers.

10. Buni, "Robert Vann of the *Pittsburgh Courier*," 10; Roy Wilkins, "National Defense and Negroes," *The Crisis*, XLVI (February 1939), 49.

11. Letter, White to Roosevelt, September 15, 1939, Box C-377, NAACP Papers. Copies of the letter were sent to Roy Wilkins, Thurgood Marshall, Charles H. Houston, and William H. Hastie; Buni, "Robert L. Vann of the *Pittsburgh Courier*," 8–10.

12. Letter, General Edwin Watson to White, October 17, 1939, Box C-377, NAACP Papers.

13. Letter, William H. Hastie to White, October 26, 1939; Memorandum, Thurgood Marshall and Roy Wilkins to White, October 28, 1939; White to Roosevelt, October 29, 1939, all in boxes C-376 and C-377, NAACP Papers.

14. The text of the National Negro Congress resolution was reprinted in the *Congressional Record*, 76th Congress, 3rd Session, April 30, 1940, 5253; Horace M. Bond, "Should the Negro Care Who Wins the War?" *The Annals of the American Academy of Political and Social Science*, CCXXII (September 1942), 81–84; Adam C. Powell, Jr., "Is This A White Man's War?" *Common Sense*, XI (April 1942), 111–113.

15. Quoted in Lee, *The Employment of Negro Troops*, 49; Colonel Eugene R. Householder, Assistant Adjutant General, voiced the same sentiments to twenty black newspaper editors on December 8, 1941; he was quoted in the *Chicago Defender*, December 13, 1941.

16. Editorial, *The Pittsburgh Courier*, December 28, 1940; *The Pittsburgh Courier*, November 2, 1940; Finkle, "Forum For Protest: The Black Press and World War II," 299.

17. By Axis propaganda, King meant that unless black soldiers received fair treatment in the army, the Germans would seize the opportunity to use psychological warfare on the troops in an effort to destroy their morale, and the will to fight for the allied cause.

18. Quoted in Lee, *The Employment of Negro Troops*, 67–69. Similar warnings from R.J. Reynolds of the *Topeka Daily Capitol* were reprinted in the *Congressional Record*, 76th Congress, 3rd Session, May 28, 1940, appendix, 40–48; Elmer A. Carter, "The Negro and Nazism," *Opportunity* XVIII (July 1940), 194–195.

19. Jean Byers, *A Study of the Negro in Military Service* (Washington, D.C.: Department of Defense, 1947), 6–9; John P. Davis, "The Negro in the Armed Forces of America," in John P. Davis, editor, *The Negro Reference Book* (New Jersey: Prentice-Hall, 1966), 627; "Army Can Dodge Anti-Discrimination Clause on Selective Service System," *The Pittsburgh Courier*, November 30, 1940.

20. "Secret Army Orders Barred," *The Pittsburgh Courier*, November 23, 1940; "Army Jim Crow Orders Defied By Connecticut," *The Pittsburgh Courier*, January 4, 1941.

21. Letter, Mary McLeod Bethune to Eleanor Roosevelt, October 5, 1940, Box 151, Judge Robert P. Patterson Papers, Manuscript Division, Library of Congress, Washington, D.C.; Henry L. Stimson Diary, January 24, 1942, Yale University Library, New Haven, Connecticut; Walter White, *A Man Called White: The Autobiography of Walter White* (New York: The Viking Press, Inc., 1948), 186–187; Colonel Campbell C. Johnson, *Selective Service System: Special Groups: Special Monograph No. 10* (Washington, D.C.: United States Printing Office, 1953), 3, 94; Roy Wilkins, "No Negro Draft Board Members in Many States, Says NAACP Survey," *The Crisis* XLVIII (January 1941), 22; "U. S. Plans New Units of Race Troops," *Norfolk Journal and Guide*, July 6, 1940; Charles S. Johnson, *To Stem This Tide: A Survey of Racial Tension Areas in the United States* (Boston: The Pilgrim Press, 1943), 81; "Only Whites Are Called; Boards All White," *The Pittsburgh Courier*, January 4, 1941.

22. Byers, *A Study of the Negro in Military Service*, 17; Eli Ginzberg and Douglas W. Bray, *The Uneducated* (New York: Columbia University Press, 1953), 240–245; Colonel Noel F. Parrish, "The Segregation of Negroes in the Army Air Forces" (unpublished M.A. thesis, Air University, 1947), 10–11; War Department Pamphlet, *Command of Negro Troops* (Washington, D.C.: United States Government Printing Office, 1944), 9.

23. Stimson Diary, May 12, 1942.

24. "War Department Press Release," The Adjutant General's Office, October 9, 1940, NARG 407.

25. Byers, *A Study of the Negro in Military Service*, 80–82; Horace R. Clayton, "Fighting For White Folks?," *Nation*, CLV (September 26, 1943), 267–269; Evelyn P. Meyers, *The Case Against Jim Crow Army Demands Investigation By the U.S. Congress* (Washington, D.C.: United States Government Printing Office, 1947), 5; "President O.K.'s Strange Request As Fellowmen Fight For Equality," *Chicago Defender*, October 9, 1940.

26. *New York Age*, October 26, 1940. The letter from Jones and the resolution adopted by the National Urban League were reprinted in this black newspaper.

27. Telegrams, Citizens' Nonpartisan Committee For Equal Rights In National Defense to Roosevelt, October 20, 1940, Franklin D. Roosevelt Papers, Franklin D. Roosevelt Library, Hyde Park, New York; to War Department, October 20, 1940, Box 151, Patterson Papers.

28. Letter, Stephen Early to White, October 18, 1940, Roosevelt Papers; James C. Evans, private interview with author, 3533 Warder Street, Washington, D.C., October 6, 1974. James C. Evans was the last black American to hold the position titled civilian aide to the Secretary of War. He assumed the post in 1947.

29. Letters, White to Early and Roosevelt, October 21, 1940; Roosevelt to Randolph, Hill, and White, October 25, 1940, Roosevelt Papers.

30. *New York Amsterdam News*, October 26, 1940.

31. *New York Age*, October 12, 1940. On November 1, 1940, the "Stephen Early Incident" made headlines in the following: *New York Times, New York Amsterdam News, The Oregon Statesman, Norfolk Journal and Guide, The Washington Afro-American, The Pittsburgh Courier, The Washington Post, Chicago Defender, The Richmond Times-Dispatch, The Los Angeles Times, The Greensboro Daily News, The Vicksburg Herald, The Baltimore Sun, The New Orleans Times, The Savannah Morning News, The Montgomery Advertiser, The Boston Daily Globe, The California Eagle, The Chicago Daily News, The Philadelphia Tribune, The Houston Post, The Detroit News, The Atlanta Daily World, The Atlanta Constitution, The Philadelphia Record, The People's Voice, The Cleveland Gazette,* and *The Indianapolis News*.

32. Walter White, *A Man Called White*, 188–189; Samual A. Stouffer and Others, *The American Soldier, Adjustment During Army Life*, Volume I (New Jersey: Princeton University Press, 1949), 489–490; Richard Bardolph, *The Negro Vanguard* (New York: Vintage Books, 1959), 353; Stimson Diary, October 23, 1940; Finkle, "Forum For Protest: The Black Press and World War II," 197.

33. Bardolph, *The Negro Vanguard*, 354; Richard M. Dalfiume, *Desegregation of the United States Armed Forces: Fighting On Two Fronts, 1939–1953* (Mis-

souri: University of Missouri Press, 1969), 40–41; White, *A Man Called White*, 187.

34. Press Release, Democratic National Committee Publicity Department Colored Division, October 30, 1940; Stimson Diary, October 22, 25, 1940; Lee, *The Employment of Negro Troops*, 79; "First Race General in History of United States Army Appointed," *Norfolk Journal and Guide*, November 2, 1940.

35. Hastie, private interview with author, March 4, 1974; memorandums, Associate Justice Felix Frankfurter to Robert P. Patterson, no date, and Huntington Thomas to Patterson, October 21, 1940, Box 151, Patterson Papers.

36. Letter, Stimson to Hastie, October 25, 1940, Box 151, Patterson Papers.

37. Hastie, private interview with author, March 6, 1974; "Colonel Eugene Householder's Remarks at the Conference of Negro Newspapers Representatives," December 8–9, 1941, NARG 107; *New York Amsterdam News*, November 2, 1940; *Norfolk Journal and Guide*, November 2, 1940.

38. Stimson Diary, October 23, 28, 1940, and October 19, 1942; Editorial, *The New York Age*, November 9, 1940; Editorial, *The Cleveland Gazette*, November 2, 1940; Editorial, *The Chicago Defender*, November 2, 1940; Editorial, *Norfolk Journal and Guide*, November 2, 1940; *The Pittsburgh Courier*, November 2, 1940; Finkle, "Forum For Protest: The Black Press and World War II," 197; White, *A Man Called White*, 188–189; Bardolph, *The Negro Vanguard*, 353; Henry L. Stimson and McGeorge Bundy, *On Active Service in Peace and War* (New York: Harper, 1948), 463; Office Memorandum, "Conference of the Chicago Council of Negro Organizations With Under Secretary Robert P. Patterson," March 29, 1941, NARG 107.

39. Memorandum, Huntington Thomas to Patterson, October 21, 1940, Box 151, Patterson Papers; Hastie, private interview with author, March 6, 1974; William H. Hastie, *On Clipped Wings: the Story of Jim Crow in the Army Air Corps* (New York: National Association for the Advancement of Colored People, 1943), 1.

40. Letter, Hastie to White and Randolph, December 21, 1940, Box 264, NAACP Papers; Rackham Holt, *Mary McLeod Bethune* (New York: Doubleday and Company, 1964), 196–197.

41. Rai Ottley, *'New World A-Coming': Inside Black America* (Boston, Houghton Mifflin Company, 1943), 314–315.

42. *The Richmond Times-Dispatch*, May 17, 1942; Letter, Eddie W. Reevers to Henry L. Stimson, August 8, 1941; Letter, Charles M. Thomas to Stephen Early, March 3, 1942, Roosevelt Papers; Warren H. Brown, "A Negro Looks At The Negro Press," *Saturday Review of Literature*, XXV (December 19, 1942), 5; Finkle, "Forum For Protest: The Black Press and World War II," 172; Sheldon B. Avery, "Up From Washington: William Pickens and the Negro Struggle For Equality 1900–1954" (unpublished Ph.D. dissertation, University of Oregon, 1970), 243–246.

43. For detailed discussions of the black community's consensus on army integration see Rai Ottley, *'New World A-Coming': Inside Black America* (Boston: Houghton Mifflin Company, 1943); William H. Hastie, *On Clipped Wings: the Story of Jim Crow in the Army Air Corps* (New York: NAACP, 1943); Richard J. Stillman, *Integration of the Negro in the U.S. Armed Forces* (New York:

Frederick A. Praeger, 1968); Richard M. Dalfiume, *Desegregation of the United States Armed Forces, 1939–1953* (Missouri: University of Missouri Press, 1969); Phillip McGuire, "Black Civilian Aides And The Problems of Racism And Segregation In The United States Armed Forces: 1940–1950" (unpublished Ph.D. dissertation, Howard University, 1975); Neil A. Wynn, *The Afro-American and the Second World War* (New York: Holmes & Meier Publishers, 1976); A. Russell Buchanan, *Black Americans in World War II* (Santa Barbara, California: ABC-Clio Press, 1977); Alan M. Osur, *Blacks In The Army Air Forces During World War II* (Washington, D.C.: United States Printing Office, 1977).

44. Ottley, "The Negro Press," *Command Ground* (Spring 1943), 11–16, Ottley; *'New World A-Coming'*, 269–270.

45. Quoted in Dwight MacDonald, "The Novel Case of Winfred Lynn," *The Nation*, CLVI (February 20, 1943), 263.

46. Memorandum of Law, United States ex rel. Winfred W. Lynn against Colonel John W. Downer, William H. Hastie Papers, Howard University Law School, Washington, D.C.; Gerald R. Gill, "Religious, Constitutional, and Racial Objections to the United States Involvement in World War II 1939–1945," (unpublished M. A. thesis, Howard University, 1974), 52; MacDonald, "The Novel Case of Winfred Lynn," 263–264.

47. Quoted in S.P. Breckinridge, "The Winfred Lynn Case Again: Segregation in the Armed Forces," *Social Service Review*, XVIII (September, 1944), 370; MacDonald, "The Novel Case of Winfred Lynn," 264–270; MacDonald, "The Supreme Court's New Moot Suit," *The Nation*, CLIX (July 1, 1944), 13–14; Letter, Winfred L. Kerr, chairman of the Lynn Committee To Abolish Segregation In The Armed Forces, to Hastie, April 4, 1944, Hastie Papers.

48. MacDonald, "The Novel Case of Winfred Lynn," 268.

49. Byers, *A Study of the Negro in Military Service*, 6–9; Davis, "The Negro in the Armed Forces of America," 627; "Army Can Dodge Anti-Discrimination Clause on Selective Service System," *The Pittsburgh Courier*, November 30, 1940.

1

Uncle Sam's Boys

If there ever were a time that all racial prejudices and
hatred should be put aside, now it is at hand, and the
country should be unified in every possible respect. The
emergency has become so great until Congress has
passed a Draft Bill to draft men for the first time during
peace-time in the history of the country into the armored
forces. Both White and Colored men are being called up
and everybody is doing his or her bit to cooperate.
Negroes like the Whites are quitting their jobs to increase the military strength of this Nation, because we
all think that a nation worth being in is worth fighting
for. But in view of this so called unity and National
emergency the age-old Monster of Prejudice has raised
his head high in the Army.

A Private

Under the Selective Service Act of 1940, Uncle Sam's black
boys registered for the armed forces in record numbers. Never
before had America witnessed such black patriotism in peace-
time. For the first time in military history, blacks had greater opportunities to serve their country. Because of the nondiscriminatory clause of
the Selective Service Act, which prohibited discrimination in the selection
and training of men based on race and color, most black troops thought
that the "armed forces of democracy" would accept their soldiery on an
equal basis. But as soon as the soldiers were mustered into the services,
most of them were faced with a rising tide of prejudice and racial
discrimination.

Having joined up, black troops experienced many problems that were
unique to them. Often they were transferred from post to post to avoid
mixing them with white troops, subjected to delayed personnel action,
relegated to dilapidated and segregated recreational facilities, overtly

1

made to feel inferior, and denied entry to special schools and training classes. Denials of entrance to the Army's specialist schools soon became the soldiers' most frequent complaint.

In a letter to Judge William H. Hastie (first black civilian aide to Secretary of War Henry L. Stimson), for example, Private Gilbert A. Cargill, an aviation pilot trainee, opines "I received a letter from the Army Air Corps base at Maxwell Field, Alabama, asking me to report there on or about Dec. 1, 1942, to take further training in the Army Instructor School maintained at that field. When I reported to this field, I was not permitted to enter the school solely because I was a Negro."[1]

Another soldier was told by a local draft board in Texas that blacks "were not accepted in the army as volunteer office candidates." In response, Private Aeron D. Bells asks Hastie, "Will you kindly tell me whether this is local prejudice, or an official order from Washington. I am sure you will agree with me when I say that the situation is 'Confusing' for I fail to see why I WILL BE FORCED TO SHED MY BLOOD on democracy's battlefields as a Private, and am refused to volunteer as an officer candidate to fulfill the same job."[2]

Besides the few who entered, getting the army's special schools to accept more blacks became an almost impossible task. The heads of these schools and the Army's general staff usually responded to the inquiries made by Hastie and Assistant Civilian Aide Truman K. Gibson, Jr., that a particular school did not accept blacks because of its location or that there was no demand for additional black personnel. At the same time, however, the Army needed more trained specialists.[3]

Blacks were excluded from the Army's specialist schools largely because of a quota system within each field, which included such specialties as civilian pilot training, aviation mechanics, photography, intelligence, bomb disposal, foreign language and area studies, aerial and field artillery observation, law, and engineering. Ironically, the Army opened these schools to black enlisted men, but prejudice and racial discrimination was so widespread that few of those who managed to graduate actually were able to apply their specialized skills to aid the country in the national struggle.[4]

Judge Hastie was aware of the Army's restrictive use of blacks but went ahead with his plans to increase the number receiving specialized training. His hope was that they would be utilized in integrated army units. To achieve his objective, Hastie counted on the black press, black and white national and local leaders, black national self-help organizations, public schools, colleges, and universities to advertise the opening of special training classes to qualified blacks.[5]

A few black troops subsequently entered some of the schools; however, the total number was relatively small, and most were trained at segregated facilities. In fact, the trainees never reached the 10 percent black population ratio the Army purportedly sought to achieve. In some instances, blacks were told that state laws prevented them from training at some schools. For example, Private Richard Bennett was transferred from Grenier Field, New Hampshire, to Oklahoma A & M College for clerical training only to be refused admission because the Oklahoma Constitution and other state statutes did not permit blacks and whites in the same classroom.

The same situation occurred at the University of Virginia at Charlottesville.[6] Gibson protested these denials, but the Army's legal staff upheld the states. To avoid further charges of discrimination, the soldiers involved were transferred to Sheppard Field, Wichita Falls, Texas, where race was not a factor in their training.[7]

In spite of these and other setbacks, Hastie and Gibson continued their efforts to get more blacks trained and used as army specialists. For instance, in July 1942, Hastie suggested to General I. H. Edwards, Assistant Chief of Staff for Air, that the Army Air Corps train blacks as aerial observational pilots. His recommendation was aborted before he had a chance to make a case for his proposal. Hastie had wanted blacks who failed to qualify as pursuit pilots at Tuskegee Training Base (a segregated training facility for blacks), particularly those who had successfully completed the primary course, to be used as field artillery observational pilots. General Edwards responded that field artillery observational pilots were at full capacity, and that it was not the policy of the War Department to use personnel in other piloting endeavors who had failed any aspect of the training curriculum. Four months later, Hastie asked the Assistant Secretary of War for Air, Robert A. Lovett. for a policy ruling on the matter. Lovett replied, through his Air Corps executive, that the training and usage of blacks depended solely on the Commanding General of the Army Ground Forces and on vacancies in the Air Corps observational units.[8]

In foreign language and area studies training, Gibson, who succeeded Hastie as civilian aide in 1943, discovered that blacks were being rejected. On August 17, 1943, he complained to Assistant Secretary of War John J. McCloy, who was in charge of black troop affairs, that a few blacks who had managed to enter this program were symbols of tokenism, and that the policy should be corrected to admit qualified blacks on a much greater scale. McCloy referred Gibson's memo to Colonel Herman Beukema, Director of Specialized Training Programs, and to Beukema's deputy director, Lieutenant Colonel T. D. Palmer, for comment. On August 20, these men replied that it was the Army's policy to use blacks based on the requests from the Ground Services and Air Command. Infantry Colonel J. S. Leonard informed McCloy that "the relative small number of blacks requested by the Commands for foreign language and area studies is due to the fact that it is not known where Negro troops will serve overseas, and therefore impossible to plan on their training." McCloy replied to Gibson on August 25 that the reports from Colonels Beukema, Palmer, and Leonard indicated that the Army had reached its quota of blacks for foreign language and area studies training. This explanation, of course, contradicted that of Colonel Leonard, who days earlier had given McCloy a quite different reason for the small number of blacks accepted for the program. McCloy, however, failed to pass this information on to Gibson.[9]

At Davis-Monthan Field in Tucson, Arizona, black troops voiced other complaints. They protested that their housing facilities were covered with black tar paper while the barracks for white soldiers were painted white. And at Camp Davis, North Carolina, blacks charged that only black soldiers were required to take blood tests for venereal diseases.[10]

In addition to these grievances, Gibson, responding to a soldier's charge at Fort Benning, Georgia, of discrimination in post theaters, sent a memo to the adjutant general and subsequently asked for a policy decision on the matter because it was his understanding that any member of the armed forces could attend any facility on a military post. Adjutant General Miller G. White, without Gibson's knowledge, sent the memo to the commanding general of Fort Benning who advised him that no discrimination existed at the fort. Meanwhile, Sergeant L. A. Guenther of the War Department's general staff prepared a memo for General White. Guenther suggested to White that Gibson "be advised that, while the War Department's policy governing recreational facilities provides that such facilities are for the benefit of all personnel regardless of race, it does not prohibit a post commander from allocating recreational facilities on an 'area' for 'unit' basis if in his judgement such allocations will better serve the needs of his particular command."[11]

Blacks stationed at Camp Gordon Johnston, Florida, demonstrated another way Uncle Sam's black boys were treated. A soldier commented, "We cannot go to the church services on the camp. We have to be told when we can go and worship God, the service clubs are off limit for us because a Staff Sgt. went over with some more of our comrades in the Co. to get a couple of sandwiches and were told by a civilian worker we don't serve colored, and Sir this is an Army Post."[12]

The efforts of Hastie and Gibson and the grievances of the black soldiers created uneasiness in the War Department, but the department clung to its official policy of segregation and its unofficial policy of racial discrimination. Attempts to end or mitigate the prejudice in the armed services only confirmed the War Department's belief that blacks in and out of uniform wanted to create a social revolution, and the segregationist attitude of the armed forces remained basically the same throughout World War II. In the early stages of the war, the Army's general staff insisted that:

> Every effort should be made by the War Department to maintain in the Army the social and racial conditions which exist in Civil life in order that the normal customs of white and colored personnel now in the Army may not be suddenly disrupted. The Army can, under no circumstances, adopt a policy which is contrary to the dictates of a majority of the people. To do so would alienate the people from the Army and lower their morale at a time when their support of the Army and high morale are vital to our national needs.[13]

Statements such as the above became the military norm and reflected the general attitude of the armed forces. Although the Selective Service

Act of 1940 specifically banned racial discrimination, black troops found themselves in a precarious position. On the one hand, they took advantage of the greater opportunities provided by the act to serve. On the other, their letters express discontent over the way they were treated. "I was in hopes I could become an airplane mechanic, but the field doesn't seem to be open to negro soldiers" indicates the sentiments of many of Uncle Sam's black boys.[14]

NOTES

1. Letter, Gilbert A. Cargill to William H. Hastie, December 21, 1942, Civilian Aide to the Secretary of War Subject File, 1940–1947, National Archives Record Group 107 (hereafter cited as NARG).

2. Letter, Aeron D. Bells to Hastie, May 20, 1942, Civilian Aide to the Secretary of War Subject File, 1940–1947, NARG 107.

3. Judge William H. Hastie, private interview with author, 1701 Popla Lane, N.W., Washington, D.C., March 8, 1974; Letter, Hastie to author, October 8, 1974; James C. Evans, private interview with author, 3533 Warder Street, N.W., Washington, D.C., July 23, 1974; Letter, Howard D. Gould, Director, Department of Industrial Relations and Research, Chicago Urban League, to Gibson, November 9, 1943; Letter, Lieutenant Colonel Hugh V. Robnett, Bomb Disposal School, Aberdeen Proving Ground, Maryland, to Gibson, February 15, 1944, all in Civilian Aide to the Secretary of War Subject File, 1940–1947, NARG 107.

4. Ibid.

5. Letter, Hastie to Walter White, August 16, 1941; Letter, John W. Davis, President of West Virginia State College, to Hastie, January 3, 1941; Letter, Charles M. Ashe, flight instructor for Lincoln University of Missouri for the Civilian Pilot Training College Program, to Hastie, January 9, 1941; Letter, Garnet C. Wilkinson, First Assistant Superintendent for the District of Columbia Public Schools, to Hastie, December 16, 1941; Letter, Harold F. Smith, Director of the Lower Division, Fisk University, to Hastie, July 2, 1942, all in Civilian Aide to the Secretary of War Subject File, 1940–1947, NARG 107.

6. Letter, Nora Bennett to Hastie, December 7, 1942; Civilian Aide to the Secretary of War Subject File, 1940–1947, Judge William H. Hastie, private interview with author, March 8, 1974.

7. Memorandum, Colonel George A. Brownell to Gibson, February 24, 1943; Memorandum, Gibson to Charles Poletti, Special Assistant to the Secretary of War, March 5, 1943, Civilian Aide to the Secretary of War Subject File, 1940–1947, NARG 107.

8. Memorandum, Hastie to Edwards, July 6, 1942; Memorandum, Edwards to Hastie, July 29, 1942; Memorandum, Hastie to Robert A. Lovett, November 25, 1942; Memorandum, Richard T. Coiner to Hastie, December 17, 1942, all in Civilian Aide to the Secretary of War Subject File, 1940–1947, NARG 107.

9. Memorandum, Gibson to McCloy, August 17, 1943; Memorandum, Herman Beukema and T. D. Palmer to McCloy, August 20, 1943; Memorandum, J. S. Leonard to McCloy, August 25, 1943; Memorandum, McCloy to Gibson, August 27, 1943; Memorandum, Gibson to McCloy, September 9, 1943, all in Civilian Aide to the Secretary of War Subject File, 1940–1947, NARG 107.

10. Memorandum, Gibson to Brigadier General Miller G. White, Adjutant General, June 20, 1944; Letter, Concerned Soldiers to Gibson, March 2, 1942; Letter, Carlton Shepherd to Hastie, September 30, 1942; Letter, Disgusted Soldier to P. L. Prattis, Editor of the *Pittsburgh Courier*, January 14, 1942, all in Civilian Aide to the Secretary of War Subject File, 1940–1947, NARG 107.

11. Memorandum, Gibson to White, June 10, 1944; Memorandum, Guenther to White, June 24, 1944, Military Personnel Division, General Staff, NARG 165.

12. Letter, A Negro Soldier to the *Baltimore Afro-American*, September 27, 1943, Civilian Aide to the Secretary of War Subject File, 1940–1947, NARG 107.

13. Quoted in Ulysses Lee, *United States Army in World War II: Special Studies: The Employment of Negro Troops* (Washington, D.C.: United States Government Printing Office, 1966), 140.

14. Letter, Private Laurence W. Harris to the *Pittsburgh Courier*, November 4, 1943, Civilian Aide to the Secretary of War Subject File, 1940–1947, NARG 107.

Not Accepted as Volunteer Officer Candidates

Mr. W. H. Hasty,
Negro Adviser,
Sec'y of War,   Houston, Texas
Washington, D.C.   May 20, 1942

My Dear Sir:

I am a young Negro . . . age 33 years today . . . I am a former student of Wiley College, Marshall, Texas, and more recent of Iowa University, Iowa City, Iowa. . . . A Science Major studying for the degree of M.D. until I was forced to quit due to financial reverses. At present and for the past several years I have been with the Post Office, this city. My salary $2100. At the outbreak of the war I heard a Nationwide broadcast for Volunteer Officer Candidates. Realizing that my wife and family could not exist off my salary as a Non-Com or as a private, and wishing to fulfill my obligation to my country, I inquired into the field of V.O.C. For some time I was given the old "run-a-round," but today I was told by my board (local board # 15 Selective Service) that it had been advised by it's headquarters at Austin, Texas, that NEGROES WERE NOT ACCEPTED IN THE ARMY AS VOLUNTEER OFFICER CANDI-DATES. Will you kindly tell me whether this is local prejudice, or an official order from Washington. I am sure that you will agree with me when I say that the situation is "Confusing" for I fail to see why I WILL BE FORCED TO SHED MY BLOOD on Democracy's battlefields as a Private, and am refused to volunteer as an officer candidate to fulfill the same job.

I will appreciate any light that you may be able to shed on this confused soul.

May I remain,

Respectfully Yours,

Aeron D. Bells
#4702 Vernon Street
Houston, Texas.

My Order No. is 1635
My Serial No. is 1556
Harris County Selective Service Board
Houston, Texas.

No Nearer to the Air Corps

3475th Q. M. Trk Co.
Fort Ord Calif.
November 10, 1942

Mr. William H. Hastie

Dear Sir:

It has been several months since we have passed the necessary examination and approval of the Cadet Examining Board to qualify as an aviation Cadet.

During the Course of our examination we were stationed at Fort Sill, Okla, at which time several other soldiers took the examinations and have since then received their transfers to the Air Corp; but for some unknown reason we have not received ours.

Sir, we are college men and have had Senior R.O.T.C. training. We were also members of the Enlisted Reserve Corp. Since completing our basic training in Field Artillery we have been transferred to Fort Ord California to do basic training in the Quartermaster Corp. It seems, sir, as if we are going from one basic training to another and getting no nearer to the Air Corp. We are writing you hoping you may be able to give us either and or information so as to hasten our transfer to the Air Corp. It seems with aviation playing the vital part it is we should have hardly any trouble getting in. Our papers are in Washington awaiting disposition, as is the case of all Negro applicants. We hope you can help us. We close now awaiting your answer.

Respectfully,

Pvt. Rufus R. Johnson 15317492
Pvt. Emory A. James 15317509
Pvt. Jack Housen 15317527

Coffee and Oil Don't Look So Good

Baltimore Afro-American Newspaper   Place-Alabama
To The Editor   November 23, 1942

Dear Sir:

After years of reading the Afro-American. I think it's the wise thing to write and feel that you will print in your paper the doings of a Negro soldier.

In the first place a U.S. army uniform to a colored man makes him about as free as a man in the Georgia chain gang and you know that's hell. While on a troop movement from Camp Lee, Virginia, during the long run which would carry us deeper into the black-hearted South, and take us over two days to get there, we are traveling in an ordinary day coach, sleeping in the same car and had one (1) meal to last us.

When we reached Alabama they decided we should eat and if you could see the way they threw them box lunches together, you'd know just what I'm talking about. To top it off they brought on a can of coffee. The can was a lubricating oil can and coffee and oil don't look so good. Why it was so full of oil we raised cain and made them take it back.

This also happened. There were sailors and soldiers on that same movement . . . white of course. They got off and walked around and ate like human beings while they penned us in between two freight cars so no none could see us, kept us cooped up like animals.

I am not alone in this but three hundred of us and we all feel the same. If this is Uncle Sam's Army, then treat us like soldiers not animals or else Uncle Sam might find a new axis to fight.

Signed: The Negro.

From Three Hundred Soldiers.

P.S. Would appreciate very much if this was written up in type so the World would know.

Negroes Are Not Trained at Maxwell Field, Alabama

Dr. William H. Hastie
Civilian Aide to the   8814 Blaine Avenue
Secretary of War   Cleveland, Ohio
Washington, D.C.   December 21, 1942

Dear Dr. Hastie:

I am writing this letter to inform you of an instance of discrimination that I encountered recently at the hands of the U.S. Army Air Corps. Before citing the case I shall give you a brief background.

Since June, 1941, I have been a student in aviation courses given by the Civil Aeronautics Administration designed to furnish pilots for the armed services. Upon completion of my course in November, 1942, I received a letter from the Army Air Corps base at Maxwell Field, Alabama, asking me to report there on or about Dec., 1, 1942, to take further training in the Army Instructor School maintained at that field.

When I reported to this field, I was not permitted to enter the school solely because I was a Negro. The man to whom I talked at Maxwell Field (Mr. Feest, Room 125, Austin Hall) told me that Negroes were not trained there.

I am sending this brief outline of the situation in order that you may take appropriate measures to correct this injustice or in order that you may tell me what I should do to achieve the same result.

Yours sincerely,

Gilbert A. Cargill

Help Is Wanted

Pittsburgh Courier Publishing Company
2628 Centre Ave.
Pittsburgh, Pa.
February 10, 1943
    (Editor)
Dear Sir:

When you read this letter I hope it bring action, for there is much action
needed here and it's needed at once. I have been here in this camp now a
month. I came from Camp Stewart, Ga. It was about 97 fellows from Camp
Stewart that came here. Before comming here we were in the Artillery units
which is considered one of the high branches of the service. After the riot at
Stewart some of the fellows were put into the guard house with 10 years and
they didn't have any thing to do with the riot. You being the editor of the
Pittsburgh Courier know that Camp Stewart was nothing but a slave camp for
the colored, but we did have some discharges. Some of were sent to Kansas
some here the rest are still in Stewart. We all came here in grade only to be
put driving trucks in the Q.M. There has'nt been any of the white outfits
broken up like this. Were we doing our job to good. So good that we were
taking all the credit from the white's. Most of the fellows sent here had I.Q.
over 110 and had plenty of guts and since also. Now we are driving trucks
where it does it take so much brain to drive a dam truck. Some of the fellows
here are from the 369th the 100th and from the 372. All of these units are
suppose to be creack colored units, yet the men they send out on a cadre are
now driving trucks. This camp we are at now is the worist camp we have ever
been to. It is Camp Berkeley, Texas near the town of Abilene, Texas 12 miles
from the Camp. There is a swimming pool here in the colored area and the
colored use it on Mon. and Fri only. They have a show whre the colored go
and you sit on the out side to see the picture if it rain's there is'nt any picture.
Most of the fellows we brought here with us like to play basketball we have no
where to play but out on the hard ground. They have a field house here and
we can't even use it to practice to play basketball. Out of all the camp's we
have been to we were given week end passes and three day passes. Here you
get a pass every night until 11:00 clock and you don't even leave here until
6:30. They have two busses for the colored one leaves at 6:30 and the other
at 7:30 and it takes about a half hour to get to town. The colored busses don't
run on Mon and Fri. and the white busses won't pick you up if there is'nt but

one soldier on the buss. And if you don't go to town you can't go to the
service club because they don't have one for the colored. They get paper from
the white service club and put it in the hut. This is some of it am writing on.
We don't have a P.X. like the whites you can get only 1 bottle of beer 1 box
of ice cream. You can't use the white P.X.'s but still they can use yours and
get as much as they want. Every week they have what you call a show. A
bunch of fool get outside in the boxing ring and make fool's of the rest of us.
They start to talking about the girls in Abilene. Such things as Boy I met one
of them gals in Abilene and I looked at her head and I could see her brain.
They talk about the girl like it was heir fault. The fellows who do that are the
fellows who have been here 4 months. And the whites just love it, they die
laughing at them. Anything the white men say here Lt.'s or Pvt. they do what
ever they say. When we came here they had all of us out talking to us. We
asked them a question and they talk about something else. We ask them so
many questions it makes their heads swim, because they are'nt use to being
asked the sort of questions we ask them. They wonder if we are crazy, they try
to pull some stuff and the fellows strighten them out because they know the
rules. Now that they see that their trying to do all they can. The officers had a
habit of callen the fellows boys. If they wanted something they would say hay
boy do this or that. One day all of us were in a room together a 1st Sgt asked
the Lt were in the book's did it say that you could call a soldier a *boy* and he
did'nt know what to say. Why? Because the fellows we found here did'nt care
what they called them or what they said but we do. If we want to say
something to one or another we get to the side to say it because the one that
have been here for some time will tell every thing you say — and they are
supposa to be our people. There is a fellow here named Russell Hubbard he
usa to be a Sgt but now he is a Pvt and we have'nt been here a month yet!
You should send somebody here to talk to him he can tell you every thing and
we'll back him up. He asked the officer why could'nt the colored work in
personal. He asked them why could the colored use their own Sgt Major in
Personal in stead of the white they have in the colored unit. He really talks up
for the fellows. He has the highest IQ. on the post 139 and they don't want
him to go to O.C.S. He had a court martial at Camp Stewart and he proved he
was right they had to let him go from the guardhouse and make him a Sgt
again. What they did'nt like was he made a Lt out of a lie on the stand.
Everything went smooth until they broke up his outfit when he came here they
had him and said that he was having bulk of his pay taken away from him
until Jan. He is a fine fellow and we need officers like him. The Pittsburgh
Courier can help him. Any thing they do thats wrong he call's their bluf and

they want to do harm to him but their afraid of what might happen. All the fellows that came with him here know and if they have it might now be trouble. They keep him on guard and every thing else but he keeps going. There is five fellows who realy stick up for us and that is Charle Louise; Christ Wilson, Herbert Smith, Harry Tyler and Russell Hubbard. The most important of them all is Russell Hubbard. He is the one that can do them the most harm. Christ Wilson is next all are Sgt.'s but Hubbard. You just got to help him and the rest of the fellows. And I'm quite sure if some one came here and talked with him we could get a lot of things straight. We are quite sure you will help.

Thank you

(HELP IS WANTED)   A Group of Soldiers

You may put this in the paper also. Just to make things better it will start the ball rolling.

Come to Macedonia and Help Us!

Dr. Adam C. Powell, Jr.
Abyssinian Baptist Church
New York City   March 15, 1943

Dear Dr. Powall:

   I am writing this letter not so much with the idea that I shall directly benefit
by it but I do want someone who is in a position of influence to know what is
happening.

   In this particular camp colored troops have a number of recreational facilities, in fact, I am sure a larger number than any other camp in this section of
the country. There is a Service Club, a theatre, a swimming pool, a Bowling
Alley, and a guest house for the visitors of the enlisted men. All are ideally
situated for our use. For post transportation we have a bus exclusively for our
use but we may use the other buses if we will sit on the rear seat. The same
condition prevails on the interurban bus. The bus exclusively for colored runs
from five to twelve midnight but we may take any bus if we use the rear seat.
The 92nd Division was stationed here when the 1st Regiment of I.R.T.C.
consisted of five Battalions of colored troops. At that time all of the office
personnel was colored except the officers. Now the 1st Regiment consists of
two white battalions and two colored battalions, but the Headquarters Detachment was manned with colored personnel. A directive ordering the replacement
of all IA cadre by 1B by the first of June is the excuse used for replacing the
Regimental Headquarters Detachment with White personnel. The claim is that
from the available colored troops there are not enough man whose physical
condition warrant their reclassification as 1B, and those that are 1B have not
the educational background to fit them for office personnel. *Here sir, is the
rub.* In addressing the white section of the Regiment the officer said: "If you
have any expert typist no matter what their physical classification is I'll try to
have them reclassified to 1B". If then he is willing or can do that for the
whites, why can't the same procedure be used for the colored? Why should all
the more remunerative and so-called "white-collar" enlisted positions be given
to the white troops? Such actions as these only lead me to believe that we, the
colored troops, are not fighting for the preservation of the democratic way of
life, but for the supremacy of the white race.

   If a program needs planning to get the colored youth into schools, please
initiate it so that future actions of this kind can be forestalled. If you can do

anything to get this Regimental Headquarters back to its former standing, colored—please do that. As an enlisted man I cannot write to the Inspector General, but if you think that my complaint warrants, please do that.

If passion has beclouded my reasoning and I have my values confused, please write and straighten me out—but as the Macedonian Church once cried to Paul, "Come to Macedonia and help us!", we are enlisting your aid.

Sincerely yours,

No Place for Recreation

Camp Shelby, Miss.

July 17, 1943

Truman K. Gibson, Jr.

To whom it may concern;

In writing this letter in regards to the treatment of colored soldiers in Camp Shelby Miss. We have no place for recreation except one place which is 3 miles away almost. We do not have anyway to get to it except to walk. We are limited duty men, and all not able to hardly do any work. When we want to go to town we can hardly get a bus. Whenever we get a bus they will only take five colored soldiers, and sometimes we have to wait about two or three hours for a bus.

Our medical treatment is poor also. The doctors treat us as if we are dogs. I have reference to all statements in the letter, and lots other things that happen around this Camp. We are in a mixed company, and the whites beat and curse the colored soldiers at times they have them put in the Camp Stockade for no reason at all.

A lot of the officers are as bad as the whites that curse us. In fact we are treated like dogs. In closing hoping there will be some changes.

Pvt. Norman Brittingham

Med. Det. Sta. Hospital

Dayroom # 3 Co. C.

Camp Shelby, Miss.

We Don't Serve Colored Troops

7:30 p.m.
Monday evening
9-27-43

The Baltimore Afro-American

Dear Sir:

I am writing to you in behalf of my comrades and myself in which sir, to let your staff sir, know the condition in which we colored troops are treated here in this camp in Florida.

Sir, my home is in Balto., and I was born in Balto., and I served the Afro before joining the Army and if you can recall Sir, I were the first Balto. boy to be drafted into the Army and your photographer took my picture and had it publish in the front sheet because I used to be the only colored bugler in Fort Meade Sir.

The reason for that is to let myself be a little known to you, first sir, so now I will go on with the conditions in Fort Meade Sir. Well Sir, on Aug. 17, it was 8 cadres sent from Camp Sutner, N.C. to Camp Gordon Johnston, Fla., to organize a new training center for new troops just coming into the Army life and on each cadre it were consist of 26 soldiers which all were non-commissioned officers to form a company.

The first two weeks we laid around doing nothing and Sir, we had from M/Sgt. to Cpl on the cadre. The third week they started us cleaning the white officers rooms, making us they dirty beds and cleaning they latrine and are still doing that right at the present. We cannot go to the church services on the camp. We have to be told when we can go and worship God, the service clubs are off limit for us because a Staff Sgt. went over with some more of our comrades in the Co. to get a couple of sandwiches and were told by a civilian worker we don't serve colored, and Sir this is an Army Post. We had a dance for the colored troops because Buddy Johnson's Band played and our girls came from Tallahassee, Florida, 57 miles from Camp to entertain our soldiers in the field house. There were about 30 lounging chairs for our guest to relax in but the white M.P. made them get out of them so that the officers and their wives could set in them and they were white, and it was our dance. So they went out and got about 5 or 6 rows of benches and they were hard benches too, so that were the seats for our girls to sit on. Then, about a half hour later they got a rope and started roping our girls off like sheep, by that I mean they had given us one side and the white the other and then on the side we had

they took half of that and put a rope around our women and they were herded
up in the corner like a flock of sheep and the other half they gave it to white
soldiers to have to sit down and where we had to stand and talk to our women.
So practically most of us that came down here are from Balto., Washington,
Phila., Pitts., and New York, with a couple of exceptions which I know you
understand. We walked out of the dance and we demanded to see the Post
Commanding Officer and see the reason why we were jim crowed in our own
dance, but we never did see him. So that was the end of that. We are not
allowed to sit down in the P.X. We only can go in there, buy what we want and
get out.

Then, they have a lot of white civilians here that have priority over us.
They have more privileges than we colored troops. The way we are sleeping
and eating sir, I just wish there was a way that I could snap a picture and send
it to you. Then you wouldn't have to know the rest because you would
understand. Sir we sleep in sand floors with no boards or anything to bed. We
stand up and eat each meal which they call a meal, in a mess kitchen and are
feeding around 345 non-coms. The truth sir, are we are nothing but slaves for
the people here, every area we're moved into and which this are our second
place we are moved and will move shortly into another of the camp after we
finish putting up dry week, and putting down walk boards.

Sir, we do not have any running latrines. They have a group of colored
troops who go around every morning and clean out the used bucket and put
clean ones in. Sir, that is the way your boys who are somebody's sons are
treated here in this Army, and which we are supposed to be fighting for
Democracy and really I would like for you to publish that so that our people
outside can see just how we are treated, and I will know if it is published
because my sister has a year's subscription sent to me.

A Negro Soldier

Trades Not Opened to Blacks

Pvt. Laurence W. Harris
356 Av Sqdn S.P.A.A.T.
Lubbock, Texas
November 4, 1943

To: The Pittsburgh Courier

Dear Gentlemen:

I am writing to you in regards to my classification in the army. I have been in the army air corp for the past ten months. Gentlemen I do not feel, and in fact I know I am not doing the best I could to help win this war. I realize the army has a tough job trying to place each man where they think he is best fitted or will do the best of service for the armed forces.

In my civilian life I was a small tool maker. I worked for Silling and Spences Co in Hartford, Conn. Then I was doing much for the war effort, and was in hopes I could continue in the service. In the past ten months I feel as though I have been a complete failure to myself, and to the helping to win this war. Beside that my morale is very low because of the fact I have given the army ten months to reclassify me to something I could do much than what I am doing.

I was in hopes I could become an airplane mechanic, but the field doesn't seem to be open to negro soldiers.

I only hope and pray that I will hear from you soon as to what I could do, to get into some part of the service where I could use my trade.

Thanking you in advance.

Yours Very Truely,

Pvt. Laurence W. Harris

Discharge That Robs a Man of His Citizenship

Mr. William G. Nunn   Nov. 21–43
2628 Centre Ave.   Casual Bn. EUTC. Co. 8
Pittsburgh, Pa.   Camp Claiborn, La.

Dear Sir:

It has ben my entention to write on this matter, before now, but I never
gotten around to it. Here in Camp Claiborn, there are two casual co one for
white and one for colored. This is the outfit that men who are unable to do
duty are placed, and discharged. Now the troubel is that the white boys who
are discharged get. AC.D.D. or section 10 those are different type of discharges, while most of the colored soldiers get section eights a type of
discharge that robes a man of his citizenship. Since I am in this outfit I can tell
you all of the inside facts, but I don't have a chance to write that much since
it is a long story, if you are interested in exposeing this, have one of your
reporters to get in touch with me at once.

                                                              Very trully Yours,

                                                        Pvt. Marion Hill 6165

German POWs Have More Rights and Freedom

Hdgt. 36th Regt IARTC
Camp Livingston, La.
Mr. James Evans   1-12-44

Dear Sir:

Here I am again and gripes are foremost as usual. I ran into several West Va. College students and the lucky devils are awaiting transportation to their separation centers. The name of one is Earl Van Ripper[a very good piano player. The others I will try to get their names.

Today, I went to the Inspector General and he confirms what the other officers and men in classification here told me; that since my profile is "D" I have a very good opportunity of returning to the Air Forces and a better opportunity of getting into the redistribution center providing someone from such a place shall write for me through the proper manner. So sir, that seems to be the drawback now. I know no one in authority who can write for me.

While here, I can go to no school nor do I actually put to work the stuff I have learned. So this I.G. urges me to get into the redistribution center now while I have the chance or into the Air Force again.

That still calls for someone to send a request for me. Since I have been here, some few colored and many whites have returned to Air Force and other branches and some whites to the redistribution centers to work, but they seemed to have had the required help.

The Negro troops are getting 6 wks. trng. then a 5 day furlough, then P.O.E. Sometimes I will tell you about what goes on. Mr. Evans, this is a hell hole. Believe it or not, but the German P.W.'s here have more rights and freedom.

The cycle of training here is suppose to cease around the middle of March. What will happen to me I don't know as I am no trainee, not specialized enough for a discharge even though they are hollering for skilled workers in plants and I could do better there; here, I am carried as overhead as an assistant IEE director. None of the officers or men have ever studied IEE and are not cooperative much. The A.S.F. has its own interpretation of IEE and the poor E.M. gets no benefits out of it.

So as the I.G. and other officers here told me, I hope it is possible for you to get someone to get me into the redistribution center up there while I have the opportunity now. Then what I have learned can be followed up and carried out. One of the officers told me I should try to get out of here by the last or before the last of this month. Why? I don't know; I am trying to find out. Well sir, there is the story. My air force unit seems to be broken up and my last opportunity lies in getting someone to write for me Sir. Let me know soon what can be done. So long for awhile. Hope to tell you about this place one day when I see you.

                                        Private James Pritchett

Attacks on Black WACs

1211 - 8th Avenue

Mr. P. L. Prattis

Executive Editor

Huntington, West Va.

July 8, 1944

Dear Sir:

I am writing you in regard to the situation now existing in Camp Forrest, Tennessee; a situation which I think could be greatly relieved through the effort of your paper. The essentials of the affair are as follows: The W. A. C. detachment Section 2, with an all Negro personnel and attached to the Station Hospital, has undergone a great deal of trouble and humiliation from the White paratroopers stationed there. The W. A. C.'s are subject to attack even in their own area.

Last year, I read a most excellent news report in your paper concerning a somewhat similar affair at Camp Breckinridge, Kentucky. Your exposé of the affair did so much good that I am writing you about recent events in Camp Forrest. My informant who is an enlisted member of the detachment, has written me in several letters about the situation there. I am certain that you will feel as I do; that the situation is intolerable for the women, and a disgrace to the Army.

In one of her letters, and I quote: "Two paratroopers came into the barracks last night, down stairs where I sleep. When we woke up he was between my bed and another girls. He woke up her up kissing her. She screamed and I jumped out of bed. The rest of them did the same. He and his buddy ran out so fast it was impossible to do anything about it."

To show the gravity of the affair, I will quote at length from a recent letter: "I've been telling you all along how the men have been coming into our barracks. Well last night about 25 paratroopers came in our area and grabbed two colored boys and started dragging them down the road. The girls all ran out with broomsticks, rocks and bottles and ran after them through the woods but they never did turn the two boys loose. So they called the boys company. So the whole company came racing over in trucks, jeeps and what not as it was a quartermaster trucking company. They searched the woods high and low. I didn't know if they found the boys or not. After that 4 car loads of M.P.'s came over to guard, as they said, but only stayed about one hour. Well about 2 A.M. the paratroopers came back in taxes, got out and made a rush on our barracks again. This time we came out with knives and sticks, beat them off and alarmed the whole camp. They heard us down to the hospital. Well after that round we stayed up all night, piled our foot-lockers to the door and stood guard until morning."

As she states in her last letter: "We were all up again last night. All night from 12 to 6 A.M. this morning," and further on she states; "If things don't take a turn for the better pretty soon there are going to be a lot of A.W.O.L.'s including myself. This thing is making us all nervous wrecks. I can't take very much of this." In regard to the affair she states: "I guess there isn't anything that can be done about it. It has been reported to the N.A.A.C.P. already, one girl had guts enough to write a letter. She is being punished."

As I have been in the Army myself, and stationed in the South, I know that the letter in question had little chance of reaching the N.A.A.C.P. The Army has a method of dealing with letters from our soldiers. In this connection, I have written a letter to the New York office of the N.A.A.C.P. quoting the material above and mentioning the letter that caused the girl's punishment.

For that reason, and the one quoted above, it would be best to withhold my informant's name, especially in the event of an investigation. I might also add that I have known my informant since early in 1942, in December of which year she enlisted in the W.A.A.C. She re-enlisted in the W.A.C. has been made an acting corporal and at present wears the Good Conduct ribbon. She has married a soldier, and her husband is now serving in the South Pacific.

May I urge you to look into this affair. An interview by an agent of your with the enlisted personnel will varify the contents of this letter. There are some 185 W.A.C.'s there and I have information from only one of them. An exposé of the situation would do much good; our women need your paper's help.

Sincerely yours,

Rollins W. James, Jr.
1211 - 8th Avenue
Huntington, West Va.

Banned Black Publications

Mr. Truman K. Gibson, Jr.
Civilian Aide to the
Secretary of War   652 Ord. Am. Company
War Department   Camp Howze, Texas
Washington, D. C.   August 13, 1944

Dear Mr. Truman Gibson:

My attention has been brought to the fact that they do not allow the circulation and distribution of the Pittsburg Courier here on the post. Quite a controversy has aroused considerable confusion. Could you give me the latest War Dept. regulation on the distribution of Negro publications on military post for use in Day Room's and Service Clubs.

Could you give the official release on the Negro strength in Army.

Sincerely Yours,

Pvt. E. L. Reynolds
A.S.N. 35931780

Righting the Wrongs Heaped upon the Black Soldier

The Editor
The Pittsburgh Courier   Co. D, 47th Q.M. Regt.
Pittsburgh, Penn.   April 10, 1944

My dear Mr. Editor:

Today as never before the Nation is preparing for the greatest emergency in
the history of this country. Every man, woman, and child is being geared to
meet any possible position this country may be in. If there ever were a time
that all racial prejudices and hatred should be put aside, now it is at hand, and
the country should be unified in every possible respect. The emergency has
become so great until Congress has passed a Draft Bill to draft men for the
first time during peace-time in the history of the country into the armored
forces. Both White and Colored are being called up and everybody is doing his
or her bit to cooperate. Negroes like the White are quitting their jobs to
increase the military strength of this Nation, because we all think that a nation
worth living in is worth fighting for.

But in view of this so called unity and National emergency the age-old
Monster of Prejudice has raised his head high in the Army. Overlooking the
policy of the Army to segregate the Negroes into separate companies, the
Army as a whole is not entirely prejudiced, but here is a case where this Jim-
Crow custom is coming up.

With this fast-growing Army, with so many modern inventions that are a
part of any well-equipped Army, it has been the policy of the Army to send
members of its forces from time to time to the various factories to learn first
hand the operation and maintenance of all its equipment. I imagine this has
been working out successfully as long as only Whites were being sent, but
recently the Second and Third Armies saw fit to send two Colored Soldiers to
Akron, Ohio to attend a tire maintenance school. The Army headquarters
know that the four above mentioned soldiers were Colored, but upon arrival in
Akron they were told by Lieut. Joseph J. Poggione, the commanding Officer of
the Quartermaster Detachment in Akron that he didn't think it advisable to
have both Colored and White troops attending the same classes. In view of the
situation the Colored Soldiers were forced to return to their posts, two to Fort

Custard, Mich. and the other two to Fort Ord. Calif. The Government spent a great deal of money to send these boys so far to have to return them so soon.

The four soldiers who were the victims of this unfair decision were:

Pvt. Euliss M. Looney, Service Bn., 184th F.A.

Pvt. Joseph Nibitt, Service Bn., 184th F.A.

Pvt. Walter B. Lewis, Co. D, 47th Q.M. Regt.

Pfc. Sammie K. Banks, Co. A, 47th Q.M. Regt.

The first two were from Fort Custard, Mich. and the other two from Fort Ord. Calif.

Is there nothing that can be done to right these wrongs, or to prevent such things from happening again?

Very truly yours,

A Private

2

The Dilemma of the Black Officer

> In this battalion another colored officer and I have been
> provided with a latrine, 4 urinals (capacity 20+), 7
> wash troughs (capacity 50+), 10 showers and 16 com-
> modes. This latrine set-up is adequate for a company.
> This was given to us as our latrine. . . . White enlisted
> personnel including the instructors have been indoctri-
> nated with the idea we have no command over them. . . .
> The continuous little nasty items we are subjected to are
> quite disconcerting.
>
> Second Lieutenant Lowry G. Wright

W hy did the army disrespect black officers, question their leadership abilities, and treat them so unevenly during World War II?
The answer to this question is in the fact that black officers
were generally considered unqualified to command troops, even all-black
units. According to the military, black officers never quite measured up to
Army standards. Why? Unfortunately, they suffered from a legacy of
racist epithets. No matter how educated they were, what special training
they had, or how many years they had served, black officers were viewed
as men "past the stage of youthful daring and initiative, short on education, without self-confidence or any reason for it, poorly selected and
inadequately trained for his Army job, ridiculed by whites, uneasy with
his men and perhaps not entirely trusted by them; and convinced by all
his experience that the way to survive in the Army was to avoid 'causing
trouble.' " The black officer also had "to agree with the white man and
try not to make decisions on his own, and to employ whatever devices
would protect him from the unjust, illogical, irrational hostility of the
white Army." He "might have bars put on his shoulders or stripes on his
sleeve, but those symbols alone would not imbue him suddenly with the
skills and commanding presence needed to lead men in battle."[1]

The quotations above reflect the position of the Army toward its black
officers in World War I, but evidence reveals that this attitude changed

only reluctantly, remaining generally the same throughout the Second World War. For example, Secretary of War Stimson wrote in 1940 that "leadership is not imbedded in the negro race yet and to try to make commissioned officers to lead the men into battle—colored men—is only to work disaster to both." "Colored troops," continued Stimson, "do very well under white officers but every time we try to lift them a little bit beyond where they can go, disaster and confusion follows. . . . In the draft we are preparing to give the negroes a fair shot in every service, however, even to aviation where I doubt very much if they will not produce disaster there." Finally, Stimson noted, "nevertheless they are going to have a try but I hope for Heaven's sake they won't mix the white and the colored troops together in the same units for then we shall certainly have trouble."[2]

In spite of the fact that officer candidate schools were opened and R.O.T.C. continued for blacks in 1940, "production of black officers was very slow and it was not until 1942 that appreciable numbers of blacks were graduated." Nevertheless, "black officers constituted less than 1.9% of all officers in the military by 1945." Unfortunately "none achieved general officer or flag rank during the war."[3] Why? The Army claimed that even black troops preferred white over black officers. This was not true. The only study conducted on this question during the war concluded that a majority of black troops preferred black over white officers.[4] Had the Army promoted a policy of placing black officers in command of all the all-black Army units, the percentage of black officers may have been higher. Instead, the Army adhered to a tradition of racial discrimination against the black officer.

The problem arising from the low percentage and use of black officers in World War II was vexing to the officers themselves as well as to the War Department. It stemmed largely from reports on the performance of black officers in World War I, from Secretary Stimson's belief that black troops operated more efficiently when commanded by white officers, from the War Department's rationale that black officers were unable to get the proper respect from noncommissioned black soldiers, and from the general belief that white officers were able to obtain goods and services for their men when black officers could not.[5] More than any other factors, these were the reasons that accounted for the discrimination practiced against black officers.

Those blacks who managed to achieve officer rank faced other discriminatory problems. Rather than move toward the effective placement of black officers in the regular army, the War Department became increasingly alarmed over their growing number. The Army worried over the possibility of blacks being in command of white troops and especially of white officers. The answer to this dilemma was finally written into Army policy for the first time in April 1942.[6]

The War Department decided that black officers could on rare occasions command white enlisted men, but they would be prohibited from commanding white officers during the war crisis. One post commander even went so far as to state that no black officer could ever hope to outrank his lowest-ranked white officers. Another commander declared that white first lieutenants would be superior to a black officer with the rank of captain. In other commands blacks who managed to rise above the rank of first lieutenant were almost always stationed among units with black staffs. If a situation occurred in which a black officer outranked white officers, the army systematically instituted a shifting program. The black officer usually ended up commanding a noncombatant black service unit.[7]

The policy that no black officer would be given a command position in charge of white officers paid homage to racism and indicated the general thinking of the War Department and the officials of the officer candidate schools, even though it contradicted in spirit Secretary Stimson's assurance to Hastie that the schools would be opened on a nonsegregated and nondiscriminatory basis. Though the schools were opened, Hastie reasoned that when a black soldier graduated from a particular school and was then restricted to the command of black and white noncommissioned officers or to noncombatant service units, this reflected the paradoxical character of the Army. He believed, too, that the one difficulty with the assignment and promotion of black officers arose from the fact that white officers were routinely assigned to command duty while black officers had to wait for the War Department to indicate specifically that a particular position be filled by a black.[8]

Because Hastie hoped to strengthen his argument for the elimination of segregated Army units and facilities with the results of integrated training at the officer candidate schools, he was quick to point out the racist overtones of the War Department's announcement in 1943 that the white graduates of the schools had risen to the ranks of captains and lieutenant colonels in less than two years while no black graduate had been promoted beyond the rank of first lieutenant.[9]

A glaring example of the discriminatory promotion system is found in the records of two officers of the 93rd Division, one black, Second Lieutenant Martin Winfield, and one white, First Lieutenant Raymond Grube. Lieutenant Winfield was assigned to the 3rd Battalion of the 25th Infantry Regiment as communications officer. He received this assignment after graduating second in his class from infantry school and first in his class from communications school. During the Bougainville campaign, he worked on very difficult terrain with inadequate supplies and personnel. His commander turned in a report that indicated the high proficiency of Winfield's work on the island. When Winfield became crytography officer on Green Island, he again displayed exceptional skill and high efficiency. As late as February 1945, Winfield was still a second lieutenant. On the other hand, Lieutenant Grube was motor officer of the 1st Battalion of the 25th Infantry. As the motor officer, he illegally ordered and installed a motor on his civilian car. For this offense, Grube was court-martialled, found guilty of embezzling government property, and fined $300. One year later he was promoted to captain and given a command position.[10]

Another example of discrimination against black officers involves two blacks who attended the Judge Advocate General's Officer Candidate School. They graduated from this school with top honors but were assigned to nonlegal positions. Truman K. Gibson, Jr., protested these assignments. He complained to Assistant Secretary of War John J. McCloy that it was "a sad commentary that one of these men is wasting away as a Claims Officer at Fort Huachuca while the other has been attached in a nonlegal capacity to Selective Service Headquarters." Gibson asked McCloy to disregard the probability of discrimination but consider how useful these men would be in the administration of military justice. Gibson's reasoning apparently appealed to McCloy's sense of military efficiency, for McCloy undoubtedly put pressure on Brigadier General Russell B. Reynolds, General Staff Corps Director of the Military Personnel Division, who ordered the black officers assigned to positions more suited to their training.[11]

In numerous instances, black officers were humiliated, denied military protocol, disrespected, and forced to be "Uncle Toms." For example, a young white private from Virginia stated: "Gosh, I just had to salute a damn nigger lieutenant. Boy, that burns me up." Black officers themselves spoke of their problems, especially in the South: "To go to a nearby city is to invite trouble. Not only from civilian police but more often from the military police, who are upheld in any discourtesy, breach of discipline, arrogance and bodily assault they render the Negro officers."[12] The selections that follow vividly recreate the dilemma of the black officer in World War II.

NOTES

1. Arthur D. Barbeau and Florette Henri, *The Unknown Soldiers: Black American Troops in World War I* (Philadelphia: Temple University Press, 1974), 68–69.

2. Henry L. Stimson Diary, September 27, 1940, Yale University Library, New Haven, Connecticut.

3. Department of Defense, *Black Americans in Defense of Our Nation* (Washington, D.C.: Office of Deputy Assistant Secretary of Defense for Equal Opportunity, 1981), 33.

4. Samuel A. Stouffer and Others, *The American Soldier: Adjustment During Army Life*, Vol. I (Princeton, New Jersey: Princeton University Press, 1949), 580–582.

5. Stimson Diary, January 24, 1942; Stimson, private interview with McGeorge Bundy, Box 188, Series III, Henry L. Stimson Papers, Yale University Library, New Haven Connecticut; Henry L. Stimson and McGeorge Bundy, *On Active Service in Peace and War* (New York: Harper, 1948), 164–165; William L. White, "Negro Officers, 1917 and Now," *Survey Graphic*, XXXI (April 1942), 133; James C. Evans, private interview with author, 3533 Warder Street, N.W., Washington, D.C., October 6, 1974.

6. Memorandum, Hastie to Patterson, February 10, 1942; Patterson to Hastie, February 17, 1942, Box 151, Patterson Papers; Jean Byers, *A Study of the Negro in Military Service* (Washington, D.C.: Department of Defense, 1947), 40.

7. Byers, *A Study of the Negro in Military Service*, 41.

8. Memorandum, Hastie to Major Campbell C. Johnson, January 10, 1941, Campbell C. Johnson Papers, Moorland-Springarn Research Center, Howard University Library, Washington, D.C.; Stimson Diary, January 13, 1942; Judge William H. Hastie, private interview with author, U.S. Court of Appeals, Washington, D.C., March 6, 1974.

9. Letter, Hastie to author, October 8, 1974; Hastie, private interview with author, March 8, 1974; Hastie, "Negro Officers In Two Wars," *Journal of Negro Education*, XII (Summer 1943), 323.

10. Byers, *A Study of the Negro in Military Service*, 125–128.

11. Memorandum, Gibson to McCloy, December 14, 1944, Military Personnel Division; Directive, Reynolds to Military Personnel Division, December 28, 1944, General Staff, National Archives Record Group 165.

12. Quoted in Lucille B. Milner, "Jim Crow in the Army, *New Republic*, CX, (March 13, 1944), 340.

We Have No Command over Them

Mr. T. K. Gibson Jr.   Hdq 5th Bn STU SCU #1437
717 T St. N.W.   Camp Shelby, Miss
Washington, D.C.   May 13, 1943

Dear Mr. Gibson:

I am one of several A6D officers stationed at this camp. I admit I did not
desire to come anyplace in Mississippi, as evidenced by a letter I sent to the
Commanding General 4 So Command requesting reassignment elsewhere that
was disapproved.

However, I came here with an open mind free from any feeling as such. No
sooner, however, than I arrived things began to happen. I called the post for
transportation and arrangements were being completed when I was asked
where was I? I replied in the colored waiting room Hattiesburg Southern
Railroad Station. Retort: "You will have to get out the best you can." The
switchboard operator who seconded the teller (extension 620), refused to con-
nect me with the officer of the day or any officer on the post in authority. This
was approximately 9:00 PM Saturday night, May 6.

I brushed the incident aside and waited until 11:30 PM and took a bus into
the post.

Since being here some of the outstanding shatterens of morale are herewith
listed:

1. Messing with enlisted men—since changed

2. Inability to get public transportation to and from *time* normally. No
bus is run from town to the post for colored soldiers during the hours from
7:00 PM to 11:00 PM, and from 11:00 to 4:00 AM. Busses coming out
during day are rarities.

3. In this batallion another colored officer and I have been provided
with a latrine: 4 urinals (capacity 20+), 7 wash troughs (capacity 50+), 10
showers and 16 camodes. This latrine set-up is adequate for a company. This
was given to us as our latrine.

4. Other latrines are designated for White Enlisted Personnel Only.
Yes, there are latrines for the trainees.

5. We are separated by being placed in a whole building (two of us)
when there was adequate space in the building so designated for P.C. work.

6. White enlisted personnel including the instructors have been indoc-
trinated with the idea we have no command over them. This is evidenced by

the fact that even when we desire records we have been instructed not to go to the record clerk directly but to see the PC who is incharge, a white lieutenant, and he in charge requests the record and have them sent to us.

7. The club facilities set up for officers (club and mess) are wholly inadequate in proportion.

8. The continous little nasty items we are subjected to are quite disconcerting.

9. Enlisted (trainees) colored men are used to clear up the quarters of the permanent enlisted cadre (all white).

10. Trainees are handled like babies regard treatment and man regard work.

This is being forwarded to you because I feel in your capacity you can get some clarification of the whole.

I definitely feel that all colored cadre, including instructors in the three battalions, designated as colored training units would to a large extent clarify the existing condition. This is as true of officer personnel as enlisted personnel.

Yours for results

Lowry G. Wright
2D Lt A6D

My typewriter has been delayed and I fear I would be insulted if I requested in this battalion to use one used by Whites.

White Officers and Treatment of Black Troops

Washington and Lee University
Lexington, Va.
Aug. 23, 1943

Mr. Gibson:

In reply to your letter of August the twentieth as to my reactions toward the work here at the Special Service School. I haven't any thing but praise for this army school. Without a doubt, it is the most liberal school for it's location in the United States. It is too bad that all the officers in the armed forces can't attend this school. Why do I say this? My reason is based on these facts. There is no discrimination in the housing or quartering of officers as for living up or down stairs. The Negro officers are not put in the same platoon or company. No segregation in the mess-hall or class rooms. When the school gives a social it is for everyone. I do believe that I could have danced with a WAC officer at the last dance and nothing would have been said. (But I didn't) White and Negro Officers use the same officer's Club. Infact I am a member of the Officers' Club for I received my membership card just the other day. We swim in the same swimming pool on the same day, at the same time irrespective of color. If this can be done in Virginia where Lee (General) is as much alive today as he was eighty years ago, I am quite sure that it could be done throughout the United States in all army schools and camps. Don't lose sight of the fact that there are many southerners here attending school.

I am saying again. One of the main things missing here is someone who is a Negro to lecture to white officers on how to treat Negro troops. I have had any number of white officers who are at a loss as to how Negro troops should be treated. We, or Negro troops aren't any different from white troops but they are made different by these white officers. To me it seems as if it would be quite fitting if the war department would get out a lecture on "how Negro troops should be treated" and let that lecture be delivered by a Negro Officer who has had experience. If the lecture is gotten out by the War Department the officer need not have any experience. I am suggesting that a Negro be put on this faculty if possible.

At present I am the Special Service Officer of the 370th Infantry of the 92nd Division and have been for eight months. My work is up to par for I was congratulated by the Chief of Staff of the 92nd Division personally for doing a nice piece of work in my regiment. The nice piece of work was, winning all the events but three in a division tract meet; plus having or winning the basketball championship in the division.

Mr. Gibson, I would appreciate it very much if you would let me know if a job comes up that I am qualified to do. By profession, I am a Comprehensive Tester. Had a special course in testing and worked for three years as a tester. I would give the tests during the months that school was in session, and would help to work out the median, mode, quadtile deviation and correlations during the summer. I am qualified I believe to give the Army General Classification Test. I would appreciate your kindness in helping me secure a job of this kind.

Thanks for finding time to answer my letter.

Yours very truly,

1st Lt. Edward T. Mayfield

P.S. The WAC mentioned is white.

The Case of the Negro Officer in the U. S. Army

Mr. Carl Murphy, President   June 26, 1943
Afro-American Newspapers
SUBJECT: The case of the Negro Officer in the United States Army.

TO: TO WHOM IT MAY CONCERN

I have come before you today to plead the case of the Negro Officer in the United States Army. His responsibility to the government and the request being made to him by the Negro soldier. Our purpose is two fold and delicate. It is delicate because this government at war has not yet agreed to accept the Negro soldier as a definite part of the fighting machine. Where the laxity on the part of the Army to accept the Negro soldier lies, I do not know. History has proven, above all, that we are loyal.

Gentlemen, I would like for you to picture the position I, or any other Negro officer, holds here at Keesler Field. In the first place Keesler is reluctant to accept the Negro soldier. Instead of definitely making or upholding the War Department laws, there have been unofficial efforts down here to relegate the Negro soldier to the same position that he held in civilian life. They have tried to by-pass the question by giving him a substitute for the advantages enjoyed by the white soldier. It is my official belief that if Keesler Field left the race question alone it would solve itself. Instead, Negroes are segregated by unofficial sanction. Take for instance the War Department theatre. Here, the Negro is segregated against the orders of the War Department. Signs referring to race and creed are hung in direct difiance to regulations. The Negro soldier is seated to one side of the theatre. Yet when the theatre is crowded the white soldier comes over into the Negro section for a seat. It is my judgement that racial prejudices are being instilled and forced upon a large group of intelligent and progressive minded white soldiers. This soldier is forced not to sit with the Negro soldier uhtil the place is crowded and then the color bar is forgotten. If it can be forgotten so quickly, why is it established. This is one instance where, in my opinion, a lot of progressive thingking white soldiers see their government sanction the same thing we are fighting for.

In the case of the post exchanges, this field has attempted to solve this problem in a true Southern, undemocratic manner. It has tried like most states in solving the Negro question by giving them a substitute—an inferior substitute. They have placed a small inadequate exchange (part time) on the boundry of the Negro squadron areas. This exchange is inferior in supplies, space and facilities. Then, they have seen fit to exclude the Negroes from using the dining room of the other exchanges. Here again is a violation of the regulations.

In the case of the Service Club, this field offers the very poor substitute to its Negro soldiers—the day room. I don't have to say that this is no substitute. For a day room cannot offer the entertainment and facilities of a service club. The same situation is true of the library. Several Negro soldiers went to the library to borrow books and almost created a calamity. Although the men there invited them back at any time and acted cordial, the next morning they set up a poor excuse for a library in the day room of a Negro squadron. Gentlemen, this action could not or would not have been taken without the command of some commissioned officer.

Then, there is the most painful case of all. I a commissioned officer of the United States Army, am denied the rights and privileges of an officer. I am excluded by members of my own rank and station in the Army. I am denied the privilege to use the Officer's Club. Although members of my race are used as waiters and general help around the club, I am denied the privilege of using it. It has been a source of embarrassment for a Negro soldier working there to ask me if I am denied the privilege of the club. I ask you, gentlemen, what would you say or do if a soldier, who respected you as an officer of the Army, knew that you, an officer sworn to uphold and defend the principles of this democracy, were being denied the very thing you are and asking them to lay down their life for. How can we demand the respect of men under our command when we are not respected by members of our own rank.

Gentlemen, I have seen men come from States of the South where my race is persecuted beyond belief. I have seen them come cowed. I have seen them come with no self respect. I have seen them come eager in the belief of what their state did to them, their government would not uphold. I have heard them upon entering the Army say, that an Army post is under Federal regulations and that they would not be subjected to injustices of State rule. Yet these men have been let down by the very government they swore to uphold. They see their government inflict upon them and a large number of the white race a segregation neither one desires.

They see a great Federal government built on the principle of "Liberty and justice for all" being swayed by sectional customs and traditions that were defeated in a war seventy-five years ago.

Gentlemen, at the first touch of these injustices, the men of my race naturally turn to me, a commissioned officer, to explain the reasons and policies of the government. Am I to tell them that the great and powerful government of the United States of America is being swayed by a small state government? I ask you, gentlemen, what am I to say? Am I to admit that we are fighting for ideals for another country or people when America has not yet established these ideals at home? These are the problems of the Negro officer. He is being constantly appealed to by the men under his command to correct the injustices that exist on the post and yet, the post, knowing that these injustices do exist, take no step to correct them. What would you do?

These type of conditions seriously injure the morale of the Negro soldier and tend to give him an air of indifference that he is sure to carry with him to civilian life. I have heard it expressed openly, hundreds of times by Negro soldiers that they would just as soon give their life fighting the injustices inflicted upon him right here in the United States than to fight to correct the injustices of other people they know nothing about on foreign soil. This state of mind has been brought about by the reluctance of the federal government to uphold firmly the rights of all men.

Gentlemen, it would be foolish of me to expect that these injustices could be wiped out immediately. For that reason I am making several suggestions that would not solve the problem but would alleviate the tenseness of the situation and increase the morale of the Negro troops.

Let the government solve the problem in the Southern States just as the Negro problem has been solved in the north. I set myself up as no authority on racial relations but the north has solved its racial problem by placing in the Negro neighborhood facilities equal in every aspect to the facilities in the white neighborhood. It is a known fact that any minority group likes to be with their own people. Hence, the different nationality sections of any large city. So it would appear to me if the Army placed equal facilities within the areas occupied by Negro troops then there would be no race problem. For no soldier would have the desire to walk ten blocks to a service club when there is one across the street. Understand, gentlemen, the facilities would or should be the same or else the desire would arise for them to go to the best. If this is done then there would not have to be any restrictions because there would be no desire. You say to yourselves that this is costly. Well, gentlemen, ask any Southern state where segregation is practised and they will say it is costly.

It costs money to segregate. I cite as an example of this type of race relations the City of Chicago. Chicago has no jim crow laws. Its citizens, black or white, are free to go anywhere. But, Chicago has no trouble because long ago she understood that give the minority group its own facilities and they have no desire to leave their neighborhood. Yet Chicago restricts no one group or race.

In conclusion, I say that the Army is not only to build soldiers but useful citizens in the post war regardless of race. However, if these injustices continue to exist I am fearful that the United States shall see one tenth of her Army indifferent and somewhat disappointed in their belief of our creed, "Liberty and justice for All."

The Colored Officers Are Fed Up

Mr. C. A. Scott,   ENROUTE TO FORT HUACHUA, ARIZONA
General Manager   A Noncom in the 92nd Division
Atlanta Daily World   November 23, 1943

Dear Sir:

May I extend my heartfelt congratulations to you and your paper for the article printed awhile back concerning the 92nd Division. It really pictured quite a few existing evils that the Negro soldiers and officers are forced to come in contact with. A thousand congratulations to you.

May I add that the conditions are really appalling. This outfit is the most rotten outfit in the World. We have no program—we only walk, walk, walk. These daily hikes are made only to keep us away from the garrisons, because the program made out by Colonel Bailer's, Chief of Staff, is really unfit for an inductee.

The colored officers are fed up with it. They know that they are not being treated fairly, but there is nothing they can do. Whenever they go over bounds, they are simply re-classified. Though we have some brilliant Negro officers they are never promoted. Some of these officers hold degrees from the nation's outstanding universities, while white officers come from Ft. Benning, ignoratnt as the days are long. In a few months they are captains. The poor colored officer who is his superior in service, tact and etc. is still a Second Lt.

General Almond is rotten. Possibly the news never reached you but there are several rumors that he has been fired at by soldiers who despise him. Whenever he is introduced, there is the usual "Boo."

When General Davis inspects the P.T.U., our cripples are hidden. These are men who are walked "to death" and are physically unfit to carry on. They are really sapping the life out of the fellows. The morale is at as low an ebb as in a whore-house. Nobody gives a d—- about what happens. Unless something is done, there will be an internal revolution. They are afraid for us to have our rifles after we leave the field. They search daily for ammunition. I swear to God it is pathetic.

It is true that I am a non-commissioned officer in the outfit, but I shall withhold my name because it will only get me "busted" and a term in the guard house. I ask that you even destroy this letter after reading it. The name on the envelope may or may not be mine.

One who desires you to know

Please Help Me!

The Afro-American Newspapers   December 28, 1943

Dear Sloan:

How's the boy? I have been reading of the excellent work which you have been doing—congratulations and keep pushing.

The main reason I am writing to you is that I am confronted with a situation I cannot successfully cope with and I need help. As you probably know I am in the 92nd Division. Much has been said about the division in the Negro newspapers recently, but now the fight, which threatened to be a roaring fire, has apparently died out. Sloan, this is not the time to stop! Being in the division, and in the army too much protesting and fighting leaves me open for a charge of sedition. But you are now a part of the Negro press, our greatest fighting weapon, and are therefore in position to help me.

Prejudice is a vicious and subtle thing here in Huachuca. Discriminatory acts are performed in such a manner that there baseness is blanketed under vague military terms and "customs of the service." General Davis, recently here for investigation, turned in a report that all was well in the division. It would appear as if he is performing his job, a military figure-head, more than well.

We recently returned from a series of problems on the field, which showed the division to be ill-prepared for combat. Why? Was it the inefficient functioning of Negro officers; was it that Negro troops do not make good soldiers? No, No Sloan, none of these is the reason. The 18th Corps Commander brought out the real reason in his final critique. That reason was the inefficient functioning of the staffs in the division and those staffs are all most entirely lily white.

All this would probably be denied if made public, but these things are truths. I know.

We Negroes appear to be content with the knowledge that we now have Negro officers in the army. We must not be content with that fact alone. The 92nd and 93rd Divisions are all Negro divisions and they should be commanded by Negro officers *only*, and I mean from the division commander to the second lieutenant. The many indications of unrest in this 92nd Division is the result of the feeling that the mass of the soldiers here in Huachuca have men in this division are mostly Southerners and it is their opinion that in the army they should be no longer under command of whites since this is a Negro division.

There is much more I could say, Sloan, but excessive words are not necessary. You now know the basic facts. Please help me! See that these facts are gotten into the Afro-American and into the Spokesman. I promise you I will continue to do what little I can but help is needed from the outside and is needed desperately.

Thank you in advance and try not to let me down.

Sincerely,

A Negro Officer

No Longer Needed?

CHICAGO DEFENDER
What the People Say
3435 Indiana Avenue
Chicago, Ill.,

SERVICE CLUB
United State Army
Fort Ord, Calif.
10 January 1944

Dear Editor:

We can't understand why so many crack Negro combat units are being broken up during this period of the war. Could it be that our skilled soldiers are no longer needed to defend our great country?

We like several other of our fellow comrades have been transferred from crack combat training units to Quartermaster Truck Companies, where our specialized training is no longer needed, and where we have very little or no chance for advancement. In serveral companies here, we have skill instructors in practically every field from such organizations as: Field Artillery Replacement Training Centers of Ft. Sill, Okla., and Ft. Bragg, N.C., Infantry Training Regiment, Ft. McClellan, Ala., Infantry Replacement Training Center, Camp Wheeler, Ga., Air Base Security Bn., Camp Butler, N.C. The average cadreman here has had at least two years of specialized training in his field. Their IQ's range from 105 to 134, yet they have been denied the opportunity granted other Enlisted Men to attend Officer Candidate Schools, ASTP, and other specialized Training courses.

We feel that we could be of greater service to our country as Officers or specialized Training courses open for Negro Troops, or is it that our country is now in position to promote useless training?

A Group of Negro Officers

A Figure Head

Atty. Truman K. Gibson   Co. A 66th Med. Trg. Bn.
Civilian Aide to Secy. of War   M. R. T. C.
White House   Camp Barkeley, Texas
Washington, D. C.   Feb. 13th, 1944

Dear Mr. Gibson:

Your letter of the 20th was received and I must say it was received most
cordially. It proved evident that you are interested in acquiring equality in
army camps.

Camp Barkeley is one of the largest army camps in Texas and the only
Medical Replacement Training Center in the south. We, approximately two
hundred of us, were the first Colored to be stationed here, now however, there
are roughly over five hundred of us. The latter of which will replace us since
our training is nearing completion. None of our commissioned officers are
Colored despite the fact that located here are Officer Candidate and Medical
Administration schools. There are relatively few of our boys who attend these
schools and those who are fortunate to finish are immediately shipped to Ft.
Huachuca or elsewhere. Up until a few weeks ago, we could attend only one
theater out of five on the post. This theater was an open air theater which we
could only attend when the weather was favorable. By protest, we acquired the
right to attend any theater of our choice but are forced to contend with being
segregated. We have buses which are local and those that run to and from
camp, on the local buses we are compelled to sit in the back, threaten by the
drivers if we refuse. Despite the fact that buses run all day back and forth to
camp at regular one half hour entervals, we have only three which we may
ride. Our buses are crowded to the extent that it is practically impossible to
close the doors and yet extra buses has been refused us. The camp provides
army buses that carry soldiers to town but we aren't allowed to ride them. Our
sector is completely ostrasized from the camp proper so we rarely see the
other group. Our living quarters are terrible being formerly C.C.C. barracks,
located just in from of the camp cess pool. When I first arrived, our sector
actually looked like a garbage dump in comparison with the rest of the camp.
We spent three weeks cleaning the place before we could begin training. There
is also a quarter master outfit stationed near us, this outfit was here at least six
months before we arrived. It consist of no lest than nine companies. These
nine companies, including our two, are forced to use a small post-exchange

capable of convienely servicing no lest than three companies the most. The nearest post-office is the other side of the camp; approximately 2½ miles away. We have one service club shared by both divisions. It is poorly equipped having nothing but writting tables, a pingpong table and a piano. We don't have a library, a chapel or a chaplain. We conduct our own services in one of the poorly constructed class rooms. We have had Joe Louis to give a boxing exhibition and two dances in the three months I've been here. We were told that if we wanted entertainment we would have to provide it ourselves.

It was to my amazement, a short time ago, when I had the opportunity of visiting the German concentration camp here at Barkeley to observe a sign in the latrine, actually segregating a section of the latrine for Negro soldiers, the other being used by the German prisoners and the white soldiers. Seeing this was honestly disheartening. It made me feel, here, the tyrant is actually placed over the liberator.

Many of the existing conditions we discussed with our company commander but to no avail. Being himself a Texan and probably accoustomed to the maltreatment of Negroes, we find it extremely difficult to obtain his assistance. I was severly repremanded by the company commander, one afternoon, after a class on court martial, for asking "To who could we, as Colored soldiers turn to if we were innocently maltreated." He asked me to be specific. I spoke of the treatments we received in town, on camp buses and theaters. My question was very diplomatically ignored and after class, in his office, he called me a trouble maker and gave me an order not to even discuss the subject with the other fellows, who were aware of the existing conditions as myself. There are many reasons in my estimation which makes our company commander, Lt. Schuessle unfit for leadership.

About a month and a half ago, we had the exteem priviledge of having a Colored Colonel visit us, namely Hamilton Neal. At this particular time, we had practically no form of amusement, not even a service club. At this time the only way we could get to town which was eleven miles away, was to hitch hike or walk. Our only form of recreation was the outdoor theater in which even here we were segregated. Colonel Neal said nothing in the way of encouragement to us. We listen to him, of course, for we realized that his was a position rearly achieved by a negro. He spoke of his pleasure in viewing our i.q. records and told us we should be proud to be at camp Barkeley. I suppose Colonel Neal was sent as a moral builder but to us he completely failed in his mission, for we looked upon him as a figure head.

Although we have trained under dire handicaps, we have made an excellent record. Our talent is some of the camp's best, our basketball team, of whom much controversy was made before being allowed to enter the league, is now aspiring for first place. We have just returned off a ten day Biovauc and we received the commendation that our group simulated the problem of evacuation of casualties under battle conditions better than any group who have gone before us. If afforded the opportunity, we could be a great asset to the camp.

I realize that as a soldier there is very little I can do in remedying the conditions that exist in the outside world. I am of the opinion, the undemocratic conditions that is in army camps are caused by prejudice officials and if the right sources were informed, immediate steps would be taken for correction. I sincerely hope that from the meagre information I have given you that it might prove advantageous in your ultimate objective, of course, in writting, I couldn't tell every thing for fear of boring you or perhaps making you think of my possible exaggeration but I assure you, I have written only the concised facts.

                                                            Sincerely yours,

                                                    Pvt. Bert B. Babero

Use of the Term Nigger

SUBJECT: Conditions existing in the California Arizona   June 2, 1944
Maneuver Area affecting the Negro Soldier.

TO: The Reverend Dr. Adam Clayton Powell Jr., New York, N.Y.

1. The following is a small list of incidents which have occurred within the past few months, in California Maneuver Area which may draw to your attention the deplorable plight of the Negro soldier and Officer in the Army of the United States.

a. On August 31st 1943, a white private told a Negro Officer who had reprimanded him for not observing the ordinary military courtesy of a salute, if you would take your clothes off and lay them on the ground I would salute them but I wouldn't salute anything that looks like you. The Officer called a Captain and told him of the incident. In the presence of the private, the Captain said, "Well Lieutenant, what do you want me to do about it?" The Officer reported the matter to the major under whom he was serving immediately. The Major advised "I wouldn't make an issue of the incident if I were you." The Officer insisted on preferring a charge against the soldier. He was transferred from the post three days later. He was never notified that the soldier would be tried on any charge. Three weeks later he requested the Commanding Officer of the Post to investigate and received the information that the soldier had been tried by Summary Court and fined $18.00 and restricted to the area for 30 days. The organization was scheduled to move and did move from the area in less than one week.

b. In contrast with the above is this case. A Negro soldier on a post in this area committed a minor violation by driving five men in a jeep for a distance of about three quarters of a mile. A colonel saw him load up the vehicle and sent a white corporal in a vehicle to chase him and get his name. When the driver reached his company motor pool, the white soldier drew up and proceeded to get the information asked by the colonel. In the meantime, a Negro Corporal witnessing the proceedings asked the white Corporal, Why don't you mind your own business. You are not an M.P. The Corporal reported the incident to the Colonel who demanded disciplinary action against the Negro Corp. He was tried by Summary Court, reduced to the grade of Private, fined $12.00 per month for two months and restricted to the area for thirty days.

He was more severly dealt with for arguing with a Corp. (white) than a white boy was dealt with for insulting a Negro Officer. A Negro Officer on the post protested the sentence and within 24 hours, an attempt was made to trump up a charge against the Officer, on which to Court Martial him.

c. At another post, three Negro Soldiers have recently been Court Martialed and sent to prison for Five years, for telling a Major that they were not physically fit for a heavy laboring detail to which they had been assigned. Yet, these men had all before been recommended by the Medical Authorities for discharges because of their physical conditions.

d. On or about 20 January five other men who are in the same category as the above three were told by a Major when they protested that they could not do pick and shovel work, "If I had you Niggers in my section of the country, I'd make you work." Then about ten minutes later he threatened to Court Martial a Negro Officer because the Officer protested his statement.

e. On 31 January, this same Major told the Commanding Officer of that company of all very physically broken up men, "If any person is too sick to work he is too sick to eat, so if any man here can't work, don't feed him. Give him half rations; give him quarter rations. Feed them nothing but soup." He added that he'd come by at mealtime from time to time to see that his order was being carried out.

f. Four Negro Officers were assigned to work with this group of "Cripples" in December. When they arrived on the post they found signs on the latrines of the post "COLORED TROOPS NOT ALLOWED." These officers photographed these signs the following day. That afternoon the Commanding Officer of the post removed the signs. Later that evening he called in these Officers and told them that the post was a "Keg of Dynamite" and he wanted us to tell our boys to over-look the little insults and incidents, and not start any disturbance. They couldn't win anyway, and after all only northern Negroes are insulted by the use of the term Nigger. A Southern boy understands that the white man means no harm when he uses that term. It is needless to say that the Negroes told him that they would not carry any such message to the boys and it is needless to say that they didn't.

g. Thruout the area, military authorities have intervened to see that business places, such as beer gardens serve either white or Negro soldiers, and have used their "Off Limits" rule to enforce the Edict. The result? In each town one might find one or two Negro owned "joints" where Negro soldiers and officers must go after hours for recreation. In every other place if a Negro goes in he's told, "We don't serve colored." Throughout the large town of San Bernardino, California, up to a few weeks ago, signs were posted on the window of many business places "WE CATER TO WHITE TRADE ONLY." Those signs were removed at the request of a Priest, a Rabbi and a Negro clergyman. The army never once attempted to remove this public insult.

A Negro Soldier

Discredited Black Officers

MR. P. B. YOUNG
The Norfolk Journal and Guide   July 27, 1945

My dear Sir:

We are writing first to assure you of the general attitude of the personnel of
the Division representing you in the Pacific and to simultaneously express
concurrence in thought as expressed in your opinion of the Conference at San
Francisco. We see no logic in such conferences when within the hearts of our
contemporaries there remains that discrimination against race which nullifies
the acts put in for a show of the future. There's no use in holding the penny
before the or our eye—we must exert more and constant pressure through
existing and future contacts and channels to correct the practices going on
here—now. There is an increased fervor to depress, discredit and criticize the
Negro Officer—and a direct disregard for the ability of Medical and Dental
Officers of color to handle the Division Surgeon's Office. The members of the
Medical Department are 97% of the force now in the division with a pending
and possible reduction of that percentage by one.

The Senior Medical and Dental Officers of our race have not been given the
ordinary privilege of assuming leadership in either of the Division Medical Staff
vacancies. A general influx of white officers of company and field grades of
most all components arrive in large numbers, and to all intents and purposes
have usually, with few exceptions proved to be washouts from white organizations now at the front or desk workers fresh the states.

The length of time in service for many of the colored officers dates to the
period before Pearl Harbor. These officers are passed over, given ratings of
efficiency below their merits, are placed on prearranged flop assignments in
order to discredit them or have apparent, cause for action being brought
against them.

Neglects on the part of the various staffs (white)—regimental and higher—
have telling affect on the morale and functioning of troops of our racial strain.

Aside from being a-slap-in-the-face to the Negro Medical and Dental profes-
sions, the recent arrival of a white Surgeon to direct the service, permits us no
alternative in thought; either we are not considered competent to assume the
office and its responsibilities or the Division Staff cares to have only a lily-white
Staff—which has the spectre of racial superiority or prejudice as the cause.
We are not fighting to preserve that idealogy. The office of Dental Surgeon has

been vacant for four months, the Surgeon's Office for over a month. No attempts were made to turn these offices over to the senior Medical Dental Officers of the Division. The enlisted personnel feel these acts keenly. We cannot stand idle, we need outside help.

We therefore solicit your good offices and unbiased opinion on the matter. Request that if you find our problem sufficiently important to the race as a whole, that segment of service we represent, then contact the War Department with all the ferver of that race, through all available channels now open or to be opened.

The Division Psychiatrist now one of our officers has not been given his proper rank of Major since his appointment but several white officers have been brought in and given priority of colored officers who have been holding particular assignments without prejudice and competently.

These are only a few of the facts, if we can get them to you, for your appraisal and liquidation if possible, with a more favorable outlook for the Negro Officer in a Negro Division—(so called) but with lily-white staffs to which we must pay homage or get the benefits of a Courts-Martial whose members' minds were formed and trained in Texas, Alabama, Arkansas and Georgia.

We think that all agents should set about, *together*, and at once to curb this action.

Yours very truly,

The Officers of the 93rd Inf. Div.

3

Laborers in Uniform

> We are a group of permanent K. P.'s. We are allowed no
> other advancement whatsoever. It is true that K. P. push-
> ers (Head K. P.) are made Cpl. and Sgt. but the K. P.'s
> themselves are a miserable group that will be worked like
> slaves without any ratings to speak of. We are confined
> to this job not because we are not fit for anything else
> but because we are dark. We are referred to on this post
> as "that nigger squadron at the end of the field."
>
> 328th Aviation Squadron
> and 908th Quartermaster Company

America's involvement in the Second World War did not produce
a revolution in the way a majority of its black soldiers were
perceived, treated, and utilized. Their usage reflected what had
been the official policy of the armed forces in World War I and other
major American wars. Most of the black soldiers then as well as in World
War II were denied entry to special training schools and systematically
placed in labor and supply units.

When the U.S. finally entered the war as a fighting participant, blacks
wondered if they would be assigned to combat units or be restricted to
labor battalions. Although they were assigned to every branch of the
services opened to them, the Army confined most of the troops to the
Service Forces. Blacks comprised an overwhelming majority of the Quartermaster Corps, the Corps of Engineers, and the Transportation Corps.
These assignment practices resulted in blacks being trained almost exclusively for noncombat functions as laborers, stevedores, and servants.
They ultimately represented the physical backbone of the armed forces.
The soldiers were bridge builders, ditch diggers, latrine cleaners, potato
peelers, cooks, dock workers, trash collectors, shoeshine boys, housekeepers, dishwashers, truck drivers, etc.

Some white troops were placed in the Services Forces, but the prepon-
derance of soldiers performing menial jobs was unquestionably black. This

"black work," as it was known, was reserved for black soldiers because the military considered them less educated and more effective in these areas of deployment.

A majority of blacks who either volunteered or were drafted were indeed less educated and scored lower on the Army General Classification Test (AGCT) than a majority of the white troops. But the army disregarded pleas from blacks who had technical skills and college training, and who made passable scores on the AGCT. More often than not these soldiers were grouped with the unskilled and forced to do menial tasks while "they" complained that their skills and training were wasting away.

Blacks who volunteered for the Army Air Corps Enlistment Program can serve as a glaring example of the disproportionate number of black troops assigned to the Service Forces. The creation of black and separate aviation squadrons became an embarrassment for the Army Air Corps. These squadrons were organized when the Air Command agreed to accept 2500 black soldiers as pilot trainees. They were eventually assigned to all army air fields to be utilized as the local commanders wished. More often than not the squadrons performed menial tasks. The War Department accused William H. Hastie of blowing this issue out of proportion, but Assistant Secretary of War Robert P. Patterson indirectly confirmed Hastie's accusation. In a 1942 letter to Wilbur La Roe, chairman of the Washington Federation of Churches' Committee on Civic Affairs, Patterson revealed that blacks were indeed being used mainly as labor and maintenance crews. The letter was reprinted in the *Congressional Record*. In it Patterson admitted that the aviation squadrons provided a place for men in the Army Air Force who did not qualify for more technical duties. He went on to say that "the duties they (black) perform are to a large extent labor and housekeeping jobs that have to be done at every Air Force base." But Patterson modified his statement, explaining that "while there are no white units actually named 'aviation squadrons (separate)' there are many white headquarters squadrons which perform the same type of duties at Air Force installations."[1]

Hastie disagreed vehemently with Patterson. He believed the aviation squadrons were created to provide a place for blacks rather than mix them with the regular Air Force units. Thus he objected to Patterson's efforts to whitewash the fact that 95 percent of the blacks who had entered the Air Force had been assigned to these aviation squadrons, regardless of their ability, by announcing publicly that they did not qualify for more technical duties. Hastie had discovered that there was no attempt by the Air Command to prevent the assignment of men with superior abilities to these labor units. There was no reason to question Hastie's findings since Secretary Stimson had admitted in his diary that "the Army had adopted rigid requirements for literacy mainly to keep down the number of colored troops."[2] The scores made on the AGCT determined the placement of men in the Army Air Force.

Thus, those blacks who had the capacity to make fine noncommissioned officers were denied this privilege because of a longstanding racist tradition that was simply transferred from the larger American society to the military establishment. That tradition was based on the concept that blacks in or out of uniform were innately inferior and should be kept in their place—a place somewhere below the status of whites. This status mirrored the central theme of America's view of the black citizen: "Being a Negro and different from the white man, he, therefore, could not be expected ever to measure up to the white's standards of character and achievement and being of an inferior race, it was logical that he should be kept in an inferior place, which is his place."[3]

The selections in this chapter illustrate the complaints of black soldiers as they protested against what they considered discriminatory army practices based on the color of their skin and not on their training and skills.

NOTES

1. Letter, Patterson to LaRoe, March 13, 1942, Box 151, Judge Robert P. Patterson Papers, Manuscript Division, Library of Congress, Washington, D.C.; Congressional Record, 78th Congress, 1st Session (1943), 3691.

2. William H. Hastie, *On Clipped Wings; The Story of Jim Crow in the Army Air Corps* (New York: National Association for the Advancement of Colored People, 1943), 5–6; Henry L. Stimson Diary, May 12, 1942, Yale University Library, New Haven, Connecticut; *Congressional Record*, 78th Congress, 1st Session (1943), 3691; A. Russell Buchanan, *Black Americans in World War II* (Santa Barbara, California: ABC-Clio Press, 1977), 62.

3. Quoted in Howard E. Odum, *Race and Rumors of Race: Challenge to American Crisis* (Chapel Hill: University of North Carolina Press, 1943), 19; Samuel H. Stouffer and Others, *The American Soldier: Adjustment during Army Life* (Princeton, New Jersey: Princeton University Press, 1949), 599; Eli Ginzburg, "The Negro Soldier," in his *The Negro Potential* (New York: Columbia University Press, 1956), 79.

Slavery Is Now

78 Aviation Sqdr. (Sy)
Randolph Field, Texas
October 28, 1942

The Pittsburgh Courier

Dear Sir:

We are members of the 78 Aviation Sqdr, and its seem like we are not being treated fair. Most of us got trades of our own to help win this war.

But instead we are servant and ditch diggers and we want better, if it ever been slavery it is now, please help us because we want better.

They got us here washing diches, working around the officers houses and waiting on them, instead of trying to win this war they got us in ditches.

Please report this to the N.A.A.C.P. and tell them to do something about this slavery place, where a colored soldier haven't got a chance.

Most of us are young and want to learn something, and we even got some that, want, action to help win this war.

And the sad part about it that most of us are volunteers, but they didn't give us what we ask for, they gave us a pick.

If you want your colored brothers to get somewhere please report this to the President.

Pvt Jus Hill　　　　　　　　　　　　　　　　　　　　A Lone Soldier

No One's Fools

938th Quartermaster Plt.
Transportation Air Base
Fort Logan, Colorado,
April 26, 1943

The Pittsburgh Courier

Dear Sirs:

We are soldiers who are stationed in Fort Logan, Colorado. We would appreciate it to the highest if our little article was printed in your paper against discrimination.

We are colored soldiers who have been discriminated against terribly to the extent where we just can't possible stand any more. We're supposed to be representing part of the Army in which we're fighting for equality, justice and humanity so as all men, no matter of race, color, or creed, can be free to worship any way that they please.

Here on the Post we're treated like dogs. We work on different positions, sometimes for 9 or 10 hours daily. In the mornings we report to one particular job and at noon we are taken from the former one into a complete new one by orders of the white N.C.O.s (meaning Non-commissioned Officers) and at these jobs we work at a very tiresome task, one that is unfit for even a dog. And yet the whites which are supposed to be a labor battalion just sit down and watch us do their work.

Even in eating time we were told to remain at attention outside the messhall until the whites have finished eating, then we go and eat what's left over—food which is cold, tasteless and even sometimes dirty from sitting on tables from left overs.

Last week we marched in formation to the messhall and were immediately told by one of the white kitchenmen to remain outside in formation until the whites had eaten. Naturally we resented that remark and also resented it. The group then decided to leave this messhall without eating anything. Immediately our own N.C.O., who is a corporal, called us to attention, then we left without eating a single thing.

We all here have come from the Easten States such as New York, Brooklyn; in fact we're comprised of the entire five boroughs and we're not accustomed to discrimination and their rules.

Why can't we eat, live and be respected as the whites? We're constantly being cursed at, and mocked. But yet we too have to die as well as them, and even perhaps beside them. We have now come to the conclusion that before we'd be a slave, We'd rather be carried to our graves and go home to the Lord and be saved. In fact we'd rather die on our knees as a man, than to live in this world as a slave, constantly being kicked around by others just because we happen to be of the darker race.

People on the outside don't know how we boys, their boys, are being treated here and perhaps on some of the other bad camps near or far. That's the reason we're writing to you to please print this article to let everyone hear our story and give us a chance. Yes, that is all we ask—a chance to prove to the whole world that we colored poeple are no one's fools. Just give us a chance to show our color.

Skills Go to Waste

1240 F.F. Plat. E.U.T.C.
7th Prov. Tng. Regt.
Camp Claiborne, La.
October 14, 1943

Dear Mr. Gibson:

Please investigate the status of Negro Specialists and Technicians sent to this Camp to be assigned to units.

After spending months in school being trained to do specific jobs we land in labor battallions while our skills go to waste. Our assignments are permanent K.P., supply and other details.

Segregation at this camp is unbelievable. Negro soldiers are allowed to ride only in numbers of 5 all other seats belong to whites. The government owned and loaned busses do not accept Negro passengers at all.

We ask you to give these matters your immediate attention.

Yours truly,

Edgar B. Holt P.F.C.

Permanent KPs and Truck Drivers

328th Aviation Squadron
Richmond Afro-American   Pampa Army Air Field
503 N. 3rd St.   Pampa, Texas
Richmond, Va.   November 22, 1943

Dear Sirs:

I am writing this letter to acquaint you with the horrible and Unamerican treatment of the Negro Personnel of this field and beseeching you to please come to our rescue. Every Negro man on this post is absolutely fed up and disappointed with the bad treatment and discrimination, segregation and injustice imposed upon us. You must please understand that we do not resent serving our country (we are proud to serve), but we would like and want very much to serve it in a more important capacity than we are at this time. We can and would fight it if trained to do so, but as yet we hardly know that a gun, or tank, combat plans, a hand grenade, machine gun look like. We haven't had any drilling to speak of that could be classed as drilling. We had three (3) weeks of basic training. It takes that long to learn to do the manual of arms (arms are something we haven't even seen except a 45 on the M.P.'s side, ready to blow your brains out if you resent being treated like a dog or being called a nigger or a Black son of a b——.), much less call it Basic Training.

Here are a few of our handicaps (yes only a few). We hardly know how to enclose in this letter all the information on the matter, please print this in your paper. Please help us.

1st

We are a group of permanent K.P.'s. We are allowed no other advancement whatsoever. It is true that K.P. pushers (Head K.P.) are made Cpl. and Sgt. but the K.P.'s themselves are a miserable group that will be worked like slaves without any ratings to speak of. We are confined to this job not because we are not fit for anything else but because we are dark. We are referred to on this post as "that nigger squadron at the end of the field."

2nd

We are discriminated against in everything we do or take part in. The post theatre is divided off for the 328th. (That's our squadron). Government buildings also. In the hospital when we are improving from our ailments, we are used as K.P.'s there until released. In the Gym we are segregated even for a

Colored U.S.O. show. We are allowed (they think it's a privilege) the great
privilege of serving the Aviation Cadets at their social functions as waiters and
flunkies of all descriptions. Some times we are allowed nights to play games in
the Gym and they take these nights away from us to give dances for the
Cadets and officers or white enlisted men. At these functions we are subject to
all kinds of abusive languages. Such as Nigger, darkie, son of a b——, and
everything mentionable. (I won't censor this letter because I want you to get
the true picture).

3rd

The 908th Quartermaster Group Colored (which was formerly men of the
328th transferred, but still sleep and eat with us, and share all the hardships
and abusive treatments as usual. So everything I mentioned in this letter is
pertaining to them too. They are just truck drivers and are called the 908th
Quartermaster Company.

4th

There are men in our squadron that have passed the test for O. C. S. and
Aviation Cadet, but have not been sent away for training as they requested.
The majority of us are well educated and are fit for something other than
K.P.'s for the white cadets, officers and driving trucks.

5th

Some of us have special trades that we were working on before induction,
more important to the war effort than K.P.'s in the army. Some of the men
here have gone to Baking and Cooking Schools finished and back here doing
K.P., now for the whites. Some have gone to mechanic school and come back
here to be truck drivers. They just drive the trucks not given the opportunity
to work on them. We are sick of this treatment and disgusted with the K.P.
duty day in and day out. Then there are so many, many dirty jobs around here
that falls to our lot.

6th

We get no consideration from our commanding officers at all. He never
stands up for us when there is any racial clashes occur, although he is an
Eastern man (Boston, Mass.). He never thinks of trying to get us out of here,
or allowing us to quit the mess hall, or allow any request for transfers from
here to go through to headquarters. We have been here for ten months (the
10th day of February) and have been laborers and K.P.'s ever since. Why
can't we be given transfers closer home and given better jobs or at least
remain here and treated like citizens of the U. S. of America. Instead we are
still slaves, laborers and flunkies for the white personnel here.

7th

The bus that comes from town has a contract with this post to carry and bring the soldiers to town. There again we are segregated and discriminated against. Four seats (eight men) for Negroes if we are lucky enough to get on first. The remainder stands regardless if the bus is not completely loaded. If we don't get on first, all stand and like it, no protests for the seats allowed, take that and like it or have one of these Texas M.P.'s crack your skull with a 45 or a stick.

8th

The white civilians hate us and we in return despise them because they abuse us in anyway they see fit. The city police have mistreated our boys on many occasions and the military authorities never go to bat for us.

9th

The city police have pulled our men out of Government cars and beat them up. One of our boys locked himself inside the car and they broke the glass and took him out forcibly and beat him unmercifully. He got 30 days in the guard house and 15 days were solitary confinement, while he was sick with bruises from the terrible beating. Our commanding officer asked him about it and before he could tell his side of the story he (the officer) said "That's not the way I heard it." So the boy just shut up then and waited for his trial. The adjutant of our squadron wanted to beat him up again because the boy resented the attitude that they took toward his case.

10th

The main thing we resent about this place is the work we have to do without ratings, the segregation and discrimination for Negroes. The lack of opportunity for advancement.

So gentlemen if you will please see fit to help us in some way we the whole squadron and the 908th Quartermaster Company (Negro) will greatly appreciate it and will cooperate 100% if investigated.

Copies of this letter are being sent to Colonel B. O. Davis, the N.A.A.C.P. and the War Dept. at Washington.

Thanking You Very Much

328th Aviation Squadron and
908th Quartermaster Company.

Detailed to Burn Army and City Garbage

The Afro-American   December 1, 1943

Dear Sir: or Whom It May Concern.

I with fifteen enlisted men and one colored officer have been detailed to the city incinerator to burn army and city garbage. The city trucks having the priority.

We have no convenient place to eat our dinner. No decent latrine. We would appreciate it very much if you would put this to the proper authorities.

Please send a reporter to city of Newport News, Va., incinerator any day except Monday.

Please do not use my name for publication.

Hoping to hear from you soon.

Cpl. Russell L. Banks

Co. F, 2nd Bn.,
Newport News Command,
Newport News, Va.,
Camp Hill.

Lugging Five Gallon Cans of Gasoline

Mr. Truman K. Gibson
Civilian Aide to Sec'y of War
Pentagon Bldg.
Washington, D. C.

Pfc Robert E. Threet 36792551
3935th Q.M.S.J. Co.
213th Q. M. (55) Bn.
Camp Bowie, Texas
Dec. 12, 1943

Dear Sir:

It is to my deep regret that I must trouble your high Office, concerning an injustice melted out to me, in my placement in Our United States Army.

While at the Reception Center in Fort Custer, Michigan, I was told that my placement depended upon my education along the line of technical subjects. Needless to say, I was asked the usual routine. I explained as was recorded, that I had had three years of College education at the Dunbar Jr. College and the Jr. College extension school. I also explained that my major and minor were Mathematics and Chemistry respectively. I also gave my ability to read, write and speak or teach Spanish or Portugese. My occupation in civilian life was bricklaying and I explained all of this to the placement personnel.

I have had Algebra, plane geometry, solid geometry, analytical geometry in college, plane trigonometry, supherical trigonometry and College algebra. I have had both high school and College physics.

During my study in foreign language, I learned Spanish and Portuguese to a perfection of otheir phonetics and grammar. I speak, read and write them well.

As a soldier of the United States Of America, whose qualifications have been burried and blocked out and ignored or overlooked by my fellow citizens of America. I beg your intercession in my behalf.

Should I be forced to continue with a labor battalion or do I as qualified citizen or soldier have to continue lugging five gallon cans of gasoline. Sir, this is contrary to the President's promulgation that every man regardless of race, color or creed is entitled to view his country in the manner most beneficial to him.

Thanking you in advance,

Yours truly,

Pfc. R. E. Threet

You Would Think They Were Some White Man
Who Hated a Negro

Mr. Carl Murphy   March 10, 1943

Dear Sir:

I am a Negro in the armed forces for a period of six months and some odd
days. The Navy, I am very sorry to say, happens to be the branch of service I
am in. I would like you to have copies made of this letter and send them to be
printed in the Afro-American, as a favor to me and the boys in this Navy
Depot.

The morale of these boys is so low it is unbelievable. It is often you hear
any of these boys say they hope the war is soon over and they don't care who
wins. The Navy does not run this depot. The Virginia laws run it. If they don't
then it is a hell of a conincidence.

We are made to work eight hours a day and when we are through some of
us are so tired we don't want to even go on liberty. The boys in the Navy
stationed at Yorktown, Va., only work four hours a day. Other stations where
many Negroes are stationed are known to only work four hours a day. They
make us work eight hours a day seven days a week with only every eighth day
off. Every other night we have liberty. We don't even have a chaplain here.
You don't know anything about Sunday down here. Sunday is just like any
other day. You are made to do nothing but work. It is rumored that we are
made to work on the depot eight hours a day, seven days a week because they
don't want us in town when the white women are there shopping and walking
the streets, window shopping, and so forth.

When I first joined the Navy I thought I was getting something swell. I was
not looking for a easy spot or a bed of roses to lay in. I was looking forward to
going to sea, doing something useful but they will keep us in this hell hole for
the duration, so we can't ever go out to sea.

They have some Uncle Tom Negroes down here—young ones, that Clayton
Powell, Jr., often speaks of in his speeches. They will do anything to make a
showing for the white man. They call themselves guards. They wear guard
belts when on duty and carry a club. You would think they were some white
man who hated a Negro or maybe some white men have poisoned their minds
against their own shipmates, for they will take these clubs and hit any of these
boys down here for the least thing. For instance, there is a guard who comes
from New Orleans. He is a Negro. One day as we were getting ready to go to

work he asked one of the boys to go along with him for some reason I do not know. Anyhow, the boy told him he would be there in a minute. He turned his back to say something to a friend and this guard, whose name happens to be Valentine, hit him on the head with a club and hit him again after he went down on the ground. Since then he had hit other boys in the head. It does not matter they will hit you for anything. Simple things that you could be reported for. They won't report you; they will hit you in the head and try to knock your brains out.

I didn't join the Navy for that. If I got to get my brains knocked out let it be where I joined the Navy to be at "sea" or on some "battlefront." Lots of fellows would like to go to sea but they tell us we are here for the duration.

I wish the NAACP and the colored newspapers would do something to help us out. They helped get us the opportunity to join the Navy. Now, I hope they get us boys at this depot a break. We happen to be stationed at St. Juliens Creek, Portsmouth, Va. Those police in Baltimore don't knock Negroes in the head as much as these Negro guards here knock other Negroes in the head. We can't get transfers out of here at all. We are just stuck. I tell my mother and father, my relatives and friends I get along fine, but it is not true. I just don't want them to know.

If there are any young boys out in civilian life who want to join the Navy, or any old ones, just take my advice and stay out. You have your heaven in civilian life but you will catch hell here if you ever get sent to St. Juliens Creek. I am only talking about Negroes joining the Navy, not white boys. White boys get the breaks.

In some parts of the Navy a Negro does get a break but that is for so far and no more. Now at Hampton Institute, for instance, you could not ask for a better Captain of a ship or station than Captain Downs.

He is a fine man and I think one of the best. In fact all of the Gold Braids at Hampton treat you like a human being and not like a dog. If they had a man in charge of this station and a few men under him with Captain Downs' views and ideas, I think we Negroes would be better off. But, something like that is almost impossible.

I hope you will have this letter printed in the papers I named in this letter, the Afro-American, Pittsburgh Courier and the Chicago Defender. I want other Negro parents and people to read this letter. I hope you people on the outside will do something for us. We need help and need it bad. You and other people may think this is a lot of foolish talk but it is not and if something is not done, something dreadful is going to happen, as I have heard there was a riot almost here once but things were settled.

This is a fact that I am telling you of now. There was a general shakedown here where the Negroes stayed in their barracks. A shake-down similar to that they have in prison. They search the men here, they search the lockers, the clothes, under our bunks and our bed clothes looking for dangerous weapons. They found straight razors, knives, dirks and daggers. It is also said they found men with hand grenades, fifty calibre shells and different kinds of ammunition.

It is some good fellows here; you could not find better friends, but if something does not be done to straighten things out, things won't be what they used to be. Things are slowly coming to a head and all it needs is a little incident to light the fuse. We all want to do right and get the war over with but we want good, decent human treatment like we are men and not like slaves or dogs.

I met you and Mrs. Lillie Jackson in Baltimore. It was while you were fighting that case of that soldier who was shot on Pitcher Street by that Officer Bender. I hope you will be able to help us in some way. Maybe Truman Gibson in Washington may be able to do something for us, I don't know.

I place our pleas in your hands. I hope you and the public won't be offended but for certain reasons I am not signing my name. I hope you will understand. Hoping to see this in the paper soon, I remain, a

Disappointed Sailor in the U.S. Navy.

Dock Stevedores and Construction Battalions

The Afro-American Newspapers
Baltimore, Maryland   February 18, 1944

Mr. Editor:

You probably have received many letters of this type, but I think that after you read this letter you will be forced to at least investigate the case.

On behalf of the two hundred and forty-nine men formerly of the Third Signal Troop, 2nd Cavalry Division, Ft. Clark, Texas, I plead that our case be printed; so that our race will know the true conditions that face the colored soldiers.

January 21, this year, the 2nd Cavalry Division went on the alert for P.O.C. and probable shipment overseas. Our troop wasn't included in the order. *We later learned that we were to form a battalion and the ninth and twenty-seventh were going to be used as dock stevedores, unloading ships.* They informed us that since we were such a crack communications unit, supposedly the best in the Third Army, and too intelligent to become stevedores.

February 13, 1944 we left Ft. Clark for Camp Crowder to form a battalion along with the 159th Field Artillery Battalion also a crack Negro unit. Incidently they were rated ninety-eight per cent of being perfect in their firing tests given by an inspection team composed of Third Army officials.

We had visions of being the Cadre for an operations battalions because our troop is one-third radio operations and radio technicians. To our dismay we found that some brass hat in Washington had given orders to form a Construction Battalion. In this type battalion there isn't anyplace for radiomen. To be frank, we must toss away the months, in some cases, years of training that we have had since our entrance into the army. Of the fact that about seven hundred thousand dollars are being lost doesn't matter since the government will get more from the taxpayers.

If the colored soldiers aren't going to be able to use their training in technical fields why should they waste that time in school. That is why we are making such a fuss. We want to learn but we also want to be able to put this training to use after months of hard work in school.

Take my case for an example. From July 20, 1943 to November 13, 1943, I attended C.S.C.S. radio school and when I was released from school my classification was 766 on R.O.H.S. (radio operator high speed). I returned to my organization, the Third Signal Troop on Dec. 1, 1943 and promoted to technical fifth grade on Dec. 22.

On Jan. 21, this year, the 2nd Cavalry Div. was alerted and that is when the trouble began. They didn't want to make us a stevedore company; so they merged us with the 159 Field Artillery Bn. and gave us the glorified title of Signal Construction Bn.

My case is incidental; there is a technical sergeant that was in charge of repair maintenance for the division. He has spent years in radio, now he will probably be a construction chief.

At the present we are living in a condemned area and the sanitary facilities are outside across the street. We bathe, shave and catch cold in a poorly heated hut called a washroom or latrine. There are German prisoners here and they live better than we do.

With all this existing they even ask us about the four freedoms.

Having covered most of the important things, I am quite sure that if you have the welfare of the Negro soldier at heart, you will investigate these claims and then have them printed; so that the secrets of what the Negroes in the army endure will be revealed to the public.

For reasons that you probably know I would prefer my name to be kept out of print because I will probably be weeded out and I will be unable to continue. I remain:

Sincerely yours,

T/5 Samuel A. Connor
Co. B. 43rd Signal Const. Bn.
Camp Crowder, Missouri.

Laborers without Pay

Peterson Air Field.
214th, Aviation Sec.
July 13, 1944.
Colorado Springs, Colorado

The Pittsburg Courier.
To The Editor.

Dear Sir.

This letter is in regards to a situation as it is here in our section. Which I feel you should know about and too I feel is worth comment of course if you see fit.

The men who have been working in officers mess and quarters have been recieveing twenty dollars per month until the field was changed from bomber training station to a flight reconnance station for training.

The men now working in officers quarters and mess with the exception of cooks receive no pay. This Mr editor is a direct violation of army regulations to work an enlisted man in officers quarters or mess without pay.

The commandant of the base is named Col. Tipton. And the commander of the 214th, aviation sec. is Capt. Charles S. Adams. In writing this letter I sincerely hope you will take it under consideration, for without outside help I feel sure there will never be a correction made.

The name on the outside of the letter is assumed. In closing I want to thank you in advance for whatever steps you may take in helping us to correct the matter.

SINCERELY YOURS,

The second air force Headquarters is located in Colorado springs.

4

Illusions of Democracy

I learned early in life that for the Negro there is no
Democracy. Of course I know the principles set forth in
the Amendments and the Bill of Rights. I learned that I
knew nothing of the operation of a true democratic form
of government. I found that a Negro in civilian life has
very tough time with segregation in public places and
discrimination in industry. I knew this and I thought that
white people would react differently toward a colored
soldier.

I had heard and read of the cruel treatment given
colored soldiers and somehow, even among existing conditions of civilian life, I couldn't understand how white
people could be so down on one who wears the uniform
of the fighting forces of their country. From civilian life I
was drafted and now I prepare to fight for——the continuation of discriminatory practices against me and my
people.

A Loyal Negro Soldier

For most white Americans democracy meant equality, liberty,
fraternity, individual rights, tolerance, freedom of speech, as-
sembly and religion, military duty, and compromise. For most
black Americans democracy meant disillusionment. Black soldiers who
served in World War II epitomize this devastating, inescapable, and recurring experience. For them democracy was a grand illusion of misleading American rhetoric.

The racial prejudice heaped upon black soldiers was the bitter reality
they were forced to endure as they fought to make the world "safe for
democracy," and all mankind free to live out their fullest potential. They
were eager to fight and extremely conscious of the lofty war aims of
President Roosevelt and other American leaders, but most of them suffered from low morale throughout the war, from the actuality that they
were not being treated like other American fighting men.

Nevertheless, blacks went to war with the hope that the army would recognize their worth and solidly protect and provide for them as citizen-soldiers. They knew that in this time of national emergency their service was necessary, and they hoped that their loyalty and participation would secure for them military equality and the rewards of full citizenship at home once the war was over. The black troops believed that the hallowed principles of the Declaration of Independence and the U.S. Constitution would govern the conduct of the armed forces. The military, however, was unwilling to make the democratic rhetoric of World War II a reality for its black soldiers.

Despite the Army's uneven view and treatment of black soldiers, the soldiers understood quite clearly that racial prejudice prevented them from enjoying the optimum benefits of military life, and the moral right to function as citizen-soldiers in the "armed forces of democracy." Because they saw themselves as average and ordinary human beings who, with equal training and equal facilities, could develop like others, the soldiers pleaded with the military to accord them the same privileges and oppor-tunities accorded white soldiers.

According to the letters in this chapter, blacks loathed the idea of hav-ing to fight and die in Europe for the "four freedoms" while denied them as American soldiers. They complained that democracy for them was illusory and that they were fighting for "white folks." To these black troops "any Negro would rather give his life at home fighting for a cause he can understand than against any enemy whose principles are the same as our so-called democracy. A new Negro will return from the war—a bitter Negro if he is disappointed again. He will have been taught to kill, to suffer, to die for something he believes in, and he will live by these rules to gain his personal rights."[1]

Thus the war for black soldiers crystalized into a "Double V" cam-paign—a campaign to stop the spread of totalitarianism in Europe and to destroy the vestiges of racism in America. That black soldiers went to war believing that they were fighting to secure their rights in uniform as well as those in America cannot be denied. But their dreams were shattered, their participation became less than enthusiastic, and their letters forged a strong condemnation of American democracy.

NOTES

1. Quoted in Lucille B. Milner, "Jim Crow in the Army," *New Republic* CX (March 13, 1944), 339.

Democracy, We Shall Never Accomplish

San Marcos, Texas
Sunday Evening,
Mr. Carl Murphy   March 21, 1943

Dear Sir:

I have been in the service since January 26, 1943, and it will be more than
appreciated if you will kindly contact the NAACP, for the benefit of colored
men in this organization. My home is in Baltimore, Md., which I am very
proud to state, as there are any number of men here from Baltimore and all
points of Maryland and from all over the States.

Not in any selfishness naturally my interest points mostly to men from
Baltimore, as well as men from wherever they may come from. On the contrary, the fact remains we are in the very deep South where a colored man
doesn't have a possible chance at any field or profession he may exist. Not
getting from my subject, the very small space of time we have, there is not
one decent place of interest or entertainment for us to visit. Our post theatre,
is very much on the segregation side. We just have approximately some fifty or
sixty seats, which I will never be able to understand as regardless, we are in
uniform, because we can not possibly better our conditions. Moreover, we are
fighting for something called "Democracy" which in general we will never
receive. In order to attain peace and hold same, first we must fight for our
rights in the United States—fight with our fists as weapons and brains which
we have been attempting since the last war.

Our task here is serving officers, picking paper off the grounds or policing
the area as we call it, dressing officers beds, cleaning windows, which in my
opinion is not soldering.

Being very frank, I am more than sorry I passed the examination as it is
honestly a living "hell." My darling mother is sixty-six years old and my sister
can not work at all because of an operation. On my induction into the service
at Fort George G. Meade, Md., I wasn't granted an allotment for either of
them which I certainly tried hard to receive. Though I am a candidate for
O.C.S., I don't have the spirit to accept anything this life in the Army has to
offer me. I am disappointing a number of people in that respect. But I know
they will all understand.

Dear Sir, in closing, please alter this statement if you must however, if I had
done other than reveal the facts, I am sure they would have been much more

disappointing. So please, for my interest and the men here, the AFRO Newspaper and the freedom of the press, kindly expose this statement in any issue
of your paper and reveal same to the NAACP as well as the important public
because we are honestly fighting for not one thing but many things. I am
convinced in the field of democracy we shall never accomplish, if you desire a
picture of me one can be obtained from my mother or sister.

Sincerely,

A Negro Soldier

Fighting for the USA

The Pittsburgh Courier
Editor-in-Chief   Co B 364 Engis. Regt.
Pittsburgh, Penn.   March 6, 1943

Dear Sir:

We are the privates of the above Regt, asking for your assistance in aiding us to get an investigation of this hell hole where we are stationed. We like fighting for the U.S.A. but when we are being treated like dogs by what is called our white superior officers and their subs, the Negro non coms, there is certain privileges that we are suppose to have although we are in the Army. No Sundays off, falling out all times of the night. Never able to please no one it is *hell* living *hell* here, but when we seek information, we are thrown all most in the guard house. Thanking you for your time.

Very Truly

The Privates 364 Engis. Regt.

Fight—for Democracy?

Truman K. Gibson, Jr.
Civilian Aide to the Secretary of War
Washington, D. C.   November 5, 1943

Dear Mr. Gibson:

> And I fight—for Democracy?

Upon reading the title of this article the average reader would assume that I
am a member of the armed forces of the U.S.A. In your assumption, reader,
you are definitely correct. I was selected by the President and citizens, to fight
for a "now—existing Democracy." I am one soldier who waited to be drafted.
I didn't volunteer out. I am learning to fight to protect whatever cause for
which the Allies are fighting. I am forced to learn to be ready to kill or be
killed—for "Democracy." When fighting time arrives I will fight for ———?

I learned early in life that for the Negro there is no Democracy. Of course I
know the principles set forth in the Amendments and the Bill of Rights. I
learned that I knew nothing of the operation of a true democratic form of
government. I found that a Negro in civilian life has very tough time with
segregation in public places and discrimination in industry. I knew this and I
thought that white people would react differently toward a colored soldier.

I had heard and read of the cruel treatment given colored soldiers and
somehow, even among existing conditions of civilian life, I couldn't understand
how white people could be so down on one who wears the uniform of the
fighting forces of their country. From civilian life I was drafted and now I
prepare to fight for——The continuation of discriminatory practices against
me and my people.

I have long known that the fighting forces are composed of two divisions.
Namely, a white division composed of Germans, Jews, Italians, Dutch and all
white people of the remaining countries. (The question is: Are they loyal?) A
Negro division composed of American Negroes and all dark skin people. The
American Negro has fought in every war since the Revolutionary War. There
can be no question as to his loyalty. He is put into a division composed of the
members of his race not because of his educational qualities, his fighting
qualities or his inability to live with others, but he's put into a separate division
because of the color of his skin.

This is serious since the Negroes are trained to a large extent in Southern

States whose white civilians are more drastic in showing their dislike than in Northern white people.

I prayed that I'd be sent to a camp in my home state or that I'd be sent to some camp in a Northern State. My prayers weren't answered and I find myself at this outpost of civilization. I never wanted to be within twenty hundred miles of Alexandria, Louisiana. I am here and I can do nothing to improve my condition. Nevertheless, I prepare to fight for a country where I am denied the rights of being a full-fledged citizen.

A few weeks after my arrival, at this camp, I went to a post exchange on my regimental area. I knew that each area has an exchange but I thought that I could make my purchase at any of them. Upon entering I could feel the place grow cold. All conversation ceased. It was then that I noticed that all the soldiers and the saleswomen were white. Not to be outdone I approached the counter and was told (even before asking for the article) that, "Negroes are not served here. This post-exchange is for white soldiers. You have one near your regiment. Buy what you want there."

My answer to these abrupt and rudely made statements was in the form of a question— "I thought that post exchanges are for soldiers regardless of color, am I right?" I left this post-exchange and returned to my regimental area. I know that these saleswomen knew not the way of a true democracy.

As long as I am a soldier I fight for a mock Democracy.

I was called to report to the camp hospital for an eye examination last week. I was surprised to find the waiting room full of Negro and white soldiers who were sharing the same seats and reading the same newspapers. I was shocked. I didn't believe that the camp hospital could be so free from segregation while the camp itself was built on prejudice.

My second surprise came when registering. Each person filled out a blank and all blanks were placed in the same basket in order of the entrance regardless of the race of the entree. I was just beginning to feel proud of the hospital when a list of names were called off and my name was last on the list. I found myself in a line of sixteen (16) men, seven of whom were white. The white man gradually fell out of line and the Negroes found themselves continually waiting . . . waiting for the white soldiers to finish their examinations.

It wouldn't have been noticed had not the sergeant in charge been contented to carry only those white soldiers in the line, but he proceeded to bring more from the waiting room. When I could stand this no longer I protested.

Result: We were immediately examined and allowed to return to our regimental area. I was asked a few days later, "Don't you want to fight for the U.S.A. and its policies."

I am a soldier; I made no answer, but deep down inside I knew when I faced America's enemies I will fight for the protection of my loved ones at home.

Listen, Negro America, I am writing this article believing that it will act as a stimulant. You need awakening. Many of you have come to realize that your race is fighting on the battlefields of the world but do you know why they fight? I can answer this question.

The right on the battlefield is for your existance, not for Democracy. It is upon you that each soldier depends. In my fight my thoughts will invariably return to you who can fight for Democracy. You must do this for the soldiers because Democracy will be, and Democracy must, must be won at home—not on battlefields but through your bringing pressure to bear on Congress.

A Loyal Negro Soldier

Just Living on Borrowed Time

The Chicago Defender   January 9, 1944

To Whom It May Concern:

I being a soldier of the U.S.A., I'm sure you and our families would be interested in what occured on Sunday, January 9, 1944. Our lives were threatened because of *race prejudice*. It seems as though the colored man hasn't any rights as a soldier of the armed forces of the United States. Isn't it true we are fighting for the same cause as the white man—for democracy—which is not practiced in the land in which we serve? The rights of a man, it seems, depends on his color and we being colored gives us no rights whatsoever. Whites are treated as human beings and we are treated as slaves. We are Jim Crowed in everything we do, including officers and white soldiers are against us. As you know, we are outnumbered by ten to one and are just living on borrowed time.

If only something could be done to make us feel as though we had something to fight and die for. Now we feel as if we're here only to be slaves for the white man. We don't mind being a soldier as long we are treated like one. Now our morale is low and will not rise until something is done about this discrimination.

Signed

A Soldier

And Sunday, January 9, we prisoners were singing—you know to past the time away. Yes, we are in the stockade. We received six months for talking to some colored WACS. Well, anyway that Sunday we were singing. That helps us to do our time. Keeps us from worrying. It's about twenty eight of us colored prisoners here and about 170 white prisoners. We sleep over the white prisoners in a barrack. So they came to our door and said: "You n———s keep quiet or we will beat the h——l out of you." So we shut up. After while me and four more soldiers went to the latrine to wash up. The latrine is about forty or sixty feet from our building. So when we got to the door a crowd of white prisoners surrounded us. They had sticks and clubs. They asked us where we were from. We lied and told them the South. They said we were from the North. So one said: "Let's beat them to death and go kill the rest." We pleaded to them so hard. They told us to go back upstairs where we sleep

and tell the rest of the n——s to keep quiet. They hit us lightly and told us to
doubletime. When we got back upstairs we told the boys. So we all kept quiet.
The white major and a white lieutenant came over that night. And all they told
us was to stay up here if we didn't want to get killed. So we didn't have
anybody to help us after the officers didn't do anything. We couldn't sleep all
that night afraid they were going to come upstairs and kill us in our sleep. So
help us if you can. Because our lives are nothing down here. And just think I
have to take all this stuff for six months. I don't mind the six months at all. All
I want is safety. I wish you would write my mother about this. Her name is —
——. Don't mention my name in the paper please. For they would lynch me if
they knew I was writing to a newspaper about this.

Idealism Versus American Practice

T/5th Clarence E. Adams, 6,267,293
Mr. Carl Murphy   4295th QM Gasoline Supply Co.
Afro-American Newspapers,   Camp Breckinridge, Kentucky,
Baltimore, Maryland.   July 8, 1944.

Dear Mr. Murphy:

In response to your letter of this date, I am herewith closing the information
that I wrote you about. It is fully understood that you are not to disclose my
identity. Here is the story:

It happened on Saturday July 1, 1944. I drew a book from the Service
Club Library to read. The title of the book is "Negro Poets and Their Poems,"
by Kerlin. I had the book with me at the motor-pool where I work (I am the
dispatcher). I had finished up my work (records) for the day and was just
about ready to leave when the Company Executive Officer walked in the office.
My paraphenalia was laying on my desk including the book, so he picked up
the book and began looking through it; finally he came to this poem:
"Mulatto" by Langston Hughes. He cursed and used all-kind of vile language
about the author. He wanted to know who wrote it, where did I get the book; I
told him, and this was his reply: "Take that damn book where you got it and I
don't want to ever see anything like that around the company. The wrong
person might get a hold of it and it might cause some trouble." I said this:
"Sir, the men in the company are very intelligent and quite a few of them
spend their leisure time in reading Negro works. I am certain that this book
would make no difference to them." He said, "I don't care. I don't want books
like that around the company, because others might not be as broadminded as
you are." I said, "Yes, Sir."

I didn't take the book back as he ordered because I had not finished reading
it. On Sunday I was in Company Orderly Room and I was called into his
office, and again he asked me had I taken the book back to the library. I said,
"No, Sir." Again I was given a direct order to take the book back. I told other
members about the incident and as soon as I checked the book in at the
library another member of my organization drew it out again. I don't know
what the results are going to be.

This is the point, Mr. Murphy. Yes we are Negro Soldiers, giving our sweat,
blood, and lives for what is known as an IDEALISTIC DEMOCRACY, and here
in the midst of a world crisis we are told not to read books as that one by men

of our own race. If this sort of thing happen now, what will happen when the war is over? I am sure that it will be much worse for the Negro, of which we aren't going to stand for. A few weeks ago I gave an address before a packed chapel of officers, men and WACS. "UNDER OUR FLAG, AND AMERICAN SPEAKS." It was very militant and inspiring; so much so that I made it very uncomfortable for the white officers. Yes their faces turned all kinds of colors but there was nothing that they could do because I gave facts, dates, history, and authors. I happen to know quite a bit about the Negro, because I have and am devoting the majority of my leisure in the study of THE NEGRO.

The officer that told me to take the book back where I found it, happened to be a second lieutenant.

From time to time I will be sending you quite a bit of information of happenings here on this post; provided you want it.

Should you print this news in your paper I would appreciate a copy of it, if you will be kind enough to send me one. Whether you print it or not I still want one as they are very rare out here.

Thank you very kindly.

Respectfully Yours,

I remain,
S/T/5th Clarence E. Adams.

Neurosis on the Rise

Mr. Carter Wesley
Editor, Houston Informer   Augusta, Ga.
Houston, Texas.   August 10, 1944

Dear Sir:

If you recall I came to you once and you did all you could to assist me in
getting justice the Army was denying me. I came to you then because I
believed that you were interested in seeing the Negro youth get the justice that
the Constitution of our Government entitles him to. I'm writing you now
because I know that in this Crisis, when our boys are dying and fighting to
help preserve our Democracy, you are vitally interested in the welfare of all
American youth.

When I received that appointment for Cadet training in 1941 to Rhyan
Field, San Dieago, Cal. I realized then that if I was trained there it would
mean that the Army was not going to practice Segregation and Discrimination
in its' training of Negro pilots. You personally know the disappointment I
experienced after I was disqualified by the Army Recruiting Officers because of
a heart ailment.

Through your help I was granted another examination. I was disqualified
again. This time because of color Blindness, in spite of the fact that I passed at
least three Army color blind test preceding the test I was disqualified by.

On Oct. 12, 1942. I was inducted in the Army. I was inducted in California.
My medical examination revealed me to be in perfect health. I was fortunate
enough when I took my Classification Test to make a grade a little above
average. My interviewer suggested that I apply for O.C.S. or Aviation Cadet
Training.

I was sent from California to Jefferson Barracks, Missouri, where I took
basic training. After I finished basic training I tried to apply for OCS. I was
told by my CO that I had to wait until I was assigned to a regular outfit.
Meanwhile I was reclassified, and selected after a series of test, to go to
Teletype school. I remained in Jefferson Barracks until Jan. 22, 1943 waiting
for an opening in a teletype school. I left Jeff. Bks. Jan. 22, 1943 for
Engineer School at Ft. Belvoir, Va. I was assigned to a class in heavy equipment. I attended this school for thirty days. We were told when our classes
began that the man with the best averages would be allowed to choose between
a number of Camps and decide which camp he would like to be assigned to. I

finished with second highest average in my class of approximately fourteen
white men and three colored. I had the priviledge of choosing between Greenville, S.C., and a camp in Florida. I chose South Carolina. My hopes for an
opportunity to accomplish something in the Army were still rather high, even
though Army Discrimination had denied me the opportunity of learning to fly
and learning to operate a teletype machine. However at Ft. Belvoir I learned
something about Heavy Equipment and though this wasn't what I wanted I
was determined to make the best of it.

When I arrived in Greenville, S.C. with seven other colored fellows who
finished school at Belvoir with me; we found that we were the first Enlisted
Men assigned to an Aviation Engineer outfit. We were all specialized men. We
were interviewed and I happened to be the only one in the group that could
type a little. I was assigned to Battalion Headquarters. The other fellows were
assigned to various other jobs but none of us were put on jobs where we could
apply that knowledge which we obtained while at Ft. Belvoir.

In the course of six months I earned my present grade of Sgt. Major. I will
not tell you why now but I will say that I still wasn't satisfied. I tried to get to
OCS. I passed the Physical and I passed the OCS board but I still haven't
gotten to OCS. My application was submitted in the month of June 1943. I
was determined to get out of that outfit though and the only thing I saw to do
was to apply for Cadet Training again. I did. I passed the physical and mental
exams and was transferred out of my outfit to an Aviation Squadron on the
field, meanwhile my application papers were being sent to Washington for
approval. My papers returned from Washington about three months after my
transfer but I was rejected again for Cadet training because of my previous
record of color blindness. This was no more than I expected.

I wrote a letter to the Commanding General of the Army Air Forces asking
for another examination. My request was granted and I passed the Examination again.

I was sent to Keesler Field in Mississippi for Pre-Cadet training. There were
about one hundred and Seventy five fellows in my class. All fine fellows from
all parts of the country. Fellows with M.S. degrees, and a lot of fellows with
B.A. and B.S. degrees. We were given another Physical Examination at Keesler Field and those of us who passed the Physical were given a series of
Psychological and Psycho-motor test. Out of my class of one hundred and
seventy five men, about thirty of the fellows had left for Tuskegee when I left
the field. Possibly thirty others were waiting to go to Tuskegee. The rest of the
group was washed out for further training. Having nothing specific for the
wash-outs to do we were transferred to other organizations on the field. This

same thing had happened in each of the classes that preceded my class. Approximately Seventy percent of the fellows washed out. We were given advanced basic training. This training consisted of rigid physical Training and Cross Country runs, and lectures. It was during this training that I discovered that I wasn't the man I thought I was. My feet ached, my muscles ached and my wrist even began to bother me. For my first time during my Army Career I went on Sick Call. The Officers' diagnosis was Third Degree Pes Planus and slight Arthritus. I attended an Orthopetic Clinic for ten days. I was given arch supports for one pair of my G.I. shoes and I excused myself from all drilling and Physical Training. However I was transferred from Keesler Field as qualified for all combat duty.

About Feb. 15, 1944, I was transferred to this HELL HOLE. Daniel Field, Augusta, Georgia. This is a Replacement Depot and until a month or so ago we didn't do much of anything. However the policy changed and we began doing some more Basic Training. I tried, but I began having such severe head aches that I had three Consultations with the Psychiatrist to see if I was on the verge of Insanity. I also suffered from the same ailments I complained about at Keesler Field. Only now my nerves are in such bad condition that I must keep check on myself at all times. On the fourth of July I went on sick call again. I was so nervous that the least little thing irritated me. The Doctors Diagnosis was possible Trichinosis.

I was admitted in the hospital here. It was obvious that I was extremely nervous, but I was assigned to a bed in the ward with the other patients. The nurses and Ward boys irritated me so that I told them that their inefficiency was killing men and seemingly the only way they would believe a man was suffering would be for him to die. I was transferred out of this ward after this incident, to another ward that was supposed to be for men whose nerves were in bad order. In this ward my torture instead of my help began. I had been in the hospital three days and had hardly slept ten hours the entire time; I was given plenty sedatives. I didn't know then but I know now that I had been selected as a Guinea Pg to be tortured until I told the Experimenters every-thing they wanted to know about myself, and my opinion as to certain race questions.

I won't go into details, because I know that if I would tell you all that was imposed on me, it would sound fantastic. I will tell you however that by whatever process they used I was degenerated to the extent that my normal reflex actions were not those of a Human Being, but more like the reflex actions of an Ape. I growled and roared and I could not help myself. I was locked in a room for almost a week. Fortunately my will power kept me from going crazy. I assure you though that the officer in charge of this experiment did a damn good job of trying to drive me insane. I was even scheduled to go before a board to determine whether I was insane. Meanwhile my back was still aching so I couldn't sleep at night. Finally the Doctors decided after trying to drive me crazy that maybe my complaints were not false. They took X-rays of all possible sources of pain. I haven't seen the X-ray picture but the Officer told me that they were all negative, and they wanted to send me back to duty even though my medical record at Keesler Field should show that I am not physically qualified to do anything strenuous. After discussing my condition with one Officer I was finally granted a thirty day excuse from practically all duty. But as far as I know I am still qualified for all combat duty, Not withstanding the fact that Army Records should reveal that: I have a systolic Murmer of the heart and an enlarged heart, I stayed in 4F classification for almost a year, I have 3rd degree pes planus, I have Arthritus, I have a sprained Sacro Iliac Ligament; I suffer with hay fever and sinus trouble. If my medical Records show this (and they should) why am I still in the Army?

The Officer in charge at sick call told me that I could see my medical records, if I wrote a letter requesting that I be allowed this priviledge. My CO refused to indorse the letter because he said that he thought I wanted to start trouble. I have been transferred to another outfit here since this time. I tried to see my new CO but he refused to see me. I finally managed through persistency to talk to him. I have soldiered under this captain before and I thought once that he really had the welfare of his men at heart. I told him everything that happened to me in my experiences with the Army. I also told him what happened to me in the hospital. In the course of our conversation I implied that the only reason I had been treated this way was because I was a Negro. He Reprimanded me for the implication, but I told him that one reason I appreciated Democracy was because it gave me freedom of thought. My CO said "The Army isn't Democratic, it is Aristocratic." However he did agree to assist me in trying to see my medical records. He hasn't mentioned it since and that was three days ago. I do not believe my medical records contain all they should contain and if they don't I can prove a lot of things, because I am not the only soldier who has suffered because of the inefficiency of this hospital staff.

Sir here on Daniel Field we have some of the best material in the Army. Men, White and Colored, who are highly specialized in all fields and have been trained at Government expense. Clerks, Aviation mechanics, Radar men, Musicians, Radio men and these same men have proven themselves mentally and physically superior to other fellows. I know the Army needs these men but

some of them have been here for as long as twelve months. We have men here
who have proven their willingness to gight for Democracy by fighting, some of
them have been sent back from overseas because they were found physically
disqualified to fight. But the Doctors here don't seem to agree with the Doctors
overseas. Just a few miles from here is a German Prison Camp. Daniel Field
itself reminds me of a Japanese internment Camp I visited during my railroading days before induction. The locality of this field is nice for the purpose of
isolation.

I am not writing you because of what has been done to me by the Army. I
don't think however that murder would be too low for some Ranking Officers
in the Army. They would have murdered me here I do believe if they could
have seen an escape, beyond investigation. There are a lot of other fellows
here who are destined for the same fate, White and Colored. I know you are
not Mr. Anthony, but What the hell are these men to do under such circumstances? If the people who allow such conditions to exist constantly ignore
these conditions, what can a man do?

You know, Mr. Westley the army does a lot for a man. It makes you
understand a lot of things that probably puzzle you before you came into the
army. It makes an American understand why when the pilgrims were persecuted in Europe these people came to America seeking Freedom. You can
easily understand after being in the Army long enough why those men who
framed our Constitution included those words "Freedom, Justice, and Equality
for all." With a strong imagination you can even go back into our American
history and actually see yourself standing there at Gettysburg, feeling as President Lincoln felt when he said "It is rather for us to be here dedicated to the
great task remaining before us; that from these honored dead we take increased devotion; that this nation under God shall have a new birth of freedom,
and that government of the people, by the people, and for the people shall not
perish from the earth." Being a Negro I understand better now why when
those people were brought to America from Africa; Beaten, tortured and ex-
ploited, they still found strength to cry out in loud voices to God and sing those
spirituals they sang. I know now, why when these people were downtrodden,
beatened and tortured until their bodies ached, they still sang and prayed from
the very depts of their souls for salvation. All people who are persecuted and
enslaved sooner or later ask God for salvation.

People can't be Enslaved simply by controling their bodies. The body is only
a mechanism controled by the mind. But when a group of people allow their
minds to become enslaved you can control this group of people. The two most
popular ways of controling the minds of a group of people are: Get the group

devoted to some cause, and the other is to get the group to become victims of fear. This is how you may account for the high morale in the Armies of some countries and the low morale of Armies in other countries.

I've never told my mother anything about what has happened to me here. I know how she would feel. I'm wondering how my buddies families would feel if they really knew what actually happens to their son's here in the Army, as a result of Segregation and Discrimination. I wonder if the people who continue to advocate White Supremacy know what they are doing to their own sons on the Front. I wonder if these people realize that if it were not for Segregation and Discrimination in the Armed Forces, many Negroes would have been willing to die fighting for Democracy where White men have died. I wonder if the Armed Forces realize how much additional money, and how many additional lives it cost our Government to tolerate Segregation and Discrimination.

Mr. Westley your advice means a great deal to me now. I intend to vote in November and I would like you to advise me as to whether as I should vote for a party who has tolerated for twelve years Segregation, Discrimination and exploitation. If these people are not aware of what is going on in the Armed Forces now is the time to prove that they do not approve of such practices, and an investigation here on Daniel Field would I'm sure factually substantiate the things I have said in this letter.

I am inclosing a poem I ran across which puts in common words the kind of propaganda I listened to before I came into the Army and the propaganda I listen to now in the Army. I am also inclosing a carbon copy of the letter I wrote to the CO of the station hospital here. This is the letter my CO refused to indorse. Incidentally, this man is now adjutant of the outfit I'm in now. We also have two other white officers. One has ordered hot water thrown on a man since I've been here, and the other told one of the fellows one day that he would ram a book down his damn throat if he didn't put the book up. If this letter lacks coherrance you can easily understand why I'm confused. I have a lot to live for but I wonder if living under certain conditions is really living or existing.

Thanking you in advance for whatever advise you may give me, I remain,

Respectfully yours,

John M. Walls, Jr.
S/Sgt, A.C.

Wearing Uncle Sam's Uniform

TO: Cpl. J. H. Becton, 34462685
    Army & Navy Screen Magazine   Co. A, 371st Inf. APO 92
    By Request Dept.   Fort Huachuca, Ariz.
    New York, N. Y.   26 August 1944

Dear Dept.

I am a "negro soldier" in a combat division and there are more than fifteen
thousand "negro soldiers" in the Division, and we've been preparing for combat for more than twenty months, now the final test is on.

We have an "all negro" Division in action, and we have "negro soldiers" on
every front wearing "Uncle Sam's Uniform" and fighting for the safety of the
country the same as all other "Soldiers" of "America."

Last night, I saw the film "This is America" and there was not a single one
of "my people" in the screen, it was a film of "Whites only," why don't the
armed forces release the "negroes" and fight their own war, for if this is
"America" for "whites" only, we, the "negroes" have nothing to fight for.

Will you please give me an explanation on "This is America."

I remain,

Obligatingly yours,
/s/ Cpl. J. H. Becton

5

Biased White Officers

He, Major Sheriden, is a rough dried, leather neck
Negro hating cracker from Louisiana, who has insulted
all Negroes in general. Calls our women everything but
women. Misuse soldiers, treat us as if we were in a
forced labor camp or chain gang.

Corporal Daniell E. Williams
Sergeant Sterle Wilson
Private First Class Jasper Smith

I n performing their duties, blacks sometimes were forced to endure the verbal abuse of commissioned and noncommissioned white officers. Often these officers used racial epithets in addressing black troops largely because the War Department had not finalized an official policy on this issue. A number of white officers simply ignored the debilitating effect racial insults had on black troops. Because they were frequently used, black soldiers often reported that the morale among them was low. Attempting to redress this situation, they, with support from Civilian Aides William H. Hastie and Truman K. Gibson, Jr., urged the War Department to issue an official directive banning the use of certain words and phrases that had the effect of debasing black troops.

In their letters of protest, blacks particularly detested white officers who used the word "nigger" and other racial stereotypes when addressing them and issuing commands. These officers were often singled out by the black soldiers as "Rednecks."

Soldiers at Jackson Air Base, South Carolina, informed Judge Hastie, for example, that "the word Negro is never used here, all they call us are nigger do this, nigger do that. Even the officers here are calling us nigger." They also complained that "Lieutenant Bromberg said all Negroes need to be beaten to death."[1]

At Camp Bowie, Texas, black soldiers experienced similar treatment. The men of the 2nd Battalion wrote to the *Pittsburgh Courier* that they were jeered by white soldiers day and night, "calling us various unpleasing names as *Nigger, Snowballs,* and their *Black African Army.*" These particular troops continued, "If we ride the busses wer'e talked about like dogs and pushed and shoved around in the same manner. When we try to defend ourselves, wer'e out numbered ten to one." In an effort to get help, they asked the white senior officer of the battalion, "if a white soldier calls you nigger, curse or call you various names what to do? His answer was, to not to look at them, pay them no attention, just complertely ignore them, if necessary walk a little faster. In other words he meant for us to run and let them call us anything, and us not say nothing to them." The soldiers asked this same officer, "if a white soldier hits, kicks or pushes on you, what to do? His answer was, 'to say' 'Gwan we white man dont bother' me now. I'm a soldier just like you and you ant suppose to barther me. Ant no use for you to bother us colored soldiers, we ant going to bother you. He also says if the white soldier continue to hit you, get on out of his way, and not 'what ever we did' hit them back."[2]

In addition to this kind of officer neglect, a number of white officers spread rumors that blacks were lazy, shiftless, and descendants of animals. For instance, Jonathan Welch claimed that his commanding officers told civilians in Great Britain that blacks were descendants of monkeys. Welch lamented, "Strange as it may seem, but hard to believe that the people are told that after we stay here, we will grow tails, and we are direct descendants from monkeys. Occasionally one can find people who will still run from us . . . . our officers who are from, what is known as PECKAWOOD land, always create the problem of socializing" for us.[3]

Judge Hastie became increasingly concerned over the use of these kinds of racial references. In a 1941 conference with Secretary of War Stimson, Chief of Staff George C. Marshall, and Acting Inspector General Howard Mac C. Snyder, he called for a policy banning the use of abusive language and objected particularly to post commanders accused of racial epithets being allowed to command black troops. He suggested specifically that the War Department ban the use of the word "nigger."[4]

Secretary Stimson agreed with Hastie. In February 1942 he ordered Adjutant General R. G. Hersey to prepare a memo for the commanding generals of the Eastern Theater of Operations, the Western Defense Command, the Caribbean Defense Command, and all base commanders. The commanders were instructed to observe the following:

> Superiors are forbidden to injure those under their authority
> by tyrannical or capricious conduct or by abusive language.
> While maintaining discipline and thorough and prompt per-
> formance of military duty, all officers, in dealing with enlisted
> men will bear in mind the absolute necessity of so treating
> them as to preserve their self-respect. A grave duty rests on
> all officers and particulalry upon organization commanders
> in this respect. In this connection the use of any epithet
> deemed insulting to a racial group should be carefully
> avoided. Similarly, commanders should avoid all practices
> that the Army makes any differentiation between him and
> other soldiers.[5]

To test the effect of this new policy, Hastie asked Undersecretary of
War Patterson (Patterson became Undersecretary in 1942) in October to
recommend the removal of General John A. Warden, commander of Fort
Francis E. Warren, Cheyenne, from his command. Hastie informed Patterson that the black soldiers there were very bitter over the racist man-
nerisms of General Warden, and that he had heard him use the word
nigger while visiting the camp himself. Hastie also charged that General
Warden distributed 500 free football tickets to white soldiers only, when
he had promised a group of Cheyenne citizens that they would be dis-
persed among all the troops, including blacks stationed at the post. Hastie
was convinced that Warden's attitude toward blacks was such that his
removal from the base was essential to the well-being of both black and
white soldiers.[6]

Records did not reveal if Patterson acted on Hastie's recommendation,
but Hastie was at least able to persuade Secretary Stimson that a prohibition on abusive language and racial epithets was in the best interest of the
army, and that it would have a salutary effect on the morale of not only
black but white soldiers as well.

However, the company executive officer of Camp Breckenridge, Kentucky, either had not been informed of the Army's new policy or he
disregarded it, because five months after the policy took effect a black
soldier at the camp claimed he had been abused. Private Adams opined:

> I drew a book from the Service Club Library to read. The
> title of the book is *Negro Poets and Their Poems*, by Kerlin.
> I had the book with me at the motor pool where I work (I
> am the dispatcher). I had finished up my work (Records) for
> the day and was just about ready to leave when the Com-

pany Executive Officer walked in the office. My paraphenalia was laying on the desk including the book, so he
picked up the book and began looking through it; finally he
came to this poem: "Mulatto" by Langston Hughes. He
cursed and used all kinds of vile language about the author.
He wanted to know who wrote it, where did I get the book; I
told him, and this is his reply: "Take that damn book where
you got it and I don't want to ever see anything like that
around the company. The wrong person might get a hold of
it and it might cause some trouble."[7]

As black soldiers wrote of these kinds of racial experiences, they became more visible in the armed forces, and black *esprit de corps* was
damaged. But for the first time in U.S. military history, the army had
officially banned the use of racial epithets and insulting language. This
action was another signal that the army was, however reluctantly, making
some noteworthy shifts in race relations, although the continued protest
of some black soldiers after 1942 indicates that the directive was disregarded by some white officers.

NOTES

1. Letter, A Group of Soldiers from Jackson Air Base to Hastie, October 11, 1942, Civilian Aide to the Secretary of War Subject File, 1940–1947, National Archives Record Group 107 (hereafter cited as NARG).

2. Letter, All of the Soldiers of the 2nd Battalion to the *Pittsburgh Courier*, April 13, 1941, Civilian Aide to the Secretary of War Subject File, 1940–1947, NARG 107.

3. Letter, Jonathan Welch to Howard Murphy, Business Manager of the Afro-American Newspapers, December 10, 1943, Civilian Aide to the Secretary of War Subject File, 1940–1947, NARG 107.

4. Memorandum, Howard Mac C. Snyder to George C. Marshall, November 13, 1941, Army General Staff, NARG 407.

5. Memorandum, R. G. Hersey to the Commanding Generals, Field Forces, February 14, 1942, Army General Staff, NARG 407.

6. Memorandum, Hastie to Patterson, October 23, 1942, Civilian Aide to the Secretary of War Subject File, 1940–1947, NARG 107.

7. Letter, Clarence E. Adams to Gibson, July 8, 1942, Civilian Aide to the Secretary of War Subject File, 1940–1947, NARG 107.

Manuvers through Texas

Co. E, 25th Inf.
Camp Bowie, Texas
Pittsburgh Courier Pub. Co.   4/13/41

Dear Sirs:

I'm a soldier of the U. S. Army and a constant reader of the Pittsburgh
Courier. I've noticed that you've helped soldiers in their various jim crow
problems.

We as colored soldiers of the U. S. Army of the 25th Inf. Ft. Huachuca
Arizona, are now on manuvers through Texas, and we have a problem that we
wish you'd help us solve.

Ft. Huachuca is an exclusive colored camp with about 5,000 enlisted men.
The 2nd Battallion left Arizona on the 7th of May "to start the manuver" and
arrived at Camp Bowie Texas on May 11th to stay here for about a month.

The Army post here have approximately 22,000 white soldiers, and from
these "white" soldiers we're jeered by them both day and night, calling us
various upleasing names as *Niggers*, *Snow ball*, and their Black Affican Army.
Also they don't allow us to ride the post busses. We either have to hire a
special cab, or ride in the extreme rear of the busses. If we ride the busses
wer'e talked about like dogs and pushed and shoved around in the same
manner. When we try to defend oursselves, wer'e out numbered ten to one.
This went on for a few days "until we got tired of it." We thought we'd take
this matter up with our officers "as you understand our officers are all white."
There were various questions asked by different soldiers to the senior officer of
the 2nd Battallion (the Colonel). They were, if a white soldier calls you nigger,
curse or call you various names what to do? His answer was, to not to look at
them, pay them no attention, just completely ignore them, if necessary walk a
little faster. In other words he meant for us to run and let them call us
anything, and us not say nothing to them. Another question was, if a white
soldier hits, kicks or pushes on you, what to do? His answer was "to say"
"Gwan we white man don't bother" me now. I'm a soldier just like you and
you ant suppose to barther me. Any no use for you to bother us colored
soldiers, we ant going to bother you. He also says if the white soldier continue
to hit you, get on out of his way, and not "what ever we did" hit them back.

Also since we've been here our guards were put around the areas in which
we live, they were all given guns but not any amunation of course. All the

white soldiers have amunation. They also decided to put on colored military
Police in the colored section of town to keep down disturbance between one
another, but they have no guns or amunation, nothing but the M.P. badge not
even a club. That's in order that we don't fool with the white soldiers. The
white soldier M.P.s have pistols, clubs and amunation. They are allowed to
arrest colored soldiers, but we're not allowed to touch the white soldiers.

This is our problem, I wish that you could help us in some respect, and if
possible please publish this letter so that the rest of the country would know
how they're treating colored soldiers in the U. S. Army.

Anything that you can do to help us will be very, very much appreciated.

> Co. E, 25th Inf.
> Camp Bowie, Texas
> Signed, all the soldiers of the
> 2nd Batallion

'Negro Slaves' of Fort Leonard Wood

April 30, 1942

Dear Mr. Hastie:

We are writing you this letter as a plea in behalf of we "Negro Slaves" of Fort Leonard Wood, Missouri, to ask that you give some concern to a situation that has been, and is becoming even more intolerable. It defies the very cause for which they proclaim we, as a United Nation, are striving to make possible for all. Not only has this situation created ill-feeling, but it has also caused many soldiers to query as to the actual difference between being soldiers and being slaves.

Yesterday some of us soldiers were reading an old copy of a St. Louis paper which expressed the dissenting sentiments and attitudes of our people in regards to the use of their taxes to activate an industry which pampers to a union that connives, finesses, and finally says no to giving an opportunity to our Negro families pursuing a livelihood. You who are civilians are not alone in feeling that this war is a costly sacrifice for so false a practice. We laud your efforts and wish that we could be there to aid in the accomplishment of something that is very real.

The situation about which we are writing you is the cheap morale breaking technique used by the Commanding Officers of this camp to keep the Negro youth of Fort Leonard Wood in a servile and very much subordinate position. Fort Leonard Wood is divided into two major divisions; the regular units and the Engineer Replacement Training Center. All of the Negroes who are transferred to the Engineer Replacement Training Center, Fort Leonard Wood, Missouri, we are placed in the Seventh Group. This Seventh Group is composed solely of Negro soldier trainees. Trainees whose educational qualifications range from no formal education to second and third year graduate students. Students, who in civil life were beginning to pursue the highest of academic degrees.

The total strength of the Seventh Group numbers from three to four thousand. These soldiers are divided into four distinct groups; thirty-third, thirty-fourth, and thirty-fifth battalions. There is also a Negro band. The Seventh

Group personnel office serves as a clearing house for the Seventh Group. In the personnel office there are approximately thirty Negro clerks. The theory that is given a new clerk is that if he applies himself he will be able to work up to top positions in the personnel office. As each new clerk comes in the office he strives to become efficient to the point of necessitating promotion to the rank of corporal. Finally he is made a corporal. Then he applies himself all the more to be promoted to the grade of sergeant; and finds, much to his bewilderment, that the cannot go any higher. He immediately questions if it is that he lacks the efficiency; and is given the "brush off" that he will be promoted soon. If he pushes the reason again, though there is a vacancy, the next time he is given an answer he is also given a transfer to another camp.

In the personnel office they have one white corporal, who can barely read and write, four white sergeants, one of whom was tutored into his job by a Negro youth, one white staff sergeant and one white master sergeant. Whenever a white sergeant is transferred another white is told that he will be made sergeant providing he consents to go to work in the Seventh Group personnel. A Negro does not know enough to be placed in the vacancy created by the transfer of his superior non-commissioned officer. The Negro corporal is then forced to tutor this incumbent sergeant. It is quite obvious what the outcome of this is—the Negro is still corporal and the white boy is now sergeant. Mind you, the Seventh Group is an entirely Negro training unit except of course for positions for white non-commissioned officers that they could not otherwise place.

In none of the battalion headquarters are there any Negroes with ratings higher than that of a corporal. Of course each battalion headquarters has its staff sergeant, who of course is white. The group headquarters does not have one Negro commissioned officer. The only thing the Negro soldier is used for there is to sweep the floor or in the army vanacular, *extra duty*. The white trainees, two white master sergeants, one white technical sergeant, one white first sergeant, seventeen white staff sergeants, seven white sergeants and six white corporals.

Recently it has come of general knowledge that a special order has come out from Headquarters, ERTC, Fort Leonard Wood, Missouri, that there shall be no ratings for Negroes as master, technical, or staff sergeant. In other words, all of the ratings that pay the best money or highest in rank, are reserved for the white friends of the white officers.

We feel that if we are good enough to rain to be soldiers, we are also good enough to hold some of the high non-commissioned offices. We have constantly asked why, and received a transfer into the South as an answer. Here our hands are tied.

We implore you to give public voice to this situation that we may know why we are good enough to trek in the mud all day, but aren't good enough to handle our own records.

Yours for a Double Victory,

Men of Fort Leonard Wood

Negro Hating Cracker from Louisiana

The Pittsburgh Courier   Co. I. 469 Q. M. Regt. Trk.
Centre Avenue   Van Buren, Arkansas
Pittsburgh, Pennsylvania   June 30, 1942

Gentlemen:

I wish to bring to your attention the condition that exist here. To the third battalion of the above truck regiment stationed at Camp Maxey, Texas are up here in the cracker infested low lands of Arkansas along the river of the same name. Our mission is to do flood relief work. Which is an emergency and very important.

To the undersigned and the company as a whole have a part to play in this war, which is for the survivals of our ideals and the opportunity to carry on the fight for democracy that serves one and all equally. We are ready, willing and able but, we are not going to accept the conditions our Battalion commanders are trying to force upon us.

He, Major Sheriden, is a rough dried, leather neck Negro hating cracker from Louisiana, who has insulted all Negroes in general. Calls our women everything but women. Misuse soldiers, treat us as if we were in a forced labor camp or chain gang.

One of our soldiers who should have been in a hospital was locked in a chain which was chained to a tree so long, until his arm started to swell. He was accused of going off the post without a pass. Which he the soldier denies. His diet was bread and water, two times a day. In the German and Japanese concentration camps prisoners are not treated in that manner, prisoners are not handled in such barberic ways.

The Major told one of his Uncle Tom stooges he was going to set an example for those D.N. We would appreciate these conditions being exposed. I am sending you films which we cannot have developed here. When developed they will show you the soldier chained to a tree.

I am a western Pennsylvanian, living in the Pittsburgh district all of my life, living in Oakmont. I want the people of the Pittsburgh district to know of the sacrafices we local soldiers are making here and overseas which should inspire them to work and fight harder for victory on the home front while we are giving them victory on the battle front.

Yours for results,

Cpl. Daniell E. Williams
S/Sgt. Sterle Wilson
Pfc. Jasper Smith of
Southern California

Struck Brutally across the Face

To the Editor of *The Call and Post*
    The Call and Post Bldg.
    East 55th Street,   Keesler Field, Miss.
    Cleveland, Ohio   December 3, 1943

Dear Sir:

No doubt this article will be of interest to your readers who are concerned about conditions existing in or near army posts where Negro soldiers are stationed.

The following article is not an eye witness account. It is the consenous of statements from various soldiers who were unfortunate enough to have been "bit players" in the passing scene.

On December 1, 1943, which was the day after payday, a number of Negro soldiers, having received the customary six hour pass from the Company Commanders of their respective organizations, went into Biloxi.

In Biloxi, about two miles distance, a Negro soldier may find a change from army routine through the medium of a U.S.O., one theatre, and a few cafes.

On this particular evening that "change" was interrupted by twenty-odd white military policemen. Note: There are Negroes policing the Negro district. The whites drove into the district in jeeps armed with .45 automatics and Thompson out-machine guns.

They entered the various establishments, and reprimanded the soldiers for such minor offenses as buttons not fastened, caps tilted too much, ties loosened, and others of similar nature. They were then roughly ushered into a formation and marched to the Military Police Headquarters in Biloxi.

The lieutenant in charge gave orders to take all passes, and march the men back to Keesler Field. He told the M.P.'s to use their clubs, and if that did no good they would know what to do.

When one soldier asked (while in ranks) what was going to happen to them, he was struck brutally across the face with a club. Several others were struck either with fists, or clubs or straps.

One soldier, living in Biloxi and stationed at Keesler Field, was walking with his wife. He too, was forced into the formation leaving his wife crying as were many other colored civilians who witnessed this humiliation.

The helpless Negro M.P.'s took no part in this disgraceful mockery of democracy.

The soldiers were then marched back to Keesler Field, their names taken, and dismissed.

Several of the non-commissioned officers have made formal protests. What consideration non-commissioned officers, in good standing, will receive in the face of brutal inefficiency can be decided by the Commanding Officer in time only.

To this date nothing has been done.

Yours respectfully,

Pvt. Edward N. Lyles (35917044)
Class 700; Squad 707 1170
Training Group

Scattering Like a Pool of Animals

San Marcos, Texas
Sunday Morning

The Baltimore Afro-American   April 4, 1943

Dear Sir:

I read your very much appreciated article, and may I extend my many thanks to you and your papers and thanks again for investigating same. I sincerely hope and pray something can or will be done for the interest and welfare of all our men in the service wherever they may be, serving the same flag and country as we must, wearing the same uniform and fighting for the same freedom, we will always remain together as a group. We must work, fight, eat and think before we can do anything. Naturally, a majority always wins. As slow as I was to awake to the fact, one man alone will never win because the majority rules, to the extent they propose our time will come. I firmly believe that is correct, but I don't think we can gain any progress by sitting right waiting for any opportunity. We must fight from the bottom to reach the top. So, until we can learn to pull together in every way, we can never reach our goal.

Circumstances here are terrible, as in my previous statement I stated. It is "hell" in the Army and Texas. It isn't that I am afraid to fight, but what are we fighting for? As far as I can see we will never be a free people for the simple reason a majority rules. They either rule in or out. In this respect, mostly out, because again a majority doesn't speak up. We are supposed to be free to do as we desire, as long as we are within the law. Strange enough, we are not good enough to use the same toilets or "latrine", to dispose of waste matter from our bodies, so you can very easy observe how much we are appreciated. If there is a "hell" we are now in it and surely after our work is finished here, heaven will be our home. God only knows how we are suffering.

For now I must close but shall keep you well informed of our activities here to the best of my ability. At the present we are restricted for an indefinite period, as Thursday last some of our men refused to respond to an order issued in the usual abrupt manner using the term "Nigger." We can not go off our post unless our commanding officer escorts us. He must be with us to snap his whip as which time we are to scatter like a pool of animals fearing their master. We have but a very little privileges. We are much in the Army as we have no choice, but we are not suppose to be treated as inhumans but as able-

bodied men, which we are and we are good men in every respect and way.
Naturally good and bad in every race just the bad make it hard for the good
and the good can not over-rule the bad. For that reason we must suffer for
someone else who doesn't know how to act.

I suppose if a fatal injury had been inflicted and death was the penalty we
all would have to die, to pay for what one or two persons do. Under such
circumstances, wo until next time please continue to publish and I shall write
you again soon, in the near future. Please continue to investigate as I would
nearly give my right arm to get a discharge from the service.

Thank you kindly in advance.

I remain yours,

Protesting the Word Nigger

MEDICAL DETACHMENT, DIVISION ARTILLERY,
2nd CAVALRY DIVISION

Fort Clark, Texas
The Atlanta Daily World April 23, 1943.

Dear Editor:

I would like to know if your paper approves of a General calling his soldiers "Nigger" to their face? I think that we are in this war to fight for the rigts of all minority races, the morale of this organization will be low if our soldiers are not addressed in the right manner.

Our colored chaplain was run off this post by the General Johnson solely because he protested to him against using the word "Nigger" when referring to colored troops. I feel that it is my right and privilege to protect against the un-Godly ways that the men of the 2nd Cavalry Division are treated by their white Texas officers.

I hope that you will see that the colored people of this nation know that these conditions exist.

Believe me that these are true statements.

A Negro Soldier

You Act as Tho the World Owes You Something

                                                    Headquarters and Service Co.
                                                    388th Engineers G. S. Regt.
To: The Editor of the   Engineering Unit Training Center
Pittsburgh Courier   Camp Sutton, North Carolina
Pittsburgh, Pa.   October 15, 1943

Dear Sir:

I am writing your paper and the millions who read the Courier, of some of
the ill treatment and hardships which I and other soldiers of the Regt. had to
indure.

As I write you, I write with the interest, that you will publish whatever
portions of this letter that you find possible, as perhaps their will be portions
you will omit.

But as I am an alert believer in the quotation.

"The pen is mightier than the sword."

I shall began my letter by telling you that I served (15) fifteen months
under the command of all white officers, in the wilderness of Canada, during
the cold winter of 42-43.

When reaching our destination our officers spreaded rumors among the
people that we colored soldiers were no good, and everything they could think
of to make things hard for us, they tried to make the people believe we were
not even humans.

Of course the people themselves knew nothing of us.

The morale of regt. got so low until no one had any spirit of interest in their
work.

One of the higher ranking officers made this statement to us "you act as
tho the world owes you something" this is not even a small sample of some the
remarks made to us.

Where furloughs were granted they were only issued to their favorites, high
ranking, noncommissioned officers, whom they could influence as they desired.

We worked, sacrificed and withstood the hardships and injustices. Now having returned to the states their has been no change as yet.

After spending 15 months in the wilderness we return to recieve 15 day
furloughs, we feel as tho we should have a little more time.

I would not like to predict the destiny of the regiment, if we are taken into foreign service again, with the same groups of officers and, non Commissioned officers.

The enlisted men that comprises the regiment are all colored troops, they work ardently. But after such extremely hard times that our nerves were almost to the breaking point. One can easily understand our feelings.

But if duty so calls us to leave again, we hope it will be under different circumstances.

Sincerely,

Howard G. Conley

P.S. In printing this please withdraw the above name of signature, thanking you kindly.

Attempting to Create Pre-Civil War Days

Cpl. Jonathan Welch

Mr. Howard Murphy   33476481

Business Manager   H & S Co. 95th Engr Regt.

Afro-American Newspapers   APO 516, c/o Postmaster

Baltimore, Md.   New York, N. Y.

10 December 1943

Dear Sir:

In reply of your letter of November 15th concerning the morals of Negro troops under white officers, here is your story.

I am now a member of the Engineer Regiment, which is the familiar case of using Negroes for the laboring work, and some doing clerical work. Most of the men are untrained and know practically nothing about combat duties.

That old Southern principle of keeping Negroes as slaves is still being practiced. Working from Sun rise to Sun set and in some case into the middle of the night. Some of the men have the benefit of the doubt providing that they are good Rats. Those who run to the white officer and repeat all of the conversation that they have heard, are promised ratings as it appears to be the best way of getting advancement. The First Sergeant is from Philadelphia, Pennsylvania, and incapable of his position, repeating every incident to the Commanding Officer. The 15th Amendment of the Constitution has practically been abolished, under the careful supervision of the First Sergeant and Commanding Officer.

We are practically imprisoned at the present. Our Commanding Officer have limited our Post Boundaries to an Area 50 feet long and about 35 feet wide and we have the side of the housing area for a playground.

Our pass privileges are limited to 2 per week. In case that our friends in the nearby towns and city do not write to the Commanding Officer a letter stating that we are invited for the week-end, 24 hour passes are not issued. In order

to visit some of the members of our own organization who are about 15
minutes walk from one quarters to the other, one is required to have a pass
signing from on Charge of Quarters to the other. This is done because there
are civilians between the two quarters. In order to visit our friendly Allies who
are practically adjacent to us, this is counted as one of your passes for the
week. When one is going on pass he must be searched for weapons (knives in
particular). Only on the week-end are the members of this organization permitted to go more than 10 miles from their station.

The Red Cross is aware that we are located in this spot. Our friends have
been asked not to associate with us because they are white and we are colored.
Strange as it may seem, but hard to believe that the people are told that after
we stay here, we will grow tails, and we are direct descendents from monkeys.
Occasionally one can find people who still run from us. We have had three
pictures shown at our quarters, there has not been any such things as dances.
Not because the citizens of this beautiful land will not attend, but our officers
who are from, what is known as PECKAWOOD land always create the problem
of socializing where with some of the citizens, we are liked better than the
white American, as it has been proved that we are gentlemen.

In one of the towns nearby there was an attempted lynching by our white
troops and some Negroes were injured. As far as I know to date there has not
been anything done about this. It has been said that men of this organization
have deliberately cut white troops, but the men have only tried to protect
themselves from overwhelming odds. Men have been lined up continually for
M. P.'s and civilians to identify them as committing some crimes which are
always presented. Men have been given long terms of protecting themselves as
being tried by Courts of men who truly think that Negroes are to be done
away with and kept in prison or away from the white race altogether. Court
Martial is the morale of the officers of the organization.

United States of America is known for the freedom which we are supposed
to have. It has been President Roosevelt's policy in several of his speeches
concerning the morale of the Armed Forces overseas as well as those home,
"That if we must die, we will die for the things that we stand for and believe
in." Of course slavery was abolished in 1861, it is the policy in this branch of

the army to have it again, by having white officers mostly from Southern States over Negroes and trying to create pre-civil war days.

The people of the British Isles are willing in what way they can try and provide entertainments for us. Most of the men are wondering if they are here in prison, and, try to get something for morale, which is gone forever, our officers will lock us in our quarters as if we seem to be any too happy.

Your friend,

Jonathan Welch

P.S. Anytime you want a story I will do my best.

Mean Words to the Group

Med. Det. Sec. #2
Mr. Truman K. Gibson   Station Hospital,
Civilian Aide to the Sect of War   *Camp Sutton*, N.C.
Washington, D. C.   1 November 1943

Dear Sir:

Your letter in reply to mine forwarded you from the Courier, was a little delayed in being sent me, because I had received a transfer out of the unit, into the Med. Det. Station Hospital on this post, where the same prejudice exists, although not as great as in the 388th Engineers.

I shall begin my story from the time I joined the 388th Engineers on about 22 November 1942. There were 25 E. M. sent from the Station Hospital, Fort Huachuca, Arizona, to join the Med. Det. 388th Engineers, who were then in Canada. In the group there was one Sergeant (myself), one Tech. 3rd grade, one Tech. 4th grade, one Tech. 5th grade, and several Privates first class. We were split up in the Province of Alberta, city of Edmonton in Canada. Men were sent to various companies of the Regiment in various parts of the country. We worked in almost unbearable weather conditions. Men were freezing their hands, feet, etc., and when they would report on sick call, they would be told by our Medical Officers that nothing was wrong with them. If they were not marked "*Quarters*" on the sick book, when they were returned to their companies, they were punished by having to do a tour of extra duty.

When duty called in the morning, and men would build fires, to keep warm awaiting the remainder of the group, and when the Commanding Officer would come by and see such, he would kick the fires out, and speak mean words to the group.

Conditions of that nature existed throughout our stay there, and we were helpless to do anything about it. If such can be investigated, and corrected, we would be quite grateful and much relieved.

Respectfully yours,

Pvt. Howard G. Conley
Med. Det. Station Hosp.
Camp Sutton, N. C.

Throwing Away Discharge Papers

393-Aviation Squadron
A.A.B. Alamogordo, New Mexico
The Pittsburgh Courier   December 14, 1943

Dear Sir:

Conditions at this base being deplorable for colored soldiers, we as a group thought that your paper would be interested.

There is an instance of our present Commanding Officer throwing away a colored soldier's discharge papers. The soldier in question is still with the squadron. The proof is here.

Another instance of this Texas officer, is two soldiers were put in the Guardhouse for failure to report for duty, after working the night before.

If we demur we are threatened with the Guardhouse, or being beat up.

The whole base here is rotten with prejudice and discrimination. Most southern officers consider their war won, if he can do any thing to retarde colored soldier's morale.

At Base Headquarters conditions are much the same. The few that could, and would help our squadron are of course overruled by the southern element.

Something can, and must be done, and soon.

The Courier's reputation for printing the facts is known. Can something be done in our case?

Very truly yours,

Pvt. John S. Lyons.
393rd-Aviation Squadron.
A.A.B. Alamogordo, N. Mexico.

P.S. This is a good example of the mentality of the people in this part of the world.
Pvt. John S. Lyons

This Is the South!

.Sgt. Ben Kiser, Jr.

Mr. P. L. Prattis   Ward 22 A.

Executive Editor   Kennedy General Hospital

Pittsburgh Courier   Memphis, (15), Tenn.

Pittsburgh, 19, Penn.   June 20, 1944

Dear Sir:

This letter is being written with a purpose of extreme importance to the
Negroes stationed here at this hospital. We hope and place confidence in your
giving us the information deserved.

I have been stationed here for over two (2) months as a patient. I have not
been overseas but there are plenty of Negro boys here who have. Most of
these boys have companions who are white. They came back together. In the
time that these boys have been here they have been together. They keep in the
same wards, go to the same shows without any segregation. But when going to
the mess halls for chow they are segregated. Few of the white boys sit at the
tables allowed for colored. But the Sgt tells them to move because its not
permitted in the mess halls. The white boys disapprove of this measure and ask
why. The Sgt tells them its orders from the Lt. When we asked the Lt. he
states that this is the South. We know this is the South but also the Army. My
belief is that it can be stopped with a slight push from you. We would like for
you to give your opinion on the matter remembering an article published in the
August edition of the Courier based on a War Dept. directive banning discrimination and segregation in army camps and hospitals. We would like to have a
copy of that directive and also the numbers of it. We will appreciate all that
you can do for us.

We will be awaiting your reply with great anticipation.

Sincerely yours,

Sgt Ben Kiser, Jr.
Ward 22 A.
Kennedy General Hosp.
Memphis (15) Tenn.

Ye Shall Know Your Place

                                                      August 23rd. 1944
The Honorable Congressman   Army Medical Center
William L. Dawson   Washington, S. C.

Dear Congressman:

   Enclosed is a written account of an incident that occurred at Camp Lee
Virginia, when a group of forty eight Negro & white soldiers arrived at the
said camp, to begin the third month of their three months training course as
medical and surgical technicians.

   Even though sir, the colored soldiers in our company have the highest grade
average, we were informed today by our school commander, Major Tunick,
that in the past there had been no Negroes admitted to the advance course of
medical & surgical technicians, and there would be none selected from our
group. However fifteen per cent of the white soldiers in our class failed where
only one Negro out of thirty eight failed. .

   Dear Congressman we appeal to you whom we know as a soldier and a
fighter for the course of the common man.

                                                            Respectfully

                                        A Soldier at Walter Reed Hospital

6

Appeals to the White House

In the interest of victory for the United Nations, another
Executive Order is now needed. An Executive Order
which will lay the base for fighting for democracy in the
Armed Forces of our country. An Executive Order which
would bring about the result here at Davis-Monthan Field
whereby the Negro soldiers would be integrated into all
of the Sections on the base, as fighting men, instead of in
the segregated Section C as housekeepers.

Then and only then can your pronouncement of the
war aims of the United Nations mean to *all* that we are
"fighting to make a world in which tyranny, and aggression cannot exist; a world based upon freedom, equality
and justice; a world in which all persons, regardless of
race, color and creed, may live in peace, honor and
dignity.

Private Charles F. Wilson

During the 1940s, black Americans in and out of uniform forged
ahead toward the elimination of segregation and discrimination
in the armed forces. Their combined voices represented a
strong condemnation of army racism, and they made their feelings known
to the Roosevelts and President Harry S Truman.

But by June 1942, Judge William H. Hastie had become disillusioned
over the progress he and other black leaders were making toward redressing the grievances of black soldiers and integrating the armed
forces. He remarked privately, "I was never optimistic that it would be
possible to persuade the military to eliminate existing racial segregation
while World War II was in progress." Nevertheless, Hastie worked toward this aim. In fact, he wrote to Assistant Secretary of War John J.
McCloy that black protest against racial segregation in the armed forces
would continue despite his warnings that such agitation was more harmful
than good.[1]

The question of whether black protest was harmful did not deter the
black leadership. They made army integration and the elimination of ra-

cial abuses their highest priority during the national emergency. From 1941 to 1945, while Hastie pressed the War Department from within, the black leadership waged a public campaign. Roy Wilkins (assistant director of the National Association for the Advancement of Colored People) editorialized in the *New York Age* (a black newspaper based in Harlem, New York) that rather than save democracy and destroy Hitlerism the defense program operated deliberately to keep blacks in their places by denying them training, employment, and the opportunity to serve in the armed forces honorably. Mrs. Mary McLeod Bethune (founder and president of the National Council of Negro Women and director of the Division of Negro Affairs of the National Youth Administration in Roosevelt's administration) appealed to Mrs. Roosevelt to put pressure on the president to come to the aid of blacks. A. Philip Randolph (president of the Brotherhood of Sleeping Car Porters' Union and leader of the March-on-Washington Movement) scorned the army's racial policies on nationwide radio, while Dr. Charles H. Wesley of Howard University History Department challenged the War Department and the Executive Branch to implement the "Four Freedoms" (in January 1941, Roosevelt named four freedoms as the war aims of the U.S. and as essentials to civilization: freedom of speech, freedom of worship, freedom from want, and freedom from fear) at home in America. Walter White (executive director of the National Association for the Advancement of Colored People) and John P. Davis (national secretary of the National Negro Congress) urged President Roosevelt to meet with them in an effort to work out a solution for ending segregation and discrimination in the armed forces and in the defense plants. And Congressman Arthur W. Mitchell asked the House of Representatives to consider the patriotism and heroic military deeds of black soldiers while they sustained the War Department's racial policies. In another speech he asked if white America really concerned itself with blacks in the war effort.[2]

The comments of these national black leaders indicate that the national self-help organizations were in the vanguard of the integrationists. The big four: the National Association for the Advancement of Colored People, the March-on-Washington Movement, the National Urban League, and the National Negro Congress advocated stopping at nothing short of full integration of the armed forces. The Washington, D.C., branch of the

NAACP, for example, sent a lengthy memorandum to the War Department that spelled out in detail its views on American racism. It urged the War Department to stop paying lip service to antiquated theories of military efficiency and proposed that institutional racism be abolished in all agencies of the federal government, and in those directly or indirectly associated with it. In the same spirit the Chicago branch of the National Urban League and the Chicago Council of Negro Organizations met with Undersecretary of War Robert P. Patterson and voiced similar complaints. Patterson told the group, however, that he was disturbed over the development of national organizations opposing anything but complete integration of the armed forces.[3]

The March-on-Washington Movement wielded the most influence during this period. During the spring and early summer of 1941, it sent letters to President Roosevelt, Mrs. Roosevelt, and Secretary of War Henry L. Stimson. Its director, A. Philip Randolph, urged them to support the March on Washington by speaking to the marchers at a rally scheduled at Lincoln Memorial. Randolph maintained that fifty thousand or more blacks would move into Washington to demonstrate the need for jobs, equal opportunity, and the integration of America's army and naval forces.[4]

Meanwhile Judge Hastie requested that Secretary Stimson or some high-level official of the War Department speak briefly but candidly to the marchers about segregation and discrimination in the army and in the defense plants. Hastie suggested that the military representative be prepared to explain the following: the failure of the president to ban discrimination in defense industries; why the Senate continued to delay action on Senate Resolution 75, which called for an investigation of discriminatory practices in employment; the exclusion of blacks from the Navy, Marine Corps, and Air Corps; why the army refused to modify racial segregation; and why widespread discriminatory practices continued in Civil Service appointments.[5]

President Roosevelt, worried about the impact the threatened march on Washington might have on the nation and the democratic countries of the world, asked Mrs. Roosevelt to ask Undersecretary Patterson what could be done to prevent the march. She contacted Patterson; he recommended that she and General Edwin M. Watson (Roosevelt's aide) meet with Hastie and Randolph. Patterson prepared two memorandums; one for Mrs. Roosevelt and one for General Watson. General Watson was instructed to tell Hastie and Randolph to inform the black leadership that the War Department had implemented its policy announced in 1940; that black units had been organized in all branches of the armed forces (this was not true, according to Hastie); and that Benjamin O. Davis, Sr., had been promoted to brigadier general, something never before attained by a black American. Watson was told to say further that:

> The complaints that we have not mingled white troops and negro troops in the same units is unfounded. Such a mingling was not a part of the President's policy, and for practical reasons it would be impossible to put into operation. It would seem that Negroes might be inspired to take pride in the efficiency of Negro units in the Army, as representing their contribution to the armed forces.[6]

Patterson suggested that Mrs. Roosevelt tell Randolph that Judge Hastie had constantly advised her and the War Department on questions involving black servicemen, that by June 30, 1941, the total number of blacks in the armed forces would exceed 80,000, and that they were attending all of the regular service schools except those of the Air Corps, because a separate school would be established in this branch of the services.[7]

Randolph was sympathetic to Mrs. Roosevelt (she was considered by most black Americans as an ally in the White House) but did not abandon his plans for the march. He maintained that if the president did not issue an executive order banning segregation and racial discrimination the march would proceed. Rather than chance the disruption of a mass racial march, Roosevelt issued Executive Order 8802 in 1941. It prohibited discrimination, not segregation, in the nation's defense industries but said nothing at all about segregation and discrimination in the armed forces. Thus, Randolph's threat to lead a mass march on Washington only accomplished half of what the March-on-Washington Movement had hoped to achieve. Integration of the armed forces was yet to come. Nevertheless, "the March on Washington Committee had forced the federal government to admit publicly that blacks suffered from discrimination in employment and that the government had a responsibility to remedy it."[8]

The official remedy, however, for desegregating the nation's armed forces would not come until 1948.

While President Roosevelt acted to avoid a major racial confrontation, Mrs. Roosevelt showed compassion for the plight of black soldiers. In a 1943 letter to Assistant Secretary of War McCloy, she wrote:

> These colored boys lie side by side in the hospitals in the southwest Pacific with the white boys and somehow it is harder for me to believe that they should not be treated on an equal basis. Some of them from the south are quite evidently inferior in mentality and education. Nevertheless they do the job and they get killed just the same as the white boys.[9]

In addition to the appeals of Mrs. Roosevelt and the black leadership, black troops themselves appealed directly to the president to end segregation and racial discrimination. Because he believed that racial discrimination was inconsistent with the nation's democratic ideals, Private Charles Wilson, for example, spoke of the war aims espoused by Roosevelt but reminded him that:

> ... the picture in our country is marred by one of the strongest paradoxes in our whole fight against world fascism. The United States Armed Forces, to fight for World Democracy, is within itself undemocratic. The undemocratic policy of jim-crow and segregation is practiced by our Armed Forces against its Negro members. Totally inadequate opportunities are given to the Negro members of our Armed Forces, nearly one tenth of the whole, to participate with "equality" . . . "regardless of race and color" in the fight for our war aims.[10]

Although black soldiers voiced other major grievances, Wilson's letter demonstrates the tone of the appeals made to the Roosevelts and President Truman.

NOTES

1. Judge William H. Hastie, private interview with author, 1701 Popla Lane, N.W., Washington, D.C., March 8, 1974; Letter, Hastie to author, October 8, 1974; Memorandum, Hastie to McCloy, June 30, 1942, Civilian Aide to the Secretary of War Subject File, 1940–1947, National Archives Record Group 107 (hereafter cited as NARG).

2. Editorial, *New York Age*, March 21, 1941, Box 230, National Association for the Advancement of Colored People Papers, Manuscript Division, Library of Congress, Washington, D.C. (hereafter cited as NAACP Papers); Jervis A. Anderson, *A. Philip Randolph: A Biographical Portrait* (New York: Harcourt, Brace, Jovanovich, Inc., 1973), 243; Memorandum, "Randolph Comments on Army's Race Policy," Major James S. Tatman, Acting Chief, Analysis Branch to General F. H. Osborn, Chief, Special Service Division, Public Relations Bureau, June 14, 1943, Office of War Information, NARG 208; "Army, Navy Exclusion Is Rapped," *Pittsburgh Courier*, February 8, 1941; Letter, White to Roosevelt, March 13, 1941; Letter, Edwin M. Watson to White, April 8, 1941; Letter, White to Watson, April 11, 1941; Letter, John P. Davis to Roosevelt, April 24, 1941; Memorandum, Watson to Davis, May 1, 1941; Letter, Davis to Watson, May 7, 1941, all in the Franklin D. Roosevelt Papers, Franklin D. Roosevelt Library, Hyde Park, New York; "Negro Congress Urges New Western Front; End of J.C. in Armed Units," *Pittsburgh Courier; Congressional Record*, 77th Congress, 2nd Session (1942), Appendix 290, 2891.

3. Memorandum, District of Columbia Branch, NAACP to War Department, January 14, 1942, Army General Staff, NARG 407; Office Memorandum, "Conference of the Chicago Council of Negro Organizations with Patterson," March 28, 1941, Civilian Aide to the Secretary of War Subject File, 1940–1947, NARG 107.

4. Letter, Randolph to Roosevelt, May 29, 1941, Box 151, Robert P. Patterson Papers, Manuscript Division, Library of Congress, Washington, D.C.; Letter, Randolph to Mrs. Eleanor Roosevelt, June 3, 1941; Letter, Randolph to Henry L. Stimson, June 23, 1941, Civilian Aide to the Secretary of War Subject File, 1940–1947, NARG 107.

5. Memorandum, Hastie to Stimson, June 17, 1941, Civilian Aide to the Secretary of War Subject File, 1940–1947, NARG 107; Henry L. Stimson Diary, June 18, 1941, Yale University Library, New Haven, Connecticut.

6. Letter, Eleanor Roosevelt to Robert P. Patterson, June 10, 1941; Patterson to Watson, June 14, 1941, Box 151, Patterson Papers.

7. Memorandum, Patterson to Eleanor Roosevelt, June 13, 1941, Civilian Aide to the Secretary of War Subject File, 1940–1947, NARG 107.

8. Anderson, *A. Philip Randolph*, 257–260; Frank Freidel, *F.D.R. and the South* (Louisiana: Louisiana State University, 1965), 97; Virginius Dabney, "Nearer and Nearer the Precipice," *The Atlantic Monthly*, CCXXI (January 1943), 94: Charles E. Silbermann, *Crisis in Black and White* (New York: Random House, Inc., 1964), 65; William H. Harris, *The Harder We Run: Black Workers since the Civil War* (New York: Oxford University Press, 1982), 116–117.

9. Letter, Eleanor Roosevelt to John J. McCloy, September 29, 1943, Civilian Aide to the Secretary of War Subject File, 1940–1947, NARG 107.

10. Letter, Charles F. Wilson to President Roosevelt, May 9, 1944, Civilian Aide to the Secretary of War Subject File, 1940–1947, NARG 107.

Not Appealing for Sympathy

Mrs. Eleanor Roosevelt   374th Engineer Battalion
The Executive Mansion   Headquarters and Service Company
Washington, D.C.   January 29, 1943

My dear Mrs. Roosevelt:

I do not like to consume the time of busy people, yet I think I have a
problem that warrants consideration, that up to this point I have failed to
receive. I would like to give you my background so that you might be in a
better position to judge me and the problem that faces me.

I am thirty years old. I am the son of teacher parents. My father is at
present Dean of Men at Florida A. and M. College and is sixty seven. I
graduated from Florida A. and M. High School in 1930, and from the college
department in 1934. I taught, and was school principal for six years. I attended the University of Michigan in 1940–41 and received the master of
science degree in public health. I taught public health to teachers at Benedict
College, in Columbia, South Carolina for the summers of 1941 and 1942. I
was principal of a small high school in Florida in 1941–42 fall period. I was
inducted into the army in August 1942. In the Army General Classification
Test I scored 127.

At present I am serving as a chaplain's assistant. The work is all right, but
the chances for advancement are nil. I believe that there is a need for a
Colored Commissioned Officer to contact the Colored Service Units in camps
where these units are not numerous enough to have a chaplain assigned, to
help in building up the morale, and keeping it up. I have made many friends in
the army, since being here, because, it seems as though I have the facility of
helping them with some of their problems. My interest in public health was
directed in the channel of helping the mal-adjusted. I am a licensed minister,
and my denomination is planning to ordain me sometime in the near future. I
doubt that I could qualify under the present requirements to become a chaplain, but I do think I could do a wonderful piece of work as a morale officer in
a given area with Colored Service Units.

Many times these soldiers have problems that they are reluctant to take to a
commanding officer, because he might think it very trivial, but to that soldier it
means a lot. I have worked with young men and women, and I know some of
the problems confronting my people in the South, that cannot be solved now.

My interest is in helping to win the war, where my native ability, educational training, and excellent background might be brought into full focus.

I have at present the rank of private first class, after five months in the army. I am not appealing for sympathy, I am appealing for an opportunity to serve in a capacity with a rank that would be more commensurate with my training, intelligence, and experience and background. I am careful thinker, well liked by those with whom I work, and those who really know me.

I feel that I can be of invaluable service in some capacity as that I have mentioned. I feel that you are the one person that can help me to realize that goal. I feel that your keen understanding of the sacredness of human personality will help me.

Most respectfully yours,

Pfc. Jubie B. Bragg, Jr.
ASN 34247185

Paradox in American Democracy

33rd AAF Base Unit (CCTS(H))
Section C
DAVIS-MONTHAN FIELD
Tucson, Arizona
9 May 1944.

President Franklin Delano Roosevelt
White House
Washington, D. C.

Dear President Roosevelt:

It was with extreme pride that I, a soldier in the Armed Forces of our
country, read the following affirmation of our war aims, pronounced by you at
a recent press conference:

"The United Nations are fighting to make a world in which tyranny, and
aggression cannot exist; a world based upon freedom, equality, and justice; a
world in which all persons, regardless of race, color and creed, may live in
peace, honor and dignity."

Your use of the word "world" means that we are fighting for "freedom,
equality, and justice" for "all persons, regardless of race, color and creed" in
our own part of the world, the United States of America, as well as all other
countries where such a fight is needed to be carried through. Your use of the
words "all persons, regardless of race, color and creed" means that we are
fighting for "freedom, equality, and justice" for our Negro American, no less
than for our white Americans, or our Jewish, Protestant and Catholic Americans, or for the subjugated peoples in Europe and China and all other lands.

And the part that our country is playing in the United Nations world
struggle against "tyranny and aggression" and for "a world based upon freedom, equality and justice", although lacking in many respects, is certainly not
one to be ashamed of.

Our driving back of the Japanese facists in the Pacific; our driving back of
the German fascists in North Africa, Sicily, and Italy, in conjunction with our
British and French Allies, freeing that part of the world from "tyranny and
aggression" as the prerequisite for bringing "freedom, equality and justice" to
the North African and Italian peoples; the tremendous preparations and planning that we as part of the United Nations have carried out so that we now
stand on the eve of the invasion, and in conjunction with our Allies, the
British, Russian, French and European Underground, on the eve of freeing the
subjugated peoples of Europe from the German fascist tyranny; the glorious

part that we played in the decisions reached at Teheran; these are vivid
records of the manner in which the war aims of the United Nations, as
pronounced by you, are being fought for by us, throughout the world.

On the home front there are vivid examples also; your issuance of Executive
Order 8802, which established the Fair Employment Practices Committee, to
fight against the discriminatory employment practices being used against
Negroes and other minority groups in the war industries; the precedent-smash-
ing decision of the United States Supreme Court, upholding the right of
Negroes to vote in the Texas Democratic Primaries; the April 10th decision of
the United States Supreme Court, against peonage, which voided a Florida
statute which makes it a crime to obtain a wage advance with intent to defraud
an employer. The court held that the statute was a violation of the 13th
Amendment and the Federal Antipeonage Act; Attorney General Biddle's clearing of the CIO Political Action Committee, against the attempts on the part of
Representative Smith of Virginia to destroy it; the establishment on the part of
our government of mixed housing projects like the Mother Cabrini Housing
Project in Chicago, where segregation because of "race, color and creed" was
done away with; the cleansing of our home front of the out and out fascists,
such as Elizabeth Dilling, Lawrence Dennis, George Sylvester Vierack, Kunze,
Pelly, and the other twenty five, who are being brought to trial by our Justice
Department; the support which you have given to the fight against the
flagrantly undemocratic poll tax as reported in the Afro-American of April the
8th: "President Roosevelt told his press conference last week that he feels the
poll tax is undemocratic."; the production by the U. S. Army Signal Corps, as
authorized by the War Department, of the film "The Negro Soldier"; these are
but a few of the many examples of the fight that the democratic forces in our
government, with your leadership, is carrying on in our country as part of the
world struggle against "tyranny" and for a "world based upon freedom, equality, and justice; a world in which all persons, regardless of race, color and
creed, may live in peace, honor and dignity."

But the picture in our country is marred by one of the strangest paradoxes
in our whole fight against world fascism. The United States Armed Forces, to
fight for World Democracy, is within itself undemocratic. The undemocratic
policy of jim crow and segregation is practiced by our Armed Forces against its
Negro members. Totally inadequate opportunities are given to the Negro members of our Armed Forces, nearly one tenth of the whole, to participate with
"equality" . . . "regarless of race and color" in the fight for our war aims. In
fact it appears that the army intends to follow the very policy that the FEPC is

battling against in civilian life, the pattern of assigning Negroes to the lowest types of work.

Let me give you an example of the lack of democracy in our Field, where I am now stationed. Negro soldiers are completely segregated from the white soldiers on the base. And to make doubly sure that no mistake is made about this, the barracks and other housing facilities (supply room, mess hall, etc.) of the Negro Section C are covered with black tar paper, while all other barracks and housing facilities on the base are painted white.

It is the stated policy of the Second Air Force that "every potential fighting man must be used as a fighting man. If you have such a man in a base job, you have no choice. His job must be eliminated or be filled by a limited service man, WAC, or civilian." And yet, leaving out the Negro soldiers working with the Medical Section, fully 50% of the Negro soldiers are working in base jobs, such as, for example, at the Resident Officers' Mess, Bachelor Officers' Quarters, and Officers' Club, as mess personnel, BOQ orderlies, and bar tenders. Leaving out the medical men again, based on the Section C average only 4% of this 50% would not be "potential fighting men."

It is also a fact that" . . . the employment of enlisted men as attendants at officers' clubs, whether officially designated as "Officers' Mess" or "Officers' Club" is not sanctioned by . . ." the Headquarters of the Army Air Forces.

Leaving out the medical men again, at least 50% of the members of the Negro Section C are being used for decidedly menial work, such as BOQ orderlies, janitors, permanent KP's and the like.

Let us assume as a basis for discussion that there are no civilians or limited service men to do the menial work on the base. The democratic way, based upon "equality and justice" would be to assign this work to both Negro and white. Instead the discriminatory and undemocratic method is used whereby all of this work is assigned to the Negro soldiers.

On the other hand suppose civilians were found to take over all of the base jobs and thus free the Negro soldiers for use as fighting men. They would not be given "on-the-job-training" to become members of the ground crew, such as is being done for the WAC members on the base, because there is no such program for Negroes at Davis-Monthan Field. They would not be trained to become aerial gunners, or bombardiers, or navigators, or pilots, or bombsight mechanics, or any of the many other specialists at Davis-Monthan Field, because there is no authorization in the Second Air Force for this training to be given to Negroes.

About 15% of the soldiers of Section C are in fighting jobs, and about another 5% are receiving "on-the-job-training" in Vehicle Maintenance. Thus we see that the maintenance of the ideology of "white supremacy" resulting in the undemocratic practices of jim-crow and segregation of the Negro members of the Armed Forces brings about the condition on Davis-Monthan Field whereby 80% of the whole Section is removed from the fighting activities on the base.

From what I read in the Newspapers, the above example from my own experience at Davis-Monthan Field, is typical of the situation throughout the Armed Forces. There is the report in an editorial on page five of the March 25th edition of the Pittsburgh Courier which states that: "Negro combat units are being constantly broken up and transferred to service units."

How can we convince nearly one tenth of the Armed Forces, the Negro members, that your pronouncement of the war aims of the United Nations means what it says, when their experience with one of the United Nations, the United States of America, is just the opposite?

Are the Chinese people to believe that we are fighting to bring them "freedom, equality, and justice", when they can see that in our Armed Forces we are not even practicing ourselves what we are preaching?

However, we leave ourselves wide open for sowers of disunity. Nothing would suit Hitler, Tojo, and our own native fascists better, than disunity. The lead editorial in the Afro-American of April the 1st entitled "Soldiers or Sissies" is a tragic example of this. The editorial after relating two cases of *tyranny* against two Negro soldiers: one in Alabama where the "civil police lynched a handcuffed, defenseless soldier when they were moving from one prison to another", and another case in Louisiana, where a "Bus driver shot and killed a New York who refused to move to a rear seat", goes on to say: "This is terrorism, and the army has no answer for it. Have the soldiers themselves an answer? There are thousands of them and only a few police or bus drivers." If the advice of that editorial were followed it could only lead to disunity and civil strife. We know that isn't the answer. Disunity and civil strife would only weaken our fight against the German and Japanese fascists, or more than that result in our defeat. A victory for the German and Japanese fascists would mean a victory for our own native fascists, who are at the bottom this whole program of "white supremacy", race hatred, jim-crowism, and segregation. It would mean victory, not defeat for the Rankins, Bilbos, Smiths, Hearsts, McCormicks, Paglers, and Dies.

Such an editorial is totally irresponsible. But decrying such an editorial will get us nowhere. The only answer is to remove the conditions which give rise to such an editorial. That means fighting for the war aims of the United Nations in our own country as well as throughout the rest of the world. That means

that we must fight against the fascist shouters of "white supremacy", against
the labor baiters, against segregation and jim-crowism, wherever these evils
show their fangs, whether in the Armed Forces, or in the civilian population.

The Public Affairs Pamphlet "The Races of Mankind" by Ruth Benedict
and Gene Weltfish, as well as many other scientific writings have exploded the
anti-democratic doctrine of "race-superiority" or "white-supremacy."

The achievements of heroes like Dorie Miller; the record of the 99th Pursuit Squadron in Italy; the records of the 24th Infantry and 93rd Infantry in
Bougainfille, disprove Secretary of War Stimson's statement in a recent letter:
"Negro units . . . . have been unable to master efficiently the techniques of
modern weapons."

The experience in training Negro and white, on a mixed basis, in the
Officers' Candidate Schools, and the Army Technical Training Schools, is proof
enough, if proof is needed, that there is no justification for the present policy
of jim-crow and segregation in the Armed Forces. The Navy can look to the
Merchant Marine for an example of democracy in action, in which the crews
are organized on a mixed basis, with Negroes and whites from North and
South eating and sleeping, working and fighting together.

Just as our government in civilian life, is carrying on a fight for the full
integration of the Negro and all other minority groups into the war effort, with
the result that Negro men and women are producing the implements of war, in
jobs from the unskilled to the most highly skilled, side by side with their white
brothers and sisters, so in the Armed Forces our government must take up the
same fight for the full integration of the Negro into all phases of our fighting
forces from the lowest to the highest.

President Roosevelt, in the interest of the war effort you issued Executive
Order 8802, which established the Fair Employment Practices Committee.
Although there is still much to be done, nevertheless this committee, against
heavy opposition, has played, and is playing a gallant role in fighting for
democracy for the men and women behind the lines, in the industries that
produce the guns, and tanks, and bombers for victory over world fascism.

With your issuance of Executive Order 8802, and the setting up of the Fair
Employment Practices Committee, you established the foundation for fighting
for democracy in the industrial forces of our country, in the interest of victory
for the United Nations. In the interest of victory for the United Nations,
another Executive Order is now needed. An Executive Order which will lay the
base for fighting for democracy in the Armed Forces of our country. An
Executive Order which would bring about the result here at Davis-Monthan

Field whereby the Negro soldiers would be integrated into all of the Sections on the base, as fighting men, instead of in the segregated Section C as housekeepers.

Then and only then can your pronouncement of the war aims of the United Nations mean to *all* that we "are fighting to make a world in which tyranny, and aggression cannot exist; a world based upon freedom, equality and justice; a world in which all persons, regardless of race, color and creed, may live in peace, honor and dignity."

Respectfully yours,

Charles F. Wilson, 36794590
Private, Air Corps.

To Prevent Slanderous Assertions

His Excellency, The President,
The White House,
Washington, D. C.

U. S. SOLDIERS HOME,
Washington, D. C.,
September 4, 1945.

My dear Mr. President:

As a retired soldier who has retained his interest in the army during all of the more than 52 years of this service, active and retired, I urgently request that you exercise your authority as Commander-in-Chief of the armed forces to direct by executive order the enlistment of Negroes and their organization into units of every branch of the regular army, to at least the full proportion they bear to that of all other races in the population; and that this policy be extended to whatever reserves or auxiliary forces may be established as the peace time army. The desirability for this is apparent for many reasons.

Fifty-two years ago when I first enlisted the maximum authorized strength of the regular army was 25,000 men, the colored contingent of which consisted of two regiments of infantry, two of cavalry and a small number of special troops, making a total of between 3,000 and 4,000 men, comprising roughly one seventh of the total strength of the army. Since that time, or since the close of the Spanish-American War, there have been many increases in the size of the regular army from time to time by the addition of new regiments, but by not one additional colored regiment; so that today the same four regiments, with a few special troops, are the only colored troops in the permanent establishment, reducing the former proportion of one seventh to one fiftieth or one sixtieth of the regular army of today.

Negroes, recognizing their right to bear arms in defense of their country the same as all other races, deplore the discrimination in denying them this privilege. They appreciate the honor of serving the army and the benefit to them of such service because of the difficulty they encounter in securing employment in civil life due to prejudice against their race.

On account of the small number of colored enlisted men in the regular army whenever there is a sudden increase in the armed forces as in this latest and in previous wars there is always an insufficient number of qualified instructors from Negro troops to properly train fresh troops or to furnish nuclei for the large increase. This deficiency place colored draftees at a great disadvantage, and is, no doubt the cause of much of the unmerited stigma placed upon them for want of intelligence and incompetence which is often heard, and which unjustifiably discredits them. Lack of knowledge of the more technical branches of the service always makes Negro troops, hurriedly inducted into those branches during a war, appear more backward than white troops, the fact of their difficulty in obtaining training in civil industry being lost sight of.

The position of enlisted men in the army may be roughly compared to that of unskilled labor for privates, and semi-skilled and white-collar workers for noncommissioned and warrant officers; and to deprive the large number of colored men of such benefits by the disproportion between the ratios of white and colored men in the army, is similar to depriving them of any other employment under the Government which is freely given to white men. Colored men are ruthlessly denied many classes of work in civil life that are always open to white men; and for the Government, also, thus to continue to discriminate against them as it has done for so many years, is indeed, to close the door of hope to them.

I have requested that this authorization be made by executive order because I know from a somewhat similar experience of many years ago that, apparently because the regiments of Negroes now in the army were first incorporated in the military establishment by authorization of Congress shortly after their emancipation and at the close of the Civil War, in the minds of many, any change in the number or branch of the service of Negroes in the regular army must also be authorized by Congress; and I hope this idea will not become a fixed policy, since it is quite obvious that no special legislation is required to give one group of citizens privileges that are the acknowledged right of another group. This fact is readily recognized in raising a temporary army in time of war; it should be practiced in the peace establishment.

If Negroes were allowed to enter all branches of the service in peace time it would obviate the practice of looking upon any innovation like the placing of them in branches of the service in which they have not heretofore been used, as an "experiment," and which is often attended with much reluctance. Although Negroes have acquitted themselves with honor, and to the satisfaction of every unprejudiced officer under whom they have served in every major war in which this nation has engaged, including the War of the Revolution, this fact seems to have been lost sight of by each new generation.

I doubt, if given the opportunity to learn, Negroes would prove to be any more inapt than whites. If they should, it might be attributed to the denial to them of the opportunity to engage in skilled occupations in civil life, or it might be attributed to their inaptitude—never to their race. In either event the onus would be upon the nation; if their backwardness is due to denial of privileges, these privileges should be granted; if to inaptitude, they are a part of the population.

If it should be decided to comply with this request no better time than now could be found to accare the enlistment of qualified men, since many colored men soon to be discharged from the army will find it difficult as usual, to obtain employment, because undoubtedly there is still going to be prejudice against employing them, and many of them would be glad to return to the army. An increase in the number of Negroes in the peace-time army would materially lower the percentage of desertions, since it is an acknowledged fact that desertions among Negroes are decidedly fewer than among whites, due, of course, to economic causes—the difficulty met by Negroes in obtaining suitable employment and their greater willingness, for that reason, to accept undersirable work or to submit to inferior treatment.

If the policy that Negroes are entitled to only a token representation in the regular army be discontinued, and inclusion of them as herein requested be carried out, their right as a component part of the army will be recognized by the public; and it will help dispel the notion that it is only as an act of generosity that they are permitted to serve, and probably prevent such slanderous assertions as have recently been made that they have made in all major wars of the nation, and statements of high ranking officers of this latest war to the contrary. It is a well-known fact that in previous years, in Congress after Congress, it has been the custom for one or more enemies of the Negro to offer a bill for the disbandment of the four Negro regiments, and to discontinue the enlistment of Negroes.

Mr. President, as this request is nothing more than for simple justice, I hope it may have your careful consideration and meet with your approval; and that it may be put into operation when the time comes for the organization of the permanent peace establishment.

I am, Sir,

Very respectfully,

PRESLY HOLLIDAY,
Q. M. Sergeant, Q. M. Corps,
Retired.

7

Cruel and Usual Punishment

Sunday June 27 our Bn. Commander threatened to take a hammer and beat a soldier's "Head in to your shoulders." Everyone stood by waiting for action. The same soldier left Sunday absent without leave and returned after being gone about 8 hours. On his return he was chained to a tree as though he was some killer or even worse. The morale of the whole outfit changed within just a few minutes and about five hundred soldiers stopped work and demanded the chaines be taken off the soldier and use proper means to handle the case.

A Negro Soldier

Camp Army Ground Southern Plantation?

Please help me! was the theme of black soldiers' complaints throughout World War II. They complained and asked for relief from being punished when too ill to work, from having to work long hours in all kinds of weather without proper clothing, from enduring life in tents without flooring, from inadequate food and feeding facilities, from shock treatment and blue discharges as punishment, and from an excessive and unusually high rate of courts-martial and sentences.

The Army's use of courts-martial to punish blacks became one of the most publicized grievances of black soldiers. Troops from Camp Livingston, Louisiana, for example, wrote letter after letter in which they indicated, "Since they can't very well hang us, they take the next steps, which is court martial, and that is better known as railroading. Now you don't stand a chance, before them. They are just like a lynch mob with a neggro to hang."[1]

Other soldiers expressed similar thoughts. For instance Private Roy Hermitt was distraught because he was put in the camp stockade, kept for one month, and tried under a general court-martial without, as he claimed, just cause. Hermitt received five years and a dishonorable discharge from the Army because he had been accused and convicted of hitting a white lieutenant in a post exchange. He contended the crime had been "planted on me because I was from a Northern State, and the person that hit the Lt. was tall man, and I answered the discription." [2]

At Fort Bragg, North Carolina, the army's cruel and usual punishment surfaced again. This time thirty-five black soldiers were said to have been treated like animals and "held as garrison prisoners for eight and nine months before being tried for small cases such as two days A.W.O.L., which is supposed to be only company punishment or restrictions. Then they are tried and given six months." Moreover, these same men had to "sleep out doors in pup tents regardless of the weather—rain sleet, snow, no matter how cold it is." This soldier continued, "What I am trying to say is I don't think it is right for them to have to sleep on the ground in such weather like dogs when there is so much shelter for everyone."[3]

This kind of punishment was often the norm rather than the exception for black soldiers. Often they received punishment far greater than was justified by their crimes or alleged crimes. A sensationalized rape incident in New Caledonia (a French island in Melanesia, in the Coral Sea) on May 2, 1943, is a case in point. Two black soldiers received life sentences because they allegedly raped a white prostitute when in fact it was reasonably proven by Judge William H. Hastie and Congressman Vito Marcantonio, attorneys for the soldiers, that she willingly consented to accept a fee for her services. Hastie and Marcantonio built their case upon the following facts: the investigating officer had concluded that the evidence did not warrant a charge of rape; the woman's testimony contained serious improprieties; the woman was an admitted prostitute; and that her medical history made her story invalid since Dr. Ginieys, examining physician, stated categorically that since Fisher and Loury, the accused black soldiers, did not have gonorrhea, and

> It would have been a medical impossibility for her gonorrhea
> condition to have been due to intercourse with Fisher and
> Loury since the lesions at the neck of the uterus found by
> me within 24 hours of the alleged rape could not have been
> caused by any contact had with any person during the pre-
> vious 24 hour period.[4]

In their pleas for clemency, Hastie and Marcantonio pointed out to Secretary of War Stimson the unjustifiable severity of the life sentences since military justice was supposed to bear a reasonable relationship to the penal law of the community where the crime was committed. They insisted that rapists were, according to Section 332 of the French Penal Code for New Caledonia, subject to five but not more than twenty years at hard labor. Hastie and Marcantonio appealed to Secretary Stimson to consider all of the evidence surrounding the case before making a decision on their plea for clemency for the black soldiers. They were resolute in their belief that the sentences represented the "Scottsboro Case" of the U.S. Army (the Scottsboro Case involved nine young black boys—ages twelve to nineteen—who were arrested in Scottsboro, Alabama, in 1931 for allegedly raping two white prostitutes on a freight train. One was freed, and the others were sentenced to die in the electric chair. The case received national and international news coverage before all eight were eventually freed by 1955).[5]

Secretary Stimson refused to grant Fisher and Loury a full pardon, but he reduced their life sentences to eight and ten years, respectively.[6]

Several other rape cases involving black soldiers caused many to believe that army judges discriminated against them in handing down heavy sentences for their crimes or alleged crimes. There was some basis for this belief, for example, in a black anti-aircraft company stationed in the South. The white officer in charge of the unit posted a notice to the effect that any type of association with white women would be considered rape, the penalty for which was death. This may have been a scare tactic; nevertheless, it dampened the morale of the black troops. It was not until February 1, 1948, however, that the War Department repealed the automatic death sentence for murder and rape.[7]

The rate at which blacks were discharged from the Army under Section VIII of Army Regulations, 615–360, Paragraph 10, Special Order #69, was indicative of another kind of cruel and usual punishment. A Section VIII dismissal from the armed forces was called a "blue discharge," which was not a dishonorable discharge but one without honor and veterans benefits. The records indicate that many black soldiers were given blue discharges without substantive provocation. For instance, Private George R. Gilbert was given a section VIII dismissal for allegedly refusing to carry out orders when he was physically unable to do so. His letter to Truman K. Gibson, Jr., in March of 1943 reflected the kinds of grounds on which black troops were given blue discharges. Gilbert contended rather disquietingly that:

> After I had been in the Army about 8½ months I started to complain about my stomach (you see I have had two operations on my stomach and they began to give me trouble). The doctors told me there wasn't anything wrong with my stomach. I also had a ureathed discharge in my penis which I had ever since I was in the Army and the doctors couldn't seem to stop it. I told my commanding officers I couldn't do any hard work so they took me before a Section VIII board. I don't think I deserve a discharge of that kind after serving (11) months of honorable service.[8]

Gilbert's case and several others were investigated by the Inspector General of the Army, but the problem of Section VIII discharges remained. Out of a total of 48,603 blue discharges from December 1, 1941, to June 30, 1945, 10,806 were issued to blacks. This would not have been an equitable percentage even if the ratio of blacks in the armed forces had been the same as that in the civilian population, but since the total strength of the armed forces' black personnel never rose above 6.5 percent the inequity was even greater, because blacks received 22.2 percent of the blue discharges issued during this period.[9]

Private First Class Lloyd Lythcott wrote about shock treatment, another example of punishment for black soldiers. In a letter to the editor of the Afro-American Newspaper Chain, Lythcott graphically detailed the horrors of his ordeal:

> You know . . . after I came back to the States they gave me "shock treatment." I'll tell you how they did it. First they lay you on a table, second they strap a band around your head, then they put a sponge in your mouth, and then they turn on a switch, you don't remember anything until the next day.
>
> I ran away from the hospital. They caught me and brought me back then they put me in a locked ward and gave me the treatment more often. Now listen to this. You know . . . when I left you I was well, only headaches. They kept me locked up in a little room for three months, couldn't see nobody or write. One day I slipped away from a guard, I made up my mind that they were not going to keep me and torture me any longer.

Remember all of this is happening in "Kentucky" where no-body can help me. Anyhow . . . I couldn't get out of there this time, so I made up in my mind to die. I remembered once when I was in the bathroom I saw a can of "lye" in there. I got a paper cup and poured some of the lye in it and mixed it with water. . . . I drank it, not because I was crazy, but because of the way those crackers treated me. I forgot to tell you they used to beat me up while I was unconscious under the shock treatment. The reason I know is because sometimes my jaw was swollen and hurt, and at other times I would have a mouse under my eye, you know, a lump. Now to make things worse, the lye I drank has taken all the enamel off my teeth and my eyes are ruined from the shock treatment. I try to be happy, but I can't. I have seen your wife twice so far. I tried to explain what happened to me, but I don't think she believes me. You see I know you will believe, because I have two black burns on each side of my temple from the electric shock treatment, and you know they were never there before.[10]

At camp after camp, black soldiers loathed these types of debilitating treatment. Their letters, saturated with pleas for help, went to the black civilian aides to the secretary of war, to black and white national leaders, to the black press, and to the national black self-help organizations. To these sources, black soldiers made such statements as "please help me to see another bright day," "I was fed soup for 11 days," "15 days on bread and water."

To summarize the thoughts of the vast majority of the black troops, as late as 1944 Private Irwin C. Conley wrote "Tomorrow on, God only knows."

NOTES

1. Letter, Private Milton Adams to William H. Hastie, May 13, 1942, Civilian Aide to the Secretary of War Subject File, 1940–1947, National Archives Record Group 107 (hereafter cited as NARG).

2. Letter, Private Roy Hermitt to *The Chicago Defender*, May 16, 1942, Civilian Aide to the Secretary of War Subject File, 1940–1947, NARG 107.

3. Letter, An Unknown Soldier of the Race to the Editor of the *Baltimore Afro-American*, March 6, 1943, Civilian Aide to the Secretary of War Subject File, 1940–1947, NARG 107.

4. William H. Hastie and Vito Marcantonio, *Petition For Clemency and Brief In Support Thereof* to Secretary of War Henry L. Stimson, Army General Staff, NARG 407, 1–17.

5. Ibid., 18–23; see Dan T. Carter, *Scottsboro; A Tragedy of the American South* (Louisiana: Louisiana State University Press, 1969).

6. Hastie and Marcantonio, *Petition*, 18–23.

7. Editorials, "Black and White Rape," April 1944, Civilian Aide to the Secretary of War Subject File, 1940–1947, NARG 107; "Army Ends Death Sentence for Murder and Rape in New Code Effective February 1," *The New York Times*, July 15, 1948.

8. Letter, Private George R. Gilbert to Truman K. Gibson, Jr., March 19, 1943; Private Pedro E. Pla to Gibson, July 5, 1943; Sergeant Nathaniel Ester to Gibson, August 14, 1943; Corporal Marshall C. Brown to Gibson, December 14, 1944; Private Edward C. Green, Jr. to Gibson, July 12, 1943, all in Civilian Aide to the Secretary of War Subject File, 1940–1947, NARG 107.

9. Memorandum, Mac C. Snyder to Gibson, August 23, 1943; Letter, Edward F. Witsell, Adjutant General, to Jesse Dedmon, Jr., Director of Veterans Affairs, NAACP, December 3, 1945, Civilian Aide to the Secretary of War Subject File, 1940–1947; NARG 107; "Blue Discharges Reach Senate 92nd Betrayed by Leadership," *Pittsburgh Courier*, November 13, 1945.

10. Letter, Private First Class Lloyd Lythcott to W. I. Gibson, October 25, 1945, Civilian Aide to the Secretary of War Subject File, 1940–1947, NARG 107.

Unfair Court Martials

Pvt. Milton Adams
Post Stockade
Camp Livingston, La.
May 13, 1942

Dear Mr. W. H. Hastie:

I am private Milton Adams of Co. B. 240th Q. M. Bn of Camp Livingston,
La. I inlisted in the army Oct 17, 1942, in Chicago, Ill. And since I been in
the Army, I never had any Trouble in the Army in or out of it in my life, untill
I came to Camp Livingston. I am asking for the help of the N.A.A.C.P. And
the Crisis. I am not writing anything against the United States Army. But I am
going to tell you what the White officers are doing to us races Soldiers down
her in camp Livingston, La. Since they can't very well hang us, they take the
next steps, which is court marital, and that is better know as rail-roading. Now
you don't stand a chance, before them. They are just like a lynch mob with a
neggro to hang. Well they do not want you down hear in the Army, and I did
not ask to come down hear I was sent down hear. Well my trouble starter
when they found out that I was from Chicago, and I have had a bad deal
every since I been hear, I have tried to get away from hear, But it was the
same old story. When we finde some places for you to go, we will let you go.
Well my Commanding Officer did not like me because, I ask him not to use
the word niggers, and he saide I was one of those smart nigger from up north.
I was tried once for a offince, and given 30 days and a $12.00 fine. Now after
I had finish my sentecens, they saide they are going to try me over again. I
wish you would look into my case. I thought they could not try any person a
second time for the same offince. I really taken all the punishment I can take I
could not get a three day pass or a furlo since I been in the army, untill my
mother pass away in April. They have just about rob me out of very pay day,
for things I have never had. There are so many more case like this, a unfair
chance. I don't know what to do now. I don't want do the wrong thing, so I
am asking for help. But I am not going to take any more of these unfair trials,

because I did three months in the stockade once for something I did not have
any thing to do with. It was because I was from Chicago, and thats way every
trial I ever had is base on the fact that I come from Chicago. So I whish you
look into this case, because I can prove everything I am telling you. I will look
forward to a answer from you in few days.

Respectfully yours,

Pvt. Milton Adams
Post Stockade
Camp Livingston, La.

Not a Fair Chance

Pvt Watason Benjan
353rd F. A. T. E. Brty.
Mr. William H. Hastie   May 15, 1942

Dear Sir:

I am writing for the help of the N.A.A.C.P. I am Pvt Watason Benjan of the 353rd, F.A.T. at camp Livingston, La. I am writing to let you know how we races Soldiers are being treated down hear in camp Livingston. Well before I came into the Army I had never been into any kind of trouble in my life. Well down hear in camp Livingston it dosen't take very much to get in to trouble down hear. I came into the Army April 17, 1941. I was told when I came into the army, that I would have a fair chance, but I have not had that chance. First I was put on $21.00 bases, and next I had one of these unfair court marital trial, for which they saide I did soming wrong, and I was given six month, and then they taken $14.00 out of my pay for six months. You are tried before a court of white officers for which you don't have a chance. Now I ask you can you support your Mother on $17.00 a month, and I really have my mother to support. These officers tell you don't need any money, and you don't have a chance in defending yourself. Its just what they say. Sir I wish you would give me some help. I am thinking you sir.

Pvt. Watason Benjan
Post Stockade
Camp Livingston, La.

Please Help Me See Another Bright Day

60th Ord. Company
Camp Livingston, Louisiana
May 16, 1942

The Chicago Defender

To Whom It May Concern:

Dear Sir, I was at one time a member of this 60th ord. co. Station at Camp
Livingston La. I served for thirteen months good service in this Company
without any trouble at all. I never had any company punishment at any time,
or even a Court Martial of the court, until finially one day on the third of
March, A Lt. was hit in a post Exchange. This was planted on me because I
was from a Nothern State, and the person that hit the Lt. was tall man, and I
answered the discription. I did have a habit of going to this post Exchange, But
at the time this man was suppose to have been hit I was on guard in my
company. This I can prove. By my Sergent of the guard, Cop. of the guard
and seven more sentres of the guard. I was picked up carried to the Camp
Stockade, Kept for one Month and tried under a general Court Martial. I
recieved 5 years, and to be dishonorably discharged from the service. I think
that you will agree with me when I tell you that it was as rotton a break as
any one ever had. The words of three Sivilians who were employed at the post
Exchange and had all reasons in the world to lie on me was the cause of me
here. This I can prove. I havent even asked any one for very much, But I beg
you if you have any power at all to please help me to see another bright day. I
have a complete record of the trial. If you are willing to help me, please
answer me as soon as you can, and I will send you my record. I am a collord
Soldier from Chicago Ill, 22 years old. Willing and able to help defend my
country. As you will soon learn This Lt. said that he didn't see the man that hit
him so he don't know. Answer me soon please.

Pvt. Roy Hermitt.

Soup for 11 Days

Pvt. Robert Hills
240 Medical. ETC
Camp Livingston, La
5-20-42

Mr. Roy Wilkins

Dear Sir:

I am writing to you for the help of the N.A.A.C.P. I am private Robert Hill of 240 Medical Datc. at Camp Livingston Who have a poore Way of expressing myself and have been in the army since 1941 the 7th day of march and Who have got a Wife and mother and One child Who have got a Woman Which love to keep up With her husband my Wife is in Alexandria, La paying $20.00 per month for rent. Who have been only drawing $21.00 very since I have been in the army Who now Remains on in the Stockade Who that the Captain did kick And no Ways to take care of my family. Although it Was really pityful enough that I Was Only getting $21.00 per month in the best of my figureing to divide it between my Wife and mother the best I could And now I have been Courtmartle And they have Forfit two thirds of my pay Which only leaves me $7.00 I taken sick and they sent me to the horspital And I were feed on Soup for 11 days Until I was discharged and When I retuned back to my company I Was Awful week And they insisted on me to Work in Which I did Work. but While on duty trying to do the best I Could I taken so Week Until I had to go in And after going in sick I Was Were laced up but it was missing a few holes by my arches on account of I suffer With falling Arches And he called the guard and I Was Carried to the guard house. And I don't Want to be courtmartle down here because the Courtmartle Isnt fair. And race soldiers do not stand a change here thats Why I am Asking the Help from you. Yours truely

Pvt. Robert Hills
240 Medical. Datc
Post Stockade
Camp Livingston, La.

15 Days on Bread and Water

To Editor: Fort Bragg, N.C.
Baltimore Afro-American   March 6, 1943

Dear Sirs:

While the meditation of reading the news in your edition of the AFRO, I find it very easy as member of the race to face the facts of some of the things that you and all members of the racial conflict.

While here in Fort Bragg, a Negro soldier among Negro soldiers, are having racial conflicts as well as all over the world. It's a great pleasure and tradition to have you of the race trying to help prejudice in all parts of the world.

Although the white people here, civilians as well as officers, treat us like dogs or slaves, as I am from Chicago, please let all the race know of things and the way in which Negro soldiers in the South are treated. I am trulying hoping. If the publication of this will cost me, if so in your paper, state that a soldier owes to the AFRO an amount. It will be gladly sent to you in the future. I am a steady reader of the AFRO. Each time it comes out. I would not like my name to be in this column because it might cause me trouble.

This is something I learned from a soldier in the battalion, I am writing about. There are thirty five men held as garrison prisoners in the 41st Engineers. We find that these men are treated more like dogs.

They sleep out doors in pup tents regardless of the weather—rain sleet, snow, no matter how cold it is. What I am trying to say is I don't think it is right for them to have to sleep on the ground in such weather like dogs when there is so much shelter for everyone.

These men are held as garrison prisoners for eight and nine months before being tried for small cases such as two days A.W.O.L., which is supposed to be only company punishment or restrictions. Then they are tried and given six months.

I also learned from one of the prisoners that they work all day until one and two o'clock in the morning. Then the other few hours they have to sleep out doors. I also learned that they don't get enough to eat and then have the nerve to put a man on bread and water in a dark cold room for 14 and 15 days. Everytime some large inspecting officer comes around to inspect the officers lead him away. That is how I know it is a racket. They also make the men get up about four o'clock and rake the grounds where the tents were. When day comes no one will know any thing about the dirty work that is going on. They also had seven men in the hospital for pneumonia in the last month or so. The whole battalion is no better than the guard house.

All of their money is taken from them.

From the way the officers put it, it seems like a game they are playing. They put a man in the guard house for nothing. It also seems to me more like they are trying to help the enemy win this war the way they are treating the Negro soldier in the 41st Engineers.

I must close. I just wanted to try to let the American people know how their sons are being treated. I don't think it right for men to be treated like dogs when they have given up their homes, loved ones, etc., to try to defend their country in this great time of need.

If there is any cost put the amount under the column and you will get the money. This is an urgent message, so please help.

Signed:

An Unknown Soldier of the Race

Chained to a Tree

The Pittsburgh Courier   Van Buren, Arkansas
To: The Editor   June 28, 1943

Dear Sir:

I feel that someone should know how colored soldiers are mistreated
throughout the southern States. Sometimes we (soldiers) wonder wheather
Washington know how we are mistreated down here or if they just don't care.

We work harder than any other soldiers and get less credit. What could
anyone expect of us? Soldiers are beginning to ask if we fight for the same
causes if there is discrimination in the purpose that we fight for?

We are now in the flooded area of Arkansas to help people rebuild their
homes, farms and help them in any way that we can; however on our arrival
here we were informed that the Jim-Crow law was inforced here and that
meant we had to stay in our places. None of the boys ever worry about being
Jim-Crowed but having it rubbed in by doing things which they think will
frighten someone is too much for human to stand.

Sunday June 27 our Bn. Commander threatened to take a hammer and
beat a soldier's "Head in to your shoulders." Everyone stood by waiting for
action. The same soldier left Sunday absent without leave and returned after
being gone about 8 hours. On his return he was chained to a tree as though he
was some killer or even worse. The morale of the whole outfit changed with in
just a few minutes and about five hundred soldiers stopped work and demanded
the chaines be taken off the soldier and use proper means to handle the case.

We not only find that the people make it hard for us but we find that the
large number of officers helping in doing so.

Colored soldiers cannot enjoy the same recreation which is provided, yet
there is very little understanding given them at all.

What part do we play in this war? Will we all be chained in the end? Or
will the Government stop so much unfairness in the south? From the looks of
things they will not wait to hang us as they did in the south after the war but
they will do it before we win the present one.

Truely yours,

A Negro Soldier

God Only Knows What Will Happen Tomorrow

Mr. Truman K. Gibson
Civilian Aide to the
Secretary of War
Washington, D.C.

Camp Stockade
Camp Livingston, La.
June 15, 1944

Dear Mr. Gibson:

It goes without saying that the white man intend for the Negro to get the worse of everything. There are five disable men here in the stockade with me. These men are from 4126 QM Trucking Co, 186 QM Mobile Bn., Camp Livingston, La. I just want to tell you how the disable colored soldier is treated here. Some of this is what I see each day. Here are five cases of which I'll describe in short.

James W. McRae, 34846600, has kidney trouble. Has had it, up and down, about 12 years. He has been in the army 8 months and his condition is bad. This man can just get around. His feet swell and he has trouble with his eyes, wear glasses and walk in about a half crouch.

Ben Rhodes, 38384037, drafted 5 Dec. 42. This man complain of a back ailment due to a strain suffered in 1925. Recovered to a certain extent. He fell Sept. 1943; has not been able to do duty since. He was hit in one of his eyes by brother during childhood. Has had trouble with eye every since. Wears shades at all times. He claims to have a weak heart. This man walks in a half crouch.

Leroy Childress, 36793017, drafted 9 June 42 has foot trouble. Couldn't finish basic training. This man is so pigeon toed until he has to twist his whole body when he walks. Bothered with sinus trouble, but hasn't had an operation. Maybe due to the twisting of his body cause him to have back trouble.

Jimmy Epps, 34619430, drafted 21 Dec. 42. 7 Feb. 43, his leg was broken playing football. Carried to hospital 8 Feb. 43 about 4 p.m. This was in Camp Davis, North Carolina. After three months of whirlpool treatment, went back to duty. After which his arches fell. A trip from Ft Bliss, Texas to Camp Beauregard, La. Aug. 11, 1943, his leg became stiff. Stayed in hospital two wks. After which he was sworn out of the Army by 1st Lt. Knowles, 2nd Lt. Griffin, and Capt. Lumbeig, medical officer. Reason, unfit for military service. He has been before CDD board four times and was discharged. New C.O. in one instance held up his discharge and had him marked duty and said nobody's getting out of the army until he got out. This soldier *drag* his right leg to get along.

Mark Wheatley, 36796591, enlisted 5 July 42. This man was wounded in the Abdomen Aug. 1943, on Guna Island, South Pacific. Sent back to States Sept. 1943. Transferred from Camp Lockett, California to Camp Livingston, La. Since wounded, has not been able to perform duty. Been drug around every since he's been in Louisiana. May 25, 1944, this man tells that he was asleep on his bunk at his Company. A surgeon and a Lt. Stubrian came and awakened him by shaking. On arising, said, "don't give me any argument and get the hell out of here." He, the soldier, immediately reported it to his company commander. Nothing was done. The C.O. promised him that he would not court martial him if he would forget about the Lt. kicking him. This man has been over seas.

These five men and I are being punished because we can't do duty. In other words we can't follow the trend of thought that the white man thinks that a Negro should be able to do. These five men were court martialed (summary) 26 May 1944. Put here in the stockade. Released in four days. Their C. O. gave them another order of which they were unable to do, and they were court-martialed summary 2 June 1944 and put back here for thirty days. These men testify that they have been made do without food for a long as three days at the time. The C.O. would not let them eat in the mess hall. They have stayed in the woods by themselves three days without food or anything to sleep on or under. Their C.O. told the Prison Officer to make it hard for them when they first came in, this last time, the Provost Sgr. would not refuse them to go out on various details. But now it's different. June 12 '44 they were carried out about 8 a.m. by vehicle about 6 or 7 miles. They were put out for the purpose of walking back. They didn't walk. They were picked up before noon and brought back, ate chow, and stayed in for the evening. June 13, 44 about 8 a.m. they were taken out about the same distance by vehicle to walk back. They were dismounted with a guard, and stayed the rest of the day without food. They were brought back about 8 p.m. were not fed. June 14, 1944 which is today. These men were carried out again and they had to stay the remainder of the day without food. That means they have eaten two meals in the past two days. Tomorrow on, God only knows.

Since I've been here these three weeks, I've been in solitary confinement, three times 24 hours each time on bread and water because I am not able to do manual labor and withstand the terrific heat from the sun. Some of these men have been in solitary confinement with me the first time. Just because of disability.

Our nerves are being shattered. They stay tense waiting to see what's next. It's enough to drive anybody psycho. A disable man is ridden, and ridden again and again. The test never end. These complaints and trouble have been bothering us from 9 to 18 months. Yet, the doctor can't find anything wrong with us. They say it is in our minds. Could be in some, but when a man can prove himself to be true, he is still made out a lie and ridden some more. They ride, the Company Commanders, to make us do wrong or say something wrong so they can have us court martialed, making our record bad. We are tied of being ridden.

Why is it they treat us this way? Is it because we're colored, or they think we're goldbricks, or they think we are fools, or some lower animal, or because they have complete advantage, or what? I do not get the outward manifestation of these commissioned officers (white) of their hatred, prejudice, jim crowism during a time like this. It is at its worse now. Race tension is high. We are all disgusted, both well and the sick, the morale is below zero. By the mere fact of seeing how the disable men is treated, they believe if any of them fall victims they're be treated the same wrong way.

Out of all my going to, staying in and coming from the hospitals, I haven't seen a tenth as many white disable as I have colored. The whites have something done. They are either place where they will be of most service, on a do nothing job of course, or discharged. While in the hospital I've had many a white to come to my room and ask me why we don't do this thing or that thing. Why we don't leave this part of the country. What could I say, but make up some flimsy excuse.

I wonder how can any man think a colored soldier can be loyal treated like we are. I don't understand. This isn't the only place like that. I can cite instance upon instance of the injustices. These I thought should be noted and something done in the way of help.

There's so much I could tell about how we are treated. I've had 40 months and 14 days todate with twenty months more or less of soldiering in the south Ala. & La. with the other time in Arizona. I haven't been nowhere North or East or extreme West. Therefore you can readily see why I am tired of Army life.

Do something for us.

Yours truly,

Irwin C. Conley

P.S. I used my company address on the envelope to get it thru. I didn't think this would go thru the stockade authorities. I wrote you two letters from here. Please let me know if you received them.

Section VIII Discharges

8-23-44
Phoenix, Arizona

To: Office of Congressman William L. Dawson
To: Whom It May Concern:

Subject: the un-fair treatment of colored troops
Stationed; at Luke Field, Arizona; because of the fact; that our boys' returning from over-seas duty; injured; sick and un-able to do duty in the army are being given Section "8" discharges from this field; and the army; this Section "8" is equivalent in most cases to a dishonorable discharge with no veterans rights. included; it goes farther; that is the intimedating and descrimenating against colored Soldiers in this Section; including every imaginable conception of the terms; This treatment is being advocated by the commanding officer of this unit. (Sec. F. 3028th A.A.F.B.U. located at Luke Field, Arizona) and carried out by other officers; or ignored by the Commander of this post and his assist's. We are asking an investigation in this matter; your immediate action will benefit man; names are being with-held for specific reasons; this letter represents the entire Negro unit Stationed here and what is actually going on; They send thanks & appreciation to you; for any action taken in their behalf;

Sincerely yours,

A Fellow American & Friend

Shock Treatment

W. I. Gibson, Editor
The Afro-American   207th AAA AW Battalion
Newspaper Chain   Army Hospital Kentucky
Baltimore, Maryland   October 25, 1945

Dear Sir:

I know I should have written you a long time ago, but I couldn't. I had so much trouble I wish I could explain everything to you but I can't. It seems that such things couldn't possibly happen. The only way you would possibly believe me is to see me. You know . . . after I came back to the States they gave me "shock treatment." I'll tell you how they did it. First they lay you on a table, second they strap a band around your head, then they put a sponge in your mouth, and then they turn on a switch, you don't remember anything until the next day.

I ran away from the hospital. They caught me and brought me back then they put me in a locked ward and gave me the treatment more often. Now listen to this. You know . . . when I left you I was well, only headaches. They kept me locked up in a little room for three months, couldn't see nobody or write. One day I slipped away from a guard, I made up my mind that they were not going to keep me and torture me any longer.

Remember all of this is happening in "Kentucky" where nobody can help me. Anyhow . . . I couldn't get out of there this time, so I made up my mind to die. I remembered once when I was in the bathroom I saw a can of "lye" in there. I got a paper cup and poured some of the lye in it and mixed it with water. . . . I drank it, not because I was crazy, but because of the way those crackers treated me. I forgot to tell you they used to beat me up while I was unconscious under the shock treatment. The reason I know is because sometimes my jaw was swollen and hurt, and at other times I would have a mouse under my eye, you know, a lump. Now to make things worse, the lye I drank has taken all the enamel off my teeth and my eyes are ruined from the shock treatment. I try to be happy, but I can't. I have seen your wife twice so far. I tried to explain what happened to me, but I don't think she believes me. You see I know you will believe me, because I have two black burns on each side of my temple from the electric shock treatment, and you know they were never there before.

My mother and family know what they did. My aunt has a lawyer working on the case. So far they haven't sent me my discharge papers or given me any pay on mustering out, either. You know when you are in the hospital you are supposed to be paid for it, and when you are home, you are supposed to get it all with your mustering out pay." . . ." you know me pretty well and you will remember that I never did go to church in Georgia, Australia or New Guinea, not even on the boat going across. You and I were never afraid of nothing. We often laughed at how the longhorn used to pray when they heard they were going overseas, at least I did, if you didn't. What I am trying to say is that I should have never laughed at them as I should have prayed too. I mocked them and that means I was mocking the Lord too, so now He's making me pay.

". . ." please don't think I was or I am a fair weather friend. I would have written you sooner if I could but my nerves were so shattered from those shock treatments that I couldn't. The first time that I went out is when your wife came to see my mother, and God may strike me dead, you are the first person that I am writing since I came from overseas. My wife is somewhere living with another man, but even that don't bother me. I just want you to know that in those twenty-six months that I have know you, you were as dear to me as a brother. I hope and wish that as soon as you receive this letter you'll be catching the next boat or plane home. Your wife loves you truly, . . . All she does is to talk about her . . . I wish I had married a nice girl like you did instead of a rotten one like I did. She was mostly the blame for my troubles. I just gave you some of the details of my troubles. I'll try to explain the whole thing when I see you. Please come to see me when you come home. I'll be looking for you. Your friend,

Pfc. Lloyd Lythcott

8

Northern Racism

Leaving the south was like coming back to God's
country.
You might readily understand my aversion when I
discovered that as far north as Penn. segregation and
discrimination is practised in the army camps. I sometimes wish I could be indifferent but I can't. Right is
right and I realize there's no such thing as half way
right. Although in comparison with conditions at camp
Barkeley, [Texas,] these here are much more favorable
but why are we segregated? Why aren't we allowed to
attend but one theater out of four on the post and why
can't we use any post exchange of our choice? I tried to
answer these questions but I'm on the ebb of becoming
neurotic.

Private Bert B. Babero

ike black Americans nationwide, black soldiers perceived the
North as "heaven" compared to the "hell" in which they
found themselves in the South. They soon realized, however,
that "jim crow" abounded in and about army camps throughout the
North. On these posts and in the surrounding towns, black troops were
never able to forget that the "color line" more often than not determined
their status even in the North.

One of the most conspicuous examples of the "army color line" occurred in Massachusetts, considered in the 1940s by blacks and whites
alike one of the most liberal states in the Union. A white soldier, writing
as late as 1944, recalled that his former company commander did not
tolerate segregation or racial discrimination in his camp, but stated that
the present commander, who was "from the land of hate has set his
southern policy which is ruining the moral[e] of every soldier who reach
this Camp" and brought "hate and discrimination to this wonderful state
of Massachusetts which I think every true American should know." This
soldier went on to write, "Some of the fine Colored soldiers go to some of

the service Clubs here on the post and are ordered out by the MPs, boys who have lived here in the New England States and have enjoyed the freedoms of living, arrive here and see such conditions existing." He continued: "The white boys dont kick at all and the white boys are ordered out of the so Called Colored service club which they protest and states that we are all fighting together why cant we at least have a soda or an Ice cream together."[1]

Judge William H. Hastie and the black leadership also wondered why black and white troops could not eat, drink, and relax together. In a conservation between Walter White, General Frederick H. Osborn (chief of the Division of Special Services), and P. L. Prattis (editor of the black *Pittsburgh Courier*), the answer to this question was spelled out in official army policy. Prattis maintained and informed Hastie that Osborn

> Even justified the Army's practice of extending social patterns based on southern prejudices to other sections of the country. He said that the War Department could only have one rule which must apply to the Army as a whole and that in as much as Negroes and Whites do not sit together in theaters in the South, it was necessary when the War Department set up a system of theaters to establish separate accommodations for Negro and white soldiers. Since the War Department could issue only one rule, it, therefore, became necessary to issue a 'Jim Crow' rule which would apply to the South and North alike, although different from the ones in the South.[2]

But was "jim crow" in the North any different from in the South? The black soldiers at Camp Adair, Oregon, thought not. For Corporal William D. Lee, the camp had "no Day Rooms no U.S.O. clubs, no Service Clubs, no Libraries, and no Entertainment What So ever. We are Sure in a H-of a place. The camp is Surrounded by Two Cities one is Albany, Oregon. Second Corwallis, Oregon. Just Ten (10) miles from each to the Camp." Lee then asked, "But what good are they? If we go up and Start a convertsation with the White Ladies the M-p's. Will Chase you in and press a charge against you The ninth Corp Area is not Suppose to be Jim Crowed its Worse out here than being way down South one thing Sure they Will have a camp Some place Where theirs plenty of Colored Ladies because they dont want you to bother theirs Also Will plan a place Somewhere for the soldiers to go after hours."[3]

Other black soldiers expressed the same sentiments as Corporal Lee. In a complaint to Judge Hastie, a trooper stationed at Boise, Idaho, wrote: "The Jim-Crowism in this city is terrible. It is even worse than the southern cities because (1) There are no colored stores of any kind here (2) There is not more than 10 to 15 colored families in the whole city which has a population of about 26,000 to 28,000 people (3) In the whole city there is not one 'not one' restaurant, beer garden, cafe or tavern which will serve a colored soldier, because we soldiers tried it last night, July 29, 1941."[4]

In contrast to Boise, black troops at La Junta Army Field, Colorado, complained they had stopped attending "the base theater on account of being discriminated against." One also claimed that "in the city of La Junta, about 5 miles from the Field are two theaters where Negroes and whites attend and there is no discrimination at any one of them." He continued, "I have attended both theaters in town and have never noticed or heard of any trouble on account of Negroes and Whites sit anywhere they please. What we Negroes here can't understand is why we are discriminated in the base theater while there is no discrimination in the city's theaters. If left alone Negroes will naturally sit with one another. They have no special desire to sit beside a White Soldier. What we don't like is the discriminating policy of the War Department."[5]

At Camp George Jordon in Seattle, Washington, blacks were told that severe weather in the East had produced a coal shortage that resulted in their being asked to use wood for heating. But the soldiers became disheartened when they learned that coal was being supplied to white soldiers only two blocks away. A black trooper asserted: "This is a true fact, for I deliver coal there every day or other soldiers from this camp on that detail."[6]

This same soldier claimed, "Other than this un-democratic policy, there is a matter of passes and sick call. For instance, the white soldiers who work at the port, where we also work, go home from the port when quitting time comes. (I'm referring *only* to the married soldiers.)" He also contended that white soldiers "have class 'A' passes, which are good at any time while not on duty. The [black] married soldiers here have to return to camp when quitting time comes, make retreat at 5:00 and can't get their passes before 6:00. They must be back before reveille in the morning. The white soldiers come straight to the port in the morning. Some have told they never go to camp except to sign the pay roll and on pay day."[7]

In 1946, though the war had ended, a black officer described to Colonel Marcus Ray (successor to Truman K. Gibson Jr., as civilian aide to the Secretary of War) the racial situation that existed at Camp McCoy in Wisconsin. Major Samuel L. Ransom pointed out that the black and white troops lived in separate barracks and ate in separate mess halls. He further informed Colonel Ray that the black men even stopped going to camp dances because they were the subjects of racial abuse. Ransom ended his letter: "On the post and off we are subjected to being called names, by both Officers and enlisted men. When we report these things, they are over looked. There is an inner tension growing among the men, they fell they would just as soon die in the guard house as in this slave camp. I think that this should be looked into as soon as possible, one man was cut in a fight the other night. Hell might break loose any minute."[8]

In the North black soldiers were reminded that army life there was not a "promised land" and that racial discrimination was a national phenomenon.

NOTES

1. Letter, A White Soldier to *The Chicago Defender*, June 22, 1944, Civilian Aide to the Secretary of War Subject File, 1940–1947, National Archives Record Group 107 (hereafter cited as NARG).

2. Letters, P. L. Prattis to Hastie and Walter White, April 14, 1942; Letter, Prattis to White, April 4, 1942; Letter, White to Osborn, April 6, 1942; Letter, Gibson to White, April 6, 1942; Letter, White to Hastie and Prattis, April 18, 1942, all in Box 264, National Association for the Advancement of Colored People Papers (hereafter cited as NAACP Papers), Manuscript Division, Library of Congress, Washington, D.C.

3. Letter, Corporal William D. Lee to the *Pittsburgh Courier*, July 28, 1943, Civilian Aide to the Secretary of War Subject File, 1940–1947, NARG 107.

4. Memorandum, Hastie to Major William Slater, Chief of the Planning and Liaison Branch, August 16, 1941, Civilian Aide to the Secretary of War Subject File, 1940–1947, NARG 107.

5. Letter, A Negro Soldier to the National Association for the Advancement of Colored People, March 19, 1945, Civilian Aide to the Secretary of War Subject File, 1940–1947, NARG 107.

6. Letter, A Very Dear Friend of Billy Rowe to the Managing Editor of the *Pittsburgh Courier*, February 5, 1945, Civilian Aide to the Secretary of War Subject File, 1940–1947, NARG 107.

7. Ibid.

8. Letter, Major Samuel L. Ramson to Colonel Marcus Ray, November 12, 1946, Civilian Aide to the Secretary of War Subject File, 1940–1947, NARG 107.

Suffering Northern Indignities

Afro-American
Newark, N. J.
May 10, 1943

Just a few words to let you hear from the soldiers out here from New Jersey and New York.

I should like very much for the people to know that all is not well out here. We are suffering all kinds of indignities in this place.

The City of Sioux Falls is very jim crowed and there are no decent places to go. At camp it is the same thing. It is not a strange thing to hear a Lieutenant or Major use the word N-----r.

We were told even before we arrived at this air base that most of us would attend the technical school but insted, what are we doing? Working in mess halls, digging ditches; in other words, this is just a labor battalion.

Please see that this statement gets in the AFRO and all the colored papers right away. It may be just the very thing to help us.

Sincerely yours,

A Soldier.

Worse Here than Down South

The Pittsburgh Courier pub. Co.   Cpl. William D. Lee
2628-Centre Avenue   1911-Q. M. Sec. S.C.V.
pittsburgh, pa.   Camp Adair Oregon
Mr. William G. Nunn: July-28-1943

Dear Sir:

pordon me at this time for taking up your utmost valuable time but its
something I just had to unload off of my chest. Couldn't exactly Call it a Story
but Some bad news from a no good Spot Since their's no reporter's out here
and in fact I guess its not kown that a Colored Camp is out here for us
Soldiers. So at present I am writeing about conditions may I say its Something
Awful no places for us to have any fun at all. No Day Rooms no U.S.O. Clubs,
no Service Clubs, no Libraries, and no Entertainment What So ever. We are
Sure in a H——of a place. The camp is Surrounded by Two Cities one is
Albany, Oregon. Second Corwallis, Oregon. Just Ten (10) miles from each to
the Camp. But what good are they? If we go up and Start a convertsation with
the White ladies the M-p's. Will Chase you in and press a charge against you
The Ninth Corp Area is not Suppose to be Jim Crowed its Worse out here than
being way down South one thing Sure they will have a camp Some place
Where theirs plenty of Colored Ladies because they dont want you to bother
theirs Also Will plan a place Somewhere for the Soldiers to go after hours. Our
First Sgt. got put in the Compound over in the City So you See we havent got
a chance I would like to know why they always Send us out to places like this
How can the colored Soldier Keep up their moral when you go in the places
over in the cities the White Soldiers look at you as thou you were a no tail
Bear or a tiger So many places a Sign reads White only But Still they Say its
not Jim Crowed. The outside world dont know half the things a colored Soldier
goes through I would like for them to know Some of the things that happen in
these Western States. We are a bunch of Soldiers that were transferred from
278. Q.M.-Ser. Bn.-Ogden, Utah. to be placed on Limited Service Seams to me
We are just Castaways Some time if you Should have a reporter out in
California please Send him Around to this no good (post) perhaps your paper
would be of some help. proven facts cant be beaten I know it build up Fort
Huachuca, Ariz. because I was out their This is Strictly a White Camp and
plenty of down dixie Boys to enforce Jim Crow. laws where if they wasnt
around we could or would have a better chance.

The facts about the whole war problems Seems to me that is a harder battle
fought in America than over Sea trying to keep the Blackman Down and thats
Something will never happen now He's to far a head of time as tiem goes by
change will be made until that day (Hell) is at hand. What has the Black Race
ever done to cause the Whites to be So bitterly Against Them?

Sincerely Your's

The Above Address:

Why Are We Segregated?

Atty. Truman K. Gibson   Co. C. grp. 2, 1st Reg.
Civilian Aid to Secy of War   Camp Reynolds, Pa.
· White House, Washington, D. C.   Mar. 13, 1944

Dear Mr. Gibson:

As you may recall I wrote you several times while at camp Barkeley, Texas.
I am at present in Pennsylvania, on the brink of embarkation for overseas
duty. Leaving the south was like coming back to God's country.

You might readily understand my aversion when I discovered that as for
north as Penn. segregation and discrimination is practised in the army camps. I
sometimes wish I could be indifferent but I can't. Right is right and I realize
there's no such thing as half way right. Although in comparison with conditions
at camp Barkeley, these here are much more favorable but why are we
segregated? Why aren't we allowed to attend but one theater out of four on
the post and why can't we use any post exchange of our choice? I tried to
answer these questions but I'm on the ebb of becoming neurotic.

I didn't start this war but I didn't hesitate to come when I believed I was
needed. When inducted I honestly believed that as a negroe, I comprised an
important part of this nation and it was my patriotic duty to avail myself when
my country was in danger of peril. My attitude now is greatly changed. I'm
indifferent toward the whole affair.

I sincerely hope that through you Mr. Gibson and others like you, that
America will be awaken unto the realization that we too are human and desire
to be treated as such and also we want to readily do our part in the progress
of the nation.

I feel sure that while we are fighting on the battlefront, you will continually
be fighting on the home front, for your fight is as great as ours. Good luck.

Yours truly,

Pvt. Bert B. Babero

Reflections of a White Soldier

The Editor
Chicago Defender
3435 Indiana Ave
Chicago Illinois   22 June 1944

Dear Sir:

The fellows are betting that you wont print this but I am betting you will and I hope you wont let me down. And as a matter of fact I hope you can run this on your front page. The following statements are true and I would swear to every one of them but for military reasons I wont sign my name.

There are Italians prisoners here in this camp which I am in at the present waiting shipment else where. These prisoners are entitled to more than the Colored soldiers stationed here on the post of soldiers awaiting shipment else where. The correct title for this is DESCRIMINATION IN MASSACHUSETTS. The reason I says descrimination in Massachusetts is because it is being born here in this camp.

Now when I first arrived here at this Camp it was Commanded by a white Colonel by the name of John R. Fountain, who would go to the farthest extent to see that all soldiers are treated alike. Now he would not stand for a colored soldier to be ordered out of a White service Club as a matter of fact there was no such thing as a white and colored service club. But Now this Camp has a Colonel in Command by the name of GUY C REXROAD who are bringing hate and discrimination to this wonderful state of Massachusetts which I think every true American should know. Some of the fine Colored soldiers go to some of the service Clubs here on the post and are ordered out by the MPs, boys who have lived here in the New england States and have enjoyed the freedoms of living, arrive here and see such conditions existing. The white boys dont kick at all and the white boys are ordered out of the so Called Colored service club which they protest and states that we are all fighting together why cant we at least have a soda or an Ice cream together.

They have an alaby which is a very good one. They say the colored boys dont want the white boys at their clubs. They are trying to avoid trouble which is to me very funny because Colonel Fountain Commanded this Post over a Year and there was never a minutes Trouble but this Officer from the land of hate has set his southern policy which is ruining the moral of every soldier who reach this Camp.

Now I am not a Colored Soldier as a matter of fact I am a white Officer but white or colored I am fighting this very same thing with the enemy so why should I put up with the same policies or adopt these hatered and apply them to the fellows who I have gone to school played with on the football teams and associated with all my life. As a matter of fact I wouldn't be living to tell this today if one of the colored boys had let me drown when I was a kid.

If there are any backbone in your press you would attack this with all you might and print it on your front pages. I will be reading your papers as I always will do and I will be looking forward to reading this story in the near future. Why not request that an investigation be made to blot out this before it take root here in Massachusetts.

I would like to state that something is going on here at this camp which I think is History. It is more like real Americanism and I really dont think there is not another place in the Country such a thing has taken place. But since this new Commanding officer has taken over it is my belief that this will soon be blotted out. If it wasn't for discrimination taking root here it would be something for the entire Country to marvel at. They say Colored cannot Command white well come and see for yourself here at Myles Standish.

A White Soldier

Help in the Interest of Humanity

268th B. U.
Aviation section B.
Peterson Field Colo.
July 25, 1944

The Pittsburgh Courier
publishing co.
To the Editor.

Dear Sir:

This letter is in regards to the same situation as you have received a few days ago.

Despite the fact that the pay of enlisted men has been stopped the amount of personnel has been cut by twenty percent.

The Colorado Non Commissioned officers have been replaced by white and the situation in general terrable. The cooks salry as of last month have been lowered.

The outfit that have taken over the field are from texas this kind of treatment of enlisted men is almost unbearable. The recreation facilities here are the poorest I have seen out of seven bases I have been stationed.

Whatever steps you may take in the interest of human treatment of the whole squadron like myself I know will be deeply appreciated.

Thanking you in advance for whatever action you may take.

Sincerely yours,

An Enlisted Man of this Station

Tired of These Undemocratic Policies

The Pittsburgh Courier,   Camp George Jordon,
c/o Managing Editor,   February 5, 1945
Pittsburgh, Pennsylvania.   Seattle, Washington.

Dear Sir:

The soldiers in this camp are entirely colored, while there are two other joint cantonments (No. II & No. III) composed of white.

During the severe storms out east, we (the colored) were informed of a terrific coal shortage and it was necessary for us to burn wood for heat, which we are still doing. However, the white soldiers who are only two blocks from us, are constantly burning coal. This is a true fact, for I deliver coal there every day or other soldiers from this camp on that detail.

Other than this un-democratic policy, there is the matter of passes and sick call. For instance, the white soldiers who work at the port, where we also work, go home from the port when quitting time comes. (I'm referring *only* to the married soldiers.) They also have class "A" passes, which are good at any time while not on duty. The married soldiers here have to return to camp when quitting time comes, make retreat at 5:00 and can't get their passes before 6:00. They must be back before reveille in the morning. The white soldiers come straight to the port in the morning. Some have told they never go to camp except to sign the pay roll and on pay day.

There have been cases when the Commanding Officer of one company restricted enlisted men under him from reporting on sick call. This is strictly against army regulations. When we do go on sick call our passes are pulled and restricted to the camp area for 3 days; yet during the time of restriction we have to work all day. Doesn't it seem logical to you that if a man is well to work all day he should be given the privilege to use his pass whether he uses it or not?

The Chaplain on the post has been informed of this and other such policies. He is colored and takes no action whatsoever. I have come to the conclusion that he is skeptical or afraid of the white officers.

I would appreciate it to the highest if you would make this a headline article in your next edition, other than taking immediate action on these unconstitutional policies by sending an investigator to this corrupt establishment.

Expecting to hear from you in the very near future, I remain

Gratefully yours,

A very *dear* friend of Billy
Rowe 3159th QM. Service Co. "D"

Negroes Will Naturally Sit with One Another

N.A.A.C.P.   Sqd. F. LJAAF
69 Fifth Avenue   La Junta, Colo.
New York, N.Y.   March 19, 1945

I am a Negro soldier and have been stationed on this field for more than 30 months. I wish to call to the attention of the officials of N.A.A.C.P. to a discrimination policy of this Field in regards to Negro soldiers at the base theater here. Negroes have been jim-crowed at this theater ever since I came here in 1942. There are 4 rows of seats or to be exact there are 28 seats for colored soldiers to sit. There are M.P.s on duty to make sure that Negroes sit in the seats designated for them. Many Negro soldiers will not attend the base theater on account of being discriminated against. In the city of La Junta, about 5 miles from the Field are two theaters where Negroes and whites attend and there is no discrimination at any one of them. I have attended both theaters in town and have never noticed or heard of any trouble on account of Negroes and Whites sit anywhere they please. What we Negroes here can't understand is why we are discriminated in the base theater while there is no discrimination in the city's theaters. If left alone Negroes will naturally sit with one another. They have no special desire to sit beside a White soldier. What we don't like is the discriminating policy of the War Department.

I am a member of N.A.A.C.P. and always will be. Many of my buddies have joined and more are going to join at the end of this month. We are glad to have the opportunity to support an organization that is 100% for our welfare.

Please advise me if there is anything that can be done to eliminate this discrimination policy at La Junta Army Field, Colo.

Thanking you very much,

A Negro Soldier

Strictly Based on Jim Crow and Racial Prejudice

Drawer 49
Fort Benjamin Harrison, Indiana
The Pittsburgh Courier   May 15, 1946

Dear Courier:

I am a constant reader of your paper, which I have had a subscription for
the past (18) months. And I am thanking you and your staff, and our fighting
boys who fought galliantly in World War II under the straining conditions that
were put before them. For the contribution you both have made in the last few
years. I know you won't enjoy the rest of this letter because we as a group of
colored boys have a lot of gripe to tell you. First, we are colored boys in this
U.S.D.B. here and the conditions we are living under are beyond expression.
We can name several incidents which has taken place and still is happening
each and every day, strictly based on Jim Crow and racial prejudice. A liberal
guard was telling us one day about some of their meetings they had. And he
said we colored boys haven't got a possible chance of surviving these conditions, if the Guards in his company carried out the order 15 they were issued.
They tell them not to take any chances on any of us. Because, we were
entergaters and incite riots. I'm sorry I can't give you the name of the Officer
who issued that order. This is not half of the hardships we undergo. These
people are Black-balling us in such a way that it is in describable. We would
like for this paper (The Pittsburgh Courier) to investigate this situation or try
your best to have some of our organizations look into this matter as soon as
possible. And see to it that, we the colored boys get more substantial consideration than we have had in the past. All we ask is fair justice be given us as
equally as the White man. Have our people forgotten about us? We're not
harden criminals. And don't have any intentions of being one. All of the boys
and myself, feel that this letter is our last hope and chance of ever getting
"Fair Justice." We would like for this paper to send a reporter to this institution and start an investigation right away. Of course I sincerely hope we are
not asking to much and asking in vain. But, remember we too contributed and
sacrificed our lives for the sake of all humanity. And in addition to that: The
working staus here is terrible. We have a lot of skilled workers here such as:
clerks, cooks, barbers, truck drivers, etc. But, we are not classified by our
skill. We're classified by color. If you're white you get the good jobs. And if
you're colored you get a pick and shovel. Also the guards are instructed to use

profane language and maltreat the colored boys. We would like to sign this letter. But in case this didn't reach you and got in the wrong hands, it would jeopardize our status. Please publish this letter in your paper. Because, we colored boys here are in distress. And in great need of help. We sincerely hope you can, and will do something about this matter. We the Colored boys here appreciate whatever can be done on our behalf. And thank you very much. We will be looking forward to this letter published in your paper. Yours truly. From the boys of this U.S.D.B. Fort Benjamin Harrison, Indiana.

Names Withheld

Hell Might Break Loose Any Minute

The Hon. Marcus Ray.
Assistant To The Secretary   St. Paul, Minnesota
of War   November 12, 1946

Dear Friend Ray.

Greetings to you and a sincere wish, for your success: in the tough assignment handed to you.

This is Major Samuel L. Ransom, of the Minnesota State Guard, a member
of the Governor's Staff and the Governor's Interracial Committee. And a
member of your own Race. I am going to give you another head ache, a group
of our boys, in Wis at Camp McCoy are in trouble. They are members of the
Task Force Frost. 3591 Trans. Corp. Here is a synopsis of their complaint.

A mixed group, 27 Negros, 53 Whites, a White C.O. and First Sgt. Off to
themselves, in separat barracks, eat separately in the mess hall. Have had no
intertainment since they have been there, but the other fellow has two dances
weekly. Gone to the dances but received so much abuse, stop going.

We would like to have our wives with us, but the people who would have us
are afraid, because of the Southerners and what they threatened to do if they
taken them in.

On the post and off we are subjected to being called names, by both Officers
and enlisted men. When we report these things, they are over looked. There is
an inner tension growing among the men, they fell they would just as soon be
in the guard house as in this slave camp. I think that this slave camp. I think
that this should be looked in to as soon as possible, one man was cut in a fight
the other night. Hell might break loose any minute. You know better how to
handle this I, but if you would rather have me look in to this, write or have
War Dept, write Maj Gen. E. A. Walsh of Minn. Or better still, have your
Inspector look in to this. What ever you want me to do, I am at your service.
But kindly act at once. Let me hear from you. There is more to this than I
have told you in this short letter.

                                                  Sincerely yours,

                                           Major Samuel L. Ransom.
                                           On the Gov's Staff.

9

The Dreaded South

And now, way down in Texas, where we're not even
good as dogs, much less soldiers, even our General on
the post hates the sight of a colored soldier. Why I ask
you, do we have to fight on the home front for our lives
then go across seas and fight again? Sure I'm giving you
real facts about Ft. Clark, Texas. Everything is true and
my buddies can tell you the same thing.
   There is a town down here called Bracketville and let
me tell you it couldn't be any worse than hell itself.

Unsigned Letter

Protests of black soldiers stationed in the South were too numerous and too frequent to be mere illusions of racial abuse. For them the reality of southern racism became an invidious form of discrimination that threatened their morale and safety. The troops blamed southern civilians and the white military police for their troubles, and considered the South "worse than hell itself."

Hardly a month passed that black soldiers did not complain about being in the South and suffering from the humiliation and abuse heaped upon them by white civilians and white military police. For instance, black soldiers at Jackson Air Base in Jackson, Mississippi, collectively reported that the "civilian polices have threated to kill several soldiers here. Some part of Mississippi, Negro soldiers are not allow to walk in town. Lieutenant Bromburg said all Negroes need to be beaten to death. He assist Civilian polices in the punishment of these Negro soldiers." Conditions became so intolerable that the men asked Judge Hastie to "please help us to be transferred out the state of Mississippi."[1]

Conflicts between black soldiers and white civilians in and about the army camps seemed never to end. At Camp Claiborne, Louisiana, a disgusted black trooper alleged, "The conditions for a Negro soldier down here is unbearable the morale of the boys is very low. Now right at this moment the woods surrounding the camp are swarming with Louisiana hoogies armed with rifles and shot guns even the little kids have 22 cal. rifles and B & B guns filled with anxiety to shoot a negro soldier." This soldier claimed the situation arose because two white women had allegedly been raped by blacks within the camp.[2]

Whether true or not, these types of racial incidents contributed to much of the civilian unrest in the South. Alarm reached such heights that white civilians began to object to the stationing of black troops in camps near their communities. White civilians residing near Moore Field, Texas, for example, protested vigorously. They urged their Congressman, Milton West, to do something about what they considered a blatant disregard for the welfare of their community. Congressman West responded by pressuring the War Department to correct the situation, and the War Department sought advice from Judge Hastie. Hastie suggested to Lieutenant General Henry H. Arnold (commanding general of the Army Air Forces) in August 1942 that the Army explore the possibility of replacing black with white troops at Moore Field. Hastie considered this the most feasible solution to a serious problem, since he believed the Army had failed to protect its black soldiers from civilian attacks.[3]

Meanwhile the situation in Texas worsened. Secretary of War Stimson eventually criticized the civilians for their attitudes toward black soldiers. He wrote in his diary that

> Texas particularly has protested against the stationing of colored troops in that State, citing the race riots that took place in the last war at Houston and the previous outbreak of the 24th Infantry in Brownsville. We are suffering from the persistent legacy of the original crimes of slavery; the section of the country, they thought, which foisted that crime upon us is that part of the country which now protests most loudly against being subjected to any of the risks which have followed the wrongdoings of their ancestors.[4]

While Stimson and the War Department staff pondered the Army's predicament, the black leadership and its white supporters continued to attack the armed forces for not protecting black soldiers from civilian mistreatment. For instance, Roy Wilkins suggested to Hastie that he specifically tell Secretary Stimson: "The chief complaint against the Army, and the one which has stirred both Negro soldiers and civilians, is that the Army has surrendered completely to local prejudices and has compelled its Negro soldiers to accept brutality and discriminatory treatment in and about the camps where they are stationed."[5]

After months of indecision, the War Department issued a policy statement on troop stationing in May 1942. The department decided that where feasible black southern troops would be assigned to units in the South and black northern troops would be assigned to units in the North. Moreover, the policy called for the Planning and Liaison Branch of the War Department to station black and white troops in and about communities with commensurate civilian populations.[6]

Hastie and Assistant Civilian Aide Truman K. Gibson, Jr., welcomed the new policy but felt it was based on the War Department's presupposition that the uneasiness of white civilians was caused chiefly by northern soldiers who had enjoyed a semblance of unrestricted civility in northern communities, and who viewed themselves differently from their southern counterparts.[7]

Whether the beliefs of the civilian aides were true or not, the Army had not adequately protected its black soldiers from southern civilian attacks. Black trooper Latrophe F. Jenkins, as late as 1944, wrote pitifully to P. L. Prattis from Alabama: "This is our last hope of receiving help from the outside world. This is the final quiet before death comes. This is the dark dreary hour before dawn, a dawn that seemed to have died for us last nite, in disillusioned expectations that we thought we'd won by our willingness and sacrifices of serving overseas for nearly two punishing years." Jenkins went on to say:

> We are now in Camp Rucker, Alabama; a name that shall live in the lives of the men that live to get out of here, just as much as the memories of Siapan, Tarawa, Pearl Harbor or any of the bloody battle fields of this war, live in the minds of the men who fought there. We are here on War Department orders. Not because we chose this theatre of war to serve in, without protection. It is the same if they had landed us on New Georgia without the support of the Navy and Air Force. Even with those great odds against us, we would rather be landed on New Georgia without protection than to be left here to die as "fatted pigs" at the mercy of the iron hearted people we are surrounded by, arms against our flesh . . . . Please take this call for mercy as the last whisper before we die.[8]

Private Jenkins' complaint against the South was one of many that involved the perennial prejudices of white civilians, white military policy, and black soldiers. Reports of black troops being mistreated, beaten, and even hanged in uniform in the South seemed to become a weekly occurrence. Blacks in and out of uniform believed white military police were either responsible or stood by while white civilians unleashed their abusive assaults on black soldiers. While the civilian aides appealed to the War Department to take preventive action, the black leadership and concerned whites sent resolutions and telegrams, made suggestions, and called for open and public investigations of these atrocities heaped upon black soldiers.[9]

On September 8, 1941, Judge Hastie, sensing a state or urgency, asked Secretary of War Stimson to issue a public statement regarding the frequent altercations between white civilians, white military police, and black soldiers. He cited incidents of violence and brutality as justification for a public announcement. Hastie also insisted that the Inspector General's investigations had failed to solve, for example, the homicides at Fort Benning, Georgia. He then reminded Stimson that nothing had been done about the shooting attack on black soldiers in the barracks at Fort Jackson, South Carolina; that the recent killings of black troops at Fort Bragg, North Carolina, had gone unsolved; and that the investigation of the civilian police attack on black soldiers in Bastrop, Louisiana, had failed to produce any substantive results. Hastie ended his memo with a strong plea for Secretary Stimson to address these matters at his next news conference.[10]

Stimson yielded to Hastie on September 25 and issued a public statement that expressed the War Department's sincere concern over the disturbances involving black soldiers, white civilians, and military police. He said, moreover, that the War Department not only was concerned in achieving justice, but it was determined to correct the causes that led to the racial conflicts in order to raise the morale of all soldiers. Stimson also spoke of the military police as respectable soldiers who should not be feared and who should maintain law and order without unnecessary force. Finally, he maintained, "Recent affrays between colored soldiers and white civilians are also under investigation. The Army will not tolerate breaches of discipline by its personnel or assaults upon soldiers engaged in line of duty. Most soldiers and civilians will meet on a plane of mutual respect and understanding. However, wrong doers whose wilful conduct is impeding the cause of the Military Program must be dealt with sternly."[11]

Hastie had hoped Stimson's announcement would at least halt the atrocities committed against blacks by white military police, but the mistreatment of black soldiers continued. In Tampa, Florida, for example, several white military policemen were reported to have severely beaten a black soldier while others and civilian authorities watched and forced a gathered crowd of black and white spectators to move on. This and other malevolent acts committed against black troops greatly disturbed Judge Hastie, and he released a prepared statement to the *New York Daily News* in June 1943 that he believed demonstrated the Army's indecisiveness regarding these matters. Hastie declared:

> At Camp Stewart, Georgia, Negro soldiers and military policemen engage in a fatal gun battle. In Centerville, Mississippi, a sheriff kills a Negro soldier. At Camp Shelby, Mississippi, two Negro soldiers lie in a hospital, wounded in an affray with highway patrolmen. The environs of Camp Shelby are more than familiar to the military authorities who have surveyed and studied that very area because of the acute problems of racial relations which confront the Army there. It is only the sensational cases of shootings, killings and rioting which attract public attention. But day by day the Negro soldier faces abuse and humiliation. In such a climate resentments, hatreds and fears and misunderstandings mount until they erupt in sensational violence. Yet, both the administration and the military authorities persist in trying to muddle through, without plan or program, hoping that somehow things will come out all right. The Army, long wedded to the mores of the South and immobilized by its traditional methods of prodecure, pursues a course of dealing with each incident as it occurs. Formal investigations and reports, an occasional court-martial, the removal of some individual from his company, the shifting of a troublesome regiment to another station—these are the Army's customary and familiar devices. The Army cannot check the increasing wave of violence by ponderous investigations of each case as it occurs. The Army itself is busy with booklets, lectures and various devices of indoctrination, teaching our soldiers how to treat the peoples of India, the South Sea Islanders, the Arabs, everyone but their fellow American soldiers. It is time that similar efforts and techniques be employed in the business of building comradeship within our own military and civilian communities.[12]

Hastie's admonitions, however, went unheeded. Just one month after the release of this statement, a black soldier revealed how he had been mistreated by a white bus driver and white military policemen. On a trip to Georgia to visit his family, Private First Class Charles Mabrey, Jr., alleged his ticket was taken and he was denied a seat on a bus because he had gotten on in front of a white woman. He claimed that when he asked for his ticket the bus driver first refused but finally returned it to him. Mabrey continued: "About that time two white military policemen walked up I asked one just why I could not ride on that particular bus. One was rather nice after I had told him of my trouble but the other one spoke up very insultingly. He said, 'You let a "nigger" talk to you like that?' He said what if I did not like the way things were he would send me to camp foot forward and that he ought to arrest me anyway."[13]

In October more of the same was reported. Private T. Nicklus was humiliated by a train conductor in Clairborne, Louisiana. In sworn testimony, Nicklus recalled how the conductor pushed and hit him. When he protested, the conductor shouted: "Give me the ticket Nigger." Nicklus reportedly said he was not a nigger, and the conductor responded in anger: "Yes, you are a nigger, a god-damn nigger. You are down below the Mason Dixon Line and you are all nigger boys down here."[14]

Like most black soldiers who wrote protest letters during World War II, Nicklus and the troops "don't want no more than to be treated like soldiers."[15] The letters that follow show why the Army's black soldiers came to dread the South.

NOTES

1. Letter, A Group of Soldiers from Jackson Air Base to William H. Hastie, October 11, 1942; Letter, Mrs. Jessie W. Greene to Hastie, October 17, 1942; Letter, Mrs. Eleanor Roosevelt to John J. McCloy, September 29, 1943; Letter, McCloy to Mrs. Roosevelt, October 2, 1943, all in Civilian Aide to the Secretary of War Subject File, 1940–1947, National Archives Record Group 107 (hereafter cited as NARG).

2. Letter, A Disgusted Negro Trooper to *The Cleveland Call and Post*, August 16, 1944, Civilian Aide to the Secretary of War Subject File, 1940–1947, NARG 107.

3. Memorandum, Henry H. Arnold to Hastie, August 15, 1942; Memorandum, Hastie to Arnold, August 18, 1942, Civilian Aide to the Secretary of War Subject File, 1940–1947, NARG 107.

4. Henry L. Stimson Diary, January 17, 1942, Yale University Library, New Haven, Connecticut.

5. Letter, Roy Wilkins to Hastie, April 26, 1942, Box 264, National Association for the Advancement of Colored People Papers, Manuscript Division, Library of Congress, Washington, D.C., Stimson Diary, January 29, 1942; Memorandum, Hastie to James A. Ulio, Adjutant General, October 21, 1941; Letter, Senator Chan Gurney to Stimson, December 17, 1942; Letter, Eleanor Roosevelt to John J. McCloy, September 30, 1943; Letter, McCloy to Mrs. Roosevelt, October 2, 1943; Letter, Matthew Thorton, Jr. to President Franklin D. Roosevelt, October 13, 1941, all in Civilian Aide to the Secretary of War Subject File, 1940–1947, NARG 107.

6. Memorandum, Adjutant General James A. Ulio to the Commanding General, Services and Supply, May 8, 1942, Army General Staff, NARG 407; Ulio to Senator Chan Gurney and Hastie, December 30, 1942, Civilian Aide to the Secretary of War Subject File, 1940–1947, NARG 107.

7. Judge William H. Hastie, private interview with author, 1701 Popla Lane, N.W., Washington, D.C., March 8, 1974; Letter, Hastie to author, October 8, 1974.

8. Letter, Latrophe F. Jenkins to P. L. Prattis, September 12, 1944, Civilian Aide to the Secretary of War Subject File, 1940–1947, NARG 107.

9. Resolution, Springfield Branch of the NAACP to Stimson and Franklin D. Roosevelt, September 14, 1941; "We Are Still Waiting," *The Washington Afro-American*, October 5, 1941; Letter, Stimson to Senator Prentise M. Brown, September 16, 1941, all in Box 230, NAACP Papers; Letter, Patterson to Walter White, September 18, 1941, Robert L. Patterson Papers, Manuscript Division, Library of Congress, Washington, D.C., Telegram, John P. Davis to Stimson, April 2, 1941; Letter, Davis to Roosevelt, September 2, 1941, John P. Davis Papers, The Schomburg Center for Research in Black Culture, New York Public Library, New York City; Letter, Congressman Arthur W. Mitchell to Stimson, February 14, 1942, Civilian Aide to the Secretary of War Subject File, 1940–1947, NARG 107; Memorandum, Davis to John J. McCloy, September 4, 1941, Army General Staff, NARG 407.

10. Memorandum, Hastie to Stimson, September 8, 1941; Memorandum, Hastie to

11. Policy Statement, Henry L. Stimson to the Personnel of the United States Armed Forces, September 26, 1941, Civilian Aide to the Secretary of War Subject File, 1940–1947, NARG 107.

12. "Soldiers Flogged By Military Police," *Norfolk Journal and Guide*, September 13, 1942; Memorandum, Major James S. Tatman, Acting Chief of the Analysis Branch, to the Director of the Office of War Information, June 14, 1943, Office of War Information, NARG 208.

13. Letter, Charlie Mabrey, Jr. to the *Atlanta Daily World*, July 21, 1943, Civilian Aide to the Secretary of War Subject File, 1940–1947, NARG 107.

14. Affidavit, William J. Clark, Acting Adjutant General, to Headquarters Company "C" Camp Claiborne, Louisiana, October 31, 1943, Civilian Aide to the Secretary of War Subject File, 1940–1947, NARG 107.

15. Letter, A Group of Soldiers from Jackson Air Base to William H. Hastie, October 11, 1942, Civilian Aide to the Secretary of War Subject File, 1940–1947, NARG 107.

For Transfer Out of Mississippi

Q.M. 34th Regt. Co. F

Subject: The Condition of the Negroes   Jackson Air Base

at Jackson Air Base   Jackson, Mississippi

Mr. William H. Hastie   October 11, 1942

Dear Sir:

We as a group of Negro soldiers, wish to be soldiers in the Army of the United States, not dogs at Jackson Air Base, nor in the State of Mississippi. I'm writing for every soldier in the service at Jackson Air Base. We are treated like wild animals here, like we are umhuman. The word Negro is never used here, all they call us are nigger do this, nigger do that. Even the officers here are calling us nigger.

Civilian polices have threated to kill several soldiers here. Some part of Mississippi, Negro soldiers are not allow to walk in town. Lieutenant Bromberg said all Negroes need to be beaten to death. He assist Civilian polices in the punishment of these Negro soldiers.

It's pitiful, harmful the way we are treated here. We are even neglected in the canteen. Our food are fixed in such a manner that we can't eat. We never get enough to eat. In the hospital we are mistreated. Please help us, we need your help.

The time has come for someone to help us here. We can't go to any one here to tell our trouble too. The word has been said before us, they don't want niggers here in this air base.

Please investigate the condition here. Pass this letter on to the War Department, to General Davis, to the NAACP also for help.

Yours sincerely,

A group of soldiers

from Jackson Air Base

We don't want no more than to be treated like soldiers. Please help us to be transferred out of state of Mississippi. We don't wish to be a desertor. We just want to better our condition.

Bracketville, Texas, Worse than Hell Itself

Philadelphia Afro American
704 South Broad Street
Philadelphia, Pa.   April 19, 1943

Dear Sirs:

I am writing you this letter in response to subscription of the Afro American
of which I have not been receiving. I hope you will take the matter in
consideration because without this paper I have no means of knowing what is
happening in my home town which is Philly.

Few civilians never have the idea of what we boys are really going through
down here in Texas, one of the worst states in this country. I've been in the
Army for sixteen months and I know what the young boys are facing that are
being drafted each and every day. I have been stationed in Mississippi and also
in Southern California. Maybe you have heard of the Desert Training Center
located at Indio, California. Yes I was there for seven months where the heat
was 150 and some days even hotter. But the boys took everything they could
dish out and more too; white boys killing their buddies and even killing themselves. I've saw equipment burned up; boys roasted in them and they tell you
to be a good soldier.

And now, way down in Texas, where we're not even good as dogs, much
less soldiers, even our General on the post hates the sight of a colored soldier.
Why I ask you, do we have to fight on the home front for our lives then go
across seas and fight again? Sure I'm giving you the real facts about Ft. Clark,
Texas. Everything is true and my buddies can tell you the same thing.

There is a town down here called Bracketville and let me tell you it couldn't
be any worse than hell itself. When you go to the movies you are jim crowed;
whites on one side and you on the other. And that's right on the post. Sure
we're fighting a war, but who starts these wars? Do the colored boys or do the
white race who think they can master the world?

If your're a man and you think a whole lot of your paper than print this
because three times to one I've got a lot more to tell that would make your
head swim. The only thing you can do is sit down and write a letter home.
Otherwise you would go crazy and I know, because I almost blew my top.

It's not that we boys don't want to fight but what are we really fighting for?
Is it to free America or throw us back ten years? Ask any real Army man and
he'll tell you that the colored soldier is the best, can do anything better than a

white boy. That's why there are so many colored boys in the Engineer and Quartermaster Corps doing the hard jobs.

I've got a wife home, a mother, father and sister and brothers. Some day I'm going back there.

General Davis was down here this week to see what makes Ft. Clark tick. I and every other soldier on this post knows what this report will be. It will read something like this,

"Boys at Ft. Clark are having time of their life."

Yes, we're having a fine time of hell. But to you and all the colored civilians that are still out there, turn this bit of news loose. Let the colored public know what their boys are really going through. That's my story so let's hear about it. Every boy down here is waiting for your answer.

About my subscription, being to my change of station, I don't think you knew my right address, it is as follows:

Black Treatment Southern Style

The Atlanta Daily World   PFC Charlie Mabrey, Jr.
Circulation Department   226th Port Company
210 Auburn Avenue   Headquarters Command C.P.E.
Atlanta, Georgia   July 21, 1943

Dear Sirs:

I am Negro soldier stationed in Charleston, South Carolina at the present. I
am writing you in regard to something that occurred while I was enroute home
on a furlough recently. On Friday, July 16, 1943 I was on my way home to
LaGrange, Georgia to visit my wife and four months-old baby. I left Charleston
about two-thirty o'clock and arrived in Augusta, Georgia about seven o'clock
where I had a rest period of about thirty minutes. The bus driver, operator of
an Atlantic Trailways bus, called all passengers to come out of the station and
reclaim their seats. I got on the bus in front of a white woman who had not
been a passenger on the bus but was ordered off by the driver who addressed
me. "Say boy get off this bus."

I immediately got off and asked him what was wrong with my ticket. He
again said for me to just get off. It was then about seven-thirty o'clock. The
driver then said, "For blowing your damn top you will leave at on-fifteen
o'clock in the morning."

When I asked for the return of my ticket he at first refused to for some
reason but finally gave it back to me. About that time two white military
policement walked up I asked one just why I could not ride on that particular
bus. One was rather nice after I had told him of my trouble but the other one
spoke up very insultingly.

He said, "You let a "nigger" talk to you like that?" He said what if I did
not like the way things were he would send me to camp foot forward and that
he ought to arrest me anyway. I told him that as he had the authority to do so
he could. I want you to publish this story and to also publish my name. I sent
a copy of this airmail to the Pittsburgh Courier but I am sending it to you. I
want everyone to know how we colored soldiers are being treated here in the
South. We all have a tough time trying to visit our loved ones here in the
south and if I have any more trouble of this kind I will begin to wonder just

what we are fighting for. Perhaps instead of White America's fighting the Nazis and Japs they are fighting the Negroes of America. All America had better wake up to the fact that it is impossible to fight a battle abroad and at home too. I thank you in advance for your trouble.

Yours with sincerely,

PFC Charlie Mabrey, Jr.

Uncle Tomming for Whitey

A disgusted Negro Trooper
1331 Engr. Gen. Sec. Rgt.
Camp Claiborne, La.
To Cleveland Call & Post   August 16, 1944

Dear Editor:

I am writing you about a very delicate matter and that is about the conditions of Camp Claiborne. The conditions for a Negro soldier down here is unbearable the morale of the boys is very low. Now right at this moment the woods surrounding the camp are swarming with Louisiana hoogies armed with rifles and shot guns even the little kids have 22 cal. rifles and B & B guns filled with anxiety to shoot a Negro soldier. All of this allegedly is supposed to have started because of two white women who are supposed to have been raped within the last week on the camp grounds which I doubt very much. Now this is the setup last week previous to this last raping that was supposed to have been committed. One of our boys caught one of the white mgrs who operates one of the P.X.'s where the fellows buy the necessities of life down here having sexual relations with one of the colored girls employed there being enraged over the indignities we suffer he taken a shot at him but missed wounding one of the Negroes guarding him. After this incident around 11 o'clock they blew us out and the officers in charges of the Neighboring companys came and had rifle inspection smelling the barrels of our guns to see if they had been recently fired to locate the individual who fired the shot at their white brother. Then our rifles were confiscated prior to this 2 or 3 Negroes have been shot but they never taken any steps like that then. So now we are at the mercy of there enraged and prejudice whites who are patrolling the neighboring woods. This camp isn't run by government regulations its controlled by the state of Louisiana and white civilians. I have heard a rumor that they have found 3 Negroe soldiers dead between Glenmore La. and Camp. I don't know just how authentic it is because they try to keep us in the dark but I wouldn't doubt it a bit. They have fellows down here in the worse of condition bent over dragging their legs when investigators from Washington come down they distributed the disable around where they could not be seen. If a fellow has a complaint to his well-being and wants to go to sick call they make him wear a fullfield pack or else put him on extra detail as punishment. Transportation from camp to town is very poor when they have every convience possible for white soldiers. We used to have dances twice a week but some of the uncle Tom's on guard duty broke that up by slapping the soldiers around. There's quite a few down here who wouldn't hesitate a minute to kill you for their big white chief. Most of the noncommission officers down here are white mouths they cut your throat with their tongue for a stripe. So you see Editor as I am taken it upon myself to be and advocate for the boys from upstate. This place is a living hell I am a Northern boy and we feel that we can't tolerate these conditions much longer. I hope there's some way the Negro people of Cleveland Detroit Chicago & New York the individuals who understand a better Way of life would instigate an investigation of this place because I see things brewing down and I am afraid that we colored soldiers are going to be the goats or victims of a one sided affair. Editor due to circumstances I wish to remain incognito. So we are looking forward to the Negro Public as a hold to make a move to counteract this injustice we are suffering and they say fight for democracy in foreign lands and Islands we have never heard of before when it doesn't exist here. So long until time brings on a change from hundreds of Negro soldiers who feel as I do.

Yours sincerely,

A disgusted Negro Trooper

The Last Whisper before We Die

HEADQUARTERS
1693rd Combat Engineers
Camp Rucker, Alabama
12 September 1944.

Dear Mr. Prattis:

This is our last hope of receiving help from the outside world. This is the final quiet before death comes. This is the dark dreary hour before dawn, a dawn that seemed to have died for us last nite, in disillusioned expectations that we thought we'd won by our willingness and sacrifices of serving over seas for nearly two punishing years.

Mr. Prattis, we've gone on this job with hung down heads and bleeding hearts, cut to our souls with the sword of injustices and Negro oppression. Being slaves of our leaders that the War Department placed over us as supervisors and not MASTERS. Being driven and down trodden worst than animals in the fields around us. Men losing their lives at the hands of power intoxicated anti-Negro MP's and Nazi minded Southern whites that take us to exercise their animosities on just as the Japs are branded for treating the Chinese. We've gone on accepting this brutal policy as our part of the Constitution as a minority. We've served faithfully, ignoring suffering and torture, standing by our country with a devotion that no other can approach, white of what not, laying down our lives on every front that this war will be a Victory for us. But then that leaves us to become terribly bewildered, because if this war is won by us, (I mean America), then who's going to help us to win ours? We are definitely not included in the Allied strength of this war, nor the citizen public of this nation, It can't be. Living day and nite in servitude. In the constant fear of our lives, being less considered than aliens or National enemies, all because of the inferior inferior insignificant fact that our skin's dark. All because we were born American Negroes and not Americans. . . . We are now in Camp Rucker, Alabama; a name that shall live in the lives of the men that live to get out of here, just as much as the memories of Siapan, Tarawa, Pearl Harbor or any of the bloody battle fields of this war, live in the minds of the men who fought there. We are here on War Department orders. Not because we chose this theatre of war to serve in, without protection. It is the same if they had landed us on New Georgia without the support of the Navy and Air Force. Even with those great odds against us, we would rather be landed on

New Georgia without protection than to be left here to die as "fatted pigs" at
the mercy of the iron hearted people we are surrounded by, arms against our
flesh. No one supports us from anywhere. We wonder if this is the pay off to
reduce the total of 13,000,000 Negroes before the Armistic. We can't find
enough premonition to solve this great puzzle. Only thing we know is, we are
here dying like dogs. Being driven to insanity every day we are spared for
more torture. Even if we ask for a small bit of justice we are beaten to death
and forgotten. We were happy over seas. We were safe too, because we
protected ourselves with our arms. We studied our enemy there, and knew his
methods of attack before he came, but here we know NOTHING! We only
know we are attacked with our hands tied, and why, we never know. In those
jungles out there we prayed and prayed to see America again, but this is
surely not what we prayed for. We had hope for tomorrow in this land that we
thrilled to see on the horizon as we arrived the first of this year, but now those
hopes are more prayers that we live to get some place else where we can see
the light of day. . . . . The sunset is closing on us fast Mr. Prattis help us if you
can. Please don't let this chance past to help rescue over a thousand Negroes
here dying with me. Get us help from out there where you are free. Please
print this where people will read it and maybe some one will come to save us.
Please take this call for mercy as the last whisper before we die. Please let us
hear from you sir. May God show you the way.

Respectfully yours,

Latrophe F. Jenkins

Five Seats for Colored Boys

The Pittsburgh Courier

Napier Field, Dothan, Alabama
29 November 1944

Dear Editor:

I've just returned from the Post Theatre. Being rather disgusted over the way I was ordered out of the Post Theatre tonight; I thought I would just write this little article to show or rather let the people back home know just how we are doing down in Alabama. It is getting to the place that all colored soldiers just have to wait until there is plenty space for all whites before they can even get a seat.

I decided to take in a movie tonight. After reaching the theatre, I found that they had only five (5) seats reserved for colored, (five seats in a row), so the usher ask me to get out, so I had to get out and perhaps wait until tomorrow. Not that I mine waiting, but just the insult I got from the usher. "Get out, there isn't any seats for you colored boys." Can you picture a personnel of approximately two hundred and seventy (270) trying to see a picture at the theatre, when only twenty-five (25) can see a picture a night. Only twenty seats per night for the colored soldiers.

The Army often practice, "keep up your morale by attending movies," our morale would be very very low if we had to see movies to keep it up in Napier Field.

This is something to laugh about. Two days ago a friend from Pittsburgh received a package from the Company he worked for before entering the army. It was a very nice package, he appreciated it to the highest. But one thing I notice on the outside of the package was; "To be mailed outside the limits of the continental United States." It was addressed to Napier Field, Dotham, Ala. We as colored soldiers at Napier Field readily agree with this company. When they mailed this package, they mailed it outside the limits of the continental United States.

Sgt. Jesse L. Wilkins

30 Days on the South Carolina Chain Gang

From the magazine "The New Republic," 25 December 1944
CORRESPONDENCE
Negroes in the Army

Sir:I should like to tell you of a recent experience of mine, as a
Negro soldier in the United States Army.

One Saturday evening I left Camp Gordon, Georgia, on pass to visit some
friends in nearby Aiken, South Carolina. I boarded a Valley Coach Line bus in
Augusta, Georgia to make the 18-mile trip to my destination. Complying with
the Jim Crow laws of the state I moved to the rear of the bus. The bus,
although crowded, was quiet and the passengers, mostly civilians, are orderly.

About eight miles from Augusta, one of the seats near the middle of the bus
was emptied when one of the passengers got off. This was an aisle seat next to
a white soldier. Standing in the aisle was a colored soldier who continued to
stand by the empty seat until the white soldier touched his arm and told him to
go ahead and sit down, he didn't mind. This the colored soldier did and the two
men engaged in conversation until the bus reached Warrenville, South Carolina. There the bus driver saw the two soldiers sitting together and ordered
the colored soldier to move. This he did without hesitation and without protest.
The white soldier was indignant and protested against the driver's action, but
he was told that the laws of the state did not permit such seating and besides,
as bus driver, he would run the bus the way he wanted it run. There was not a
single word or action from anyone on the bus.

At this same stop several colored passengers got on the bus. There was
standing room only except for one seat about three-quarters of the way to the
rear of the bus. This was occupied by an elderly white civilian who was asleep.
A middle-aged colored woman got on the bus, noticed the empty seat and
turned and asked the bus driver if he would ask the man to move to a seat in
the front which had just been emptied. The bus driver very gruffly told her no,
that he would not ask the man to move, and if she didn't like it she could get
her money back and get off the bus. She went to the front to get her refund
and as she started down the steps of the bus the driver took his fist and struck
her across the back of her head. The blow almost felled her and she half-fell,
half-staggered from the bus. Several white soldiers grabbed the driver and
prevented him from inflicting further blows. From our seats in the rear we
demanded that he cease before we ourselves used force. Not one of us did

more than raise a verbal protest. The bus driver grabbed up his money box
and left the bus. We remained seated until it was evident that he would not
move the bus.

In about 15 minutes, another bus pulled in. The driver of our bus went to
the driver of this bus and told him not to let the 11 colored soldiers on the bus
because they had created a disturbance on his bus. So we were left five miles
from our destination on an empty bus. We then asked to have the Military
Police notified, and believing that they had been, we sat on in the empty bus.
There we made our mistake, for instead of Military Police, two carloads of
county police and armed civilians pulled up and ordered us to the rear of the
bus. We were then driven directly to the county jail and locked up without
being questioned, arraigned or without any of the usual procedures. We asked
to be allowed to notify our units. We were told that they would be notified.
Later we learned that they had not been notified.

The 11 of us remained locked up from 9 p.m. Saturday until 6 p.m.
Monday. I cannot described here the condition of that jail; it was absolutely
miserable. Monday evening we were taken before a court; the bus driver was
there, but there were no other witnesses. He testified and prejured himself in
every sentence. He said that we had beaten him, that we had in general raised
a rumpus. All of this was absolutely untrue. We were then called on to give
our story. It so happened that I was called on first. I told the court everything
that I saw and heard, and told it just as it happened. The other men all
agreed, only one or two having details to add. We pleaded not guilty, but it was
evident from the start that the "trial" was a farce. The judge gave us a tongue
lashing and fined us for "disorderly conduct." I was fined $25 or 30 days on
the South Carolina chain gang, as were two other fellows. The remainder were
fined $15 or 30 days on the chain gang. We were fined $25 because we had
taken seats in front of the bus while it was empty of all other passengers and
after the driver had left it. We were sitting waiting for the Military Police, or
so we thought.

No one of us had money enough to pay his fine, so we pooled our money
and paid the fine of one of my buddies. The rest of us were loaded into cars
and taken to the county farm. En route to the farm, I was able to contact
Mrs. C—— the hostess at the colored USO. I told her that I needed $25
immediately. Asking no questions, she said that she would get it for me immediately. She got the money and brought it out to the farm and thus secured my
release, but not before I had been forced to take off my military uniform and
put on the filthy, blac, (sic) and white striped clothes of a convict and have an
iron chain riveted to my right ankle. This happened to each one of us. Mrs.

C—— came just after we had been penned up. She took me back to town and gave me a meal, my first in three days. I called my battalion at 9:45 Monday evening and that was the first time that they knew what had become of us.

I returned to camp as soon as possible and notified the commanding officers of the units to which the other men belonged. Not one of them knew the whereabouts of their missing soldiers. The men were furious when they heard what had happened to us. They collected money for the fines of the other men and early Tuesday morning went to get them. They did this of their own initiative. Our officers did nothing in behalf of the men. The men on the chain gang were found 25 and 30 miles out in the country working under armed guards. By mid-afternoon the five men in my unit had been released. The others were released as the commanders saw fit to go after them.

The entire series of events was like one long nightmare. It was an experience I shall never forget and one that I did not believe could happen in this "Great Democracy." It shook to the very core my faith in a nation where such things could receive the sanction of so many people as they do here in the South. I had to call upon every ounce of training and premilitary experience to keep from becoming bitter, and to realize that I must continue to sacrifice to be a soldier so that I may fight and if necessary give my life for my country. If I did not believe that there are some necessary adjustments so that all Americans may participate fully and freely in American life, I would be unwilling and unable to be a good soldier. We who now fight and are about to fight will contest wrong wherever it is found, abroad or as a cancer in our own nation.

Somewhere in the Deep South   Sergeant

(Serviceman's name withheld to avoid reprisals by the citizens of Aiken, South Carolina.—THE EDITORS)
CERTIFIED A TRUE COPY:
/s/ Joseph F. Lockard

10

Working with Pain

I am 42 years old have been in the army nearly 13
months Havent been able to train or do any amount of
Duty since I have been in here Due to my physcal
condition I have a Bullet in my spine Broken Ribs also
my left foot have been broken I am unable to perform
military Duty I am married The Father of 6 children one
son in the U.S. Navy one son in Law in the U.S. army I
am now in the Hospital with this same Foot Badly Broken I am Willing To Do anything I can Do To Help win
Victory but as it seem to me I am out here ruining The
Morale of the younger soldiers My pleas for Discharge
always get a Deaf Ear.

Private Richmond Walker

Black troops blamed racial discrimination for many of their troubles with physical and mental handicaps in the armed forces.
According to the soldiers, their conditions did not, as was normal procedure and practice for white soldiers, incapacitate them for military duty. For the vast majority of those physically disabled, it was either
work with pain or be subjected to some kind of punitive action. From
1943 to 1944, examples of these incidents were reported in bitter complaints. The troops tell of humiliation, of having to perform duty with
broken bones, spinal injuries, swollen feet, bleeding ulcers, and heart
trouble. They also criticized the Army for inadequate medical treatment,
poor patient care, and for being forced to endure severe pain because
military officials thought they were feigning and able to work despite their
mental and physical disabilities.

Black soldiers with physical disabilities who had to do detail were particularly bitter toward the Army. A soldier at the Dibble General Hospital
in Menlo Park, California, for example, maligned the medical staff for
inadequate patient care. Private First Class Thompson wrote: "After arriving back in the States from the South west Pacific, I have been cussed
at and dog, everything has been done to me except Killed I have been a

very sick patient and these Southern Doctors, havent giving me any kind of treatment. But they want me to do detail or else be Court Martial." Thompson went on to say: "I have served 16 months Overseas, I have tried to do but my health wont allow me to work I lost the sight out of one eye and have bleeding at the mouth all this came from vomiting There are lots of colored boys here treated the same way. But they are from the south and afraid to talk."[1]

Other black troops with similar complaints also spoke out against the way they were being mistreated. A loyal soldier from Camp Butner, North Carolina, described how a fellow trooper was forced to work despite heart trouble. This soldier claimed that Private Ben J. Aitimon should have been "classed as a Cardiac patient" because "his nerve system Around his heart is torn up Very badly." He continued: "A Civilian Doctor Says it is very dangerous of his heart taking A sosytic spasm if he contues to try to Perform Ardious training When his Heart begin to beat very rapidly." The soldier also alleged that "his Commanding Officer have told the Medical Officer of the 403rd Eng Med Dept to give all enlisted men of his Co castor oil When they come there for Medical treatements regardless What their Sickness maybe."[2]

Another soldier, at Aberdeen Proving Ground in Maryland, felt that the medical staff and his military superiors ignored him after he had been admitted to the base hospital for a lingering two-year-old ankle fracture. He related that first a cast was put on too tight, then it was cut away, and finally he was made to work while experiencing severe pain. Private Edward C. Green, Jr., stated, "While not being able to walk halfly normal I was on difficult occasions assigned to various ward chores such as climbing ladders to Wash windows—excessive standing afoot continously mopping corridors and the ward. I had not even discarded my crutches at that time. Several times while mopping the floor of the ward, I slipped and possibly hurt my ankle again." To get some relief, Private Green "consulted the Hospital Chief (at that time) Colonel Stewart and frankly pointed out to him that [he] was not receiving the best attention of the medical personnel there, and requested a 'temporary' release to secure proper treatment at [his] own expense." Instead of granting this request, Green contended, Colonel Stewart told a long, long story about one other fracture patient who had to wait 3 or 4 years to get over the ailment and still this patient has not recovered as far as walking normally is concerned. It is also an interesting fact that I do not walk normal now either."[3]

At Fort Leonard Wood, Missouri, Private DeLeon J. Wood was bitter because he was told nothing could be done for his lame arm and right hand and because he was treated like a prisoner. He lamented: "The ward that I am in has bars at all the windows infact the ward is like a jail, but doors or open, but in order to go any place I have to get a pass from a Officer who are always nurses and it seem to be a great job for me to get one. It seem to me that I am place here a some kind of prisoner, there is nothing being done about my arm and hand. The doctors comes around every morning and only ask how I feel and say good morning which I see in no way of helping my arm and hand."[4]

From Camp Hood, Texas, came other reports of black soldiers having to perform military duty with lame bodies. The troops there wondered if they were "free Negroes, or still slaves." Private John Rivers alleged that they were deliberately being worked to the point of exhaustion and hospitalization. In a glowing statement, Rivers wrote: "We as soldiers here in Camp Hood, Texas, are really being treated worse than these German prisoners here. We in the camp stockade are being beaten every day until we can't stand up; drilled all hours of the night. One soldier had a bad case of appendicitis and instead of giving this man medical care he was worked harder and beaten until his appendix burst. Then he was sent to the hospital for operation. Are we still in America or are we over in Japan or Germany?"[5]

Besides being forced to do manual labor as cripples, some black soldiers revealed they were on the brink of committing suicide due to bodily pain. Fort Harrison, Indiana, trooper, Y. Z. Perry, in a letter to the editor of the *Pittsburgh Courier*, wrote: "If I don't get out of here alive very soon I'll end it all by killing myself. I am tired of suffering. I'd rather be dead than suffer this way. . . . They keep our men in the army disabled until they die I know; it has happen here last week."[6]

Because some military officials apparently believed that most of the soldiers' charges against the Army were expressions of mere malingering (undoubtedly a few were), punitive rather than corrective procedures were allegedly taken against those troops thought guilty of feigning. A case in point occurred at Camp Ellis, Texas. There a black soldier stated that "the punishment we get for being disabled is extra duty, restriction, and worst of all we are forced to sleep on the ground on only one blanket."[7]

Similar voices were heard at Camp Davis, North Carolina. For protesting against the Army's medical care, and for asking "to be given jobs that wouldn't agrivate [their] injuries," Private Fist Class Benjamin L. Lowry contended that the black troops there "were forbidden to go on sick call," and those recommended for discharge were "told that the discharges are frozen in the Fourth Service Command but that evidently applies only to Colored, since we see the whites being discharged almost daily."[8]

To make matters even more complicated for disabled black soldiers, the Army allegedly used the threat of court-martial to force them to work. However, working under this kind of duress simply led to more black protest. For instance, a soldier stationed at Seattle, Washington, claimed he was threatened with a court-martial because he was unable and refused to work; however, he changed his mind to avoid being punished. But at other camps black troops demonstrated a will to take matters into their own hands if the Army continued to ignore their request for sick call, medical discharges, and adequate and proper medical care.[9]

While no record was found to verify whether or not black soldiers ever carried out these threats, in camp after camp their letters testify to a legacy of painful abuse and medical neglect.

NOTES

1. Roy W. Thompson to Robert Vann, April 30, 1944, Civilian Aide to the Secretary of War Subject File, 1940–1947, National Archives Record Group 107 (hereafter cited as NARG).

2. Letter, A Loyal Soldier to the *Pittsburgh Courier*, February 12, 1943, Civilian Aide to the Secretary of War Subject File, 1940–1947, NARG 107.

3. Letter, Edward C. Green, Jr., to Truman K. Gibson, Jr., July 12, 1943, Civilian Aide to the Secretary of War Subject File, 1940–1947, NARG 107.

4. Letter, DeLeon J. Wood to Truman K. Gibson, Jr., May 5, 1944, Civilian Aide to the Secretary of War Subject File, 1940–1947, NARG 107.

5. Letter, John Rivers to Carl Murphy, November 24, 1943, Civilian Aide to the Secretary of War Subject File, 1940–1947, NARG 107.

6. Letter, Y. Z. Perry to the *Pittsburgh Courier*, May 28, 1944, Civilian Aide to the Secretary of War Subject File, 1940–1947, NARG 107.

7. Judge William H. Hastie, private interview with author, U.S. Court of Appeals, Washington, D.C., March 6, 1974; Letter, A Negro Soldier to Percival L. Prattis, November 14, 1943, Civilian Aide to the Secretary of War Subject File, 1940–1947, NARG 107.

8. Letter, Benjamin L. Lowry to Truman K. Gibson, Jr., March 8, 1944, Civilian Aide to the Secretary of War Subject File, 1940–1947, NARG 107.

9. Letter, Richmond Walker to Mary McLeod Bethune, December 5, 1943; Letter, Jerry M. Miller to Truman K. Gibson, Jr., July 14, 1943; Letter, Albert S. Wilkerson to Gibson, June 5, 1944; B. E. Dixon to the *Pittsburgh Courier*, May 8, 1944, all in Civilian Aide to the Secretary of War Subject File, 1940–1947, NARG 107.

Worse than Nasism of German Brutality

To Pittsburg Courier For
Publication and N.A.A.C.P.   Feb 12, 1943

if you desire

Here is a Very Cruel Case of Predjurice to our race. Worse than Nasism of
German Brutly. Who are unable to perform Ardious duty in any place. he is A
private of the 2 Chamical Decon Co Camp Butner N.C. He should be classed
as a Cardiac paitent. His nerve system Around his heart is torn up Very badly.
A Civilian Doctor Says it is very dangerous of his heart taking a sosytic spasm
if he contues to try to Perform Ardious training When his Heart begin to beat
Very rapidly. His Civilian Doctor are willing to put up his reputation on his
diagnosis of his case. As follow (he has a very serve neritist pain. and palapa-
tion at the heart.) (Active) I am no doctor I cannot explain in exact Words of
Case. But I do believe the N.A.A.C.P. can help this pvt. his Commanding
Officer have told the Medical Officer of the 403rd Eng Med Dept to give all
enlisted men of his Co castor oil When they come there for Medical treatements regardless What their Sickness maybe. This private I writing about
Vomits after each excise or hike. he is Sick or unfit for that kind of duty, but
he is a Negro who is loyal beyond the call of duty. And do not get any
consideration about his illness. Please give this letter to the N.A.A.C.P. he is
Very nervous His Name Pvt Ben J Aitimon. you May Contact him at this
adress he can explain his case to the N.A.A.C.P.
    Pvt Ben J Aitimon
    24 Chemical Decon Co
    Camp Butner N.C.
    If any one desire to try to help the Men of the 24 Chemical Decon And
others Who have problems like ours, write Pvt Ben J Aitimon
    24 Chemical Decon Co.
    Camp Butner N.C.
    Withhold names until you all have taken step to Aid this Pvt and others
they All Will Cooperate 100% to throw this Southern Coustom from this
Company. it's too Much discrimination here.

A loyal Soldier.

Liniment Massages and Heat Ray Treatment

Quartermaster Det. # 2
A. P. G. Aberdeen, Md
July 12, 1943.

Dear Mr. Gibson,

Yours of the 29th inst., is acknowledged. I have, to the best of my ability compiled the information concerning my case. Herewith I submit the facts:

I enlisted in the Army at Baltimore, Md., 2nd of April 1941., arriving at this post for duty the same date. May 13th, 1941 I fractured my left ankle which caused me to be hospitalized for a period greater than Five (5) months. This is not my first leg fracture however, having sustained several prior to entering the Army. Apparently my injuries were received in the line of duty as my pay was not affected. On being confined to the station hospital here I received medical attention, thus; a series of local anesthatics to cause the pains to subside. Shortly afterwards my ankle was *supposedly* set and cast applied. The cast was entirely too tight and I began complaining until it was cut away for loosening. It took about 3 days to get around to this action. Meanwhile I was yet experiencing pain. I am firmly convinced that in the course of the treatment given me while in the hospital there has been a considerable amount of laxity on the part of those responsible for me while in an injured state. While not being able to walk halfly normal I was on difficult occasions assigned to various ward chores such as climbing ladders to Wash windows—excessive standing afoot continously mopping corridors and the ward. I had not even discarded my crutches at that time. Several times while mopping the floor of the ward, I slipped and possibly hurt my ankle again. I recall also on another occasion that one Pvt. Joseph Ecklinger, at that time a ward orderly attacked and knocked me to the floor with his fist which I am sure harmed the progress of my injuries somewhat. I was on crutches at the time of this incident. I reported the matter to the Adjutant of the Hospital, then, at that time. (Lt. Rauscher) who upheld the actions of the ward orderly and offered me no redress whatever. Shortly after this incident I consulted the Hospital Chief (at that time) Colonel Stewart and frankly pointed out to him that I was not receiving the best attention of the Medical personnel there, and requested a "temporary" release to enter a civilian hospital to secure proper treatment at my own expense. In the place of receiving favorable results I was told a long, long story about one other fracture patient who had to wait 3 or 4 years to get over the ailment and still this patient has not recovered as far as walking normally is concerned. It is also an interesting fact that I do not walk normal now either. My injuries are 2 years or more old and still I am suffering to a great extent, an extent that causes me to sincerely concede to the candid fact that I am physically unfit for military duty. After a long period of observation here and continual passing of the buck by hospital officials here I was finally transferred to Walter Reed General Hospital in Washington, D.C. While there nothing was done for me. I inquired all I knew how as to what could be done. No one seemed to know or care. I left there and reported at Fort Meade, Md. and then returned to Aberdeen to my company and was marked "Duty."

Within 3 or 4 days my first Sergeant, Levia Happszollera referred me to the company commander for disposition. He (the Company Commander) sent me without delay back to the station hospital here. I stayed there and received liniment massages and Heat ray treatment which caused my ankle to swell the more.

Becoming highly disgusted with the attention tendered me by the doctors, I sought other means to obtain further treatment. Insomuch as consulting civilian physicians. They instructed me that they could not or rather would not care to become interested in the case while I was still a charge of the Army. I began a period of Absence without leave. Each time that I have been court-martialed for the offense, I have plaintively brought out to the court what prompted and caused me to assume those attitudes. Again no consideration. I also requested on several occasions a Physical Exam to prove my disability. As of now this hasn't been realized.

I've tried to the point of exhaustion to interest my present Company Commander in my need for a discharge. He is prone to view me as of great worth to the service, mentally, i.e., that I am capable of the execution of clerical duties efficiently. Yet when he (the present company commander) Capt. Edw. A. Sahli picture himself so competent as to answer the Trial Judge Advocates question as to my fitness for Military Duty, he avers that I am fit when this opinion should be left up to the disposition board of the medical department here or some eminent authority on orthopedics.

Capt. Sahli has gone so far as to tell me that its no use to apply for a discharge because there are other soldiers with identical or similar ailments who are in the Army and are doing wonderfully fine. My application for discharge was turned down by Capt. Sahli. It is quite obvious that maybe some men are afflicted by or with the same ailments, and it also stands true to reason that these same men can withstand and endure the rigors of Army life while in their condition. It is altogether different as pertains myself. The constant ambulation which at different times I have been subjected to has done me more harm than good.

There is a considerable amount of paralysis in my bones completely from the dorsum of my hand to the dorsum of my feet. Inclement, or the approach of inclement weather causes this condition to become more and more serious. Today, I am doing manual labor as a result of a courtmartial conviction and secondly because I am forced to do so. I am required to do constant moving about. At night when I am relieved of detail I can feel the results of such labor insomuch that I am oft-tempted to refuse direct orders that are issued me to report on daily detail. How can an individual thus affected conduct himself in any manner other than that of a potential temperamentalist. As far as I can understand, Sick call means nothing here. You are constantly reporting your complaint—A period of passing the buck is incurred—If you should be *lucky* to get to the desired clinic, the Doctor in charge warns you to not ever come back. Yet all the while, your condition is just the same.

Sir, I turn to you as the second to the last step in this matter. I am fair with myself in realizing that my condition will not allow me to endure much more. I would rather a thousand times, to have my leg cut off than to suffer as I am. To get to the point. The way I am going now will soon merit me—possibly a maximum federal sentence or its equivalent—a Dishonorable Discharge just because I am honestly trying to fight for that which belongs to me—A means to correct my difference or a discharge which will permit me to secure the same elsewhere at my expense. If this cannot be accomplished then my last means is to engage Civilian Counsel to institute proceedings in Court to my welfare. Already I have been advised by the Legal Assistance Officer at this post that I could reach this measure or step if so desired.

In addition to the above I have entered correspondence with one Attorney at Law. B. Harris Henderson—231 St. Paul Place. Baltimore, Md. as regards this matter. I am delaying instructions for him to proceed pending the outcome of your findings if you should find it necessary to investigate my case. I have also, as of this writing become satisfied that I have tried to the best of my knowledge and ability to have the "powers that be" (on this post) become interested in my plea. Seemingly I have failed in my undertakings.

I wrote the Commanding General in reference to myself. No reply has been received yet. I requested the occasion to take my case to the Commanding General of this post. His chain of command refused to hear me. The officer who has charge of me now, has refused me an interview before the commanding general here. I see no further use in my playing or masquerading under a *sham* and deceiving myself thereby to the point of belief that I will prove a bona-fide soldier when the odds are heavily stacked against me. I recall and always will, the occasion one Captain Hamburger of this command remonstrated and told me that regardless of what efforts I launched to become a soldier, I never would, or never was, nor would ever become a soldier. I accepted this officers assertions modestly, but not to the end of affirmation of his remarks, for it stands to reason and without discrimination that my "Army Service Record" and Report of Efficiency portrays that I have not under any circumstances whatever, assumed the standards an efficient soldier enjoys as a matter of merit.

I am intelligent enough to realize that my inefficiency as a soldier is not predicated upon or culminated by the desire of one Pvt. Green to become so. I profess soundly that my condition has caused me to fail as a soldier. Maybe its not my place to say this, but its an ease my conscience to state it. I can only see myself advance in the Army as a *liability* instead of an *asset* due to no fault of my own.

Sir, whatever action in my behalf you may be successful in instigating will be greatly considered timely and despairingly necessary for the curtailment of "distasteful events" which obviously are in the making.

I shall be exceedingly glad to receive a reply from you at your earliest convenience. Meanwhile I shall blend every effort to make your endeavors worthy insofar as "keeping on the bean."

Further, I swear that the testimony and statements given in this document to be the sole truth as verified by my signature.

Gratefully Yours,

Edward C. Green, Jr.
Pvt. U.S.A. 2m. Det. # 2, A.P.G. Md.

Varicose Veins

Med. Det. Bldg. 322
Station Hospital
Camp Shelby, Miss.
July 16, 1943

Mr. Truman K. Gibson, Jr.
Civilian Aide to the Secretary of War

Dear Sir:

In regards to my wife's letter. I am writing you some of the things that go on in this camp. first I will tell you some of the mistreatment. that we get and receive here. I have had the doctor at the infirmary to tell me that there wasent anything wrong with me and if I didnt go on back to work I would be put in the stockade. I suffer with severe headakes & I have varicose vains. When I was first sent over here. the doctor told me. there was nothing they could do for my ailment. But give me something to ease the pain. and they even stop doing that for me. When I was at home I could do for my self. and for the last couple of months. I have been buying asprins my self. Now for some of the things that have happen to a couple of boys I know. one of them was beat up at one of the mess halls. by three white fellows. and when they were taken to the Commanding officer over the detatchment. he gave the Colored boy a week of extra duty. and the others were let go. the other boy was struck by the first Sgt. one Sunday morning. because he didnt say yes sir to him. there are lots more complaints right here. But the boys are afraid of being punish. there are some of the boys. their homes are around here. they like it. and say they are getting along better now than they ever have. We have 600 or more colored boys in thies detatchment. and one staff sgt. and out of the 1200 Whites. there are numbers of first sgts. beside the other 5 grades of non Com's.

And Sir. I would like to get out if possible. I know there is Jobs that are open in civilian life. I can also and will do if I am allowed a chance. I have a clean civilian record. and also an army one. up until now. and It would be a great please and I would be very greatful to you. if you can help me in any way. I thank you very much for answering my wife's letter. in regards to this information. and I truly hope there will be something done about it. as I remain.

Respectfully Yours.

Jerry M. Miller

Treated Worse than Japs

1333 G. S. Regt.
Camp Ellis, Texas
November 14, 1943

Dear Mr. Prattis:

I have wrote to the Pittsburgh Courier before about the way the disabled Negro soldier is treated here at Camp Ellis. Sir the sick and disabled soldier is treated worst than a Jap, or German Prisoner ever dreamed of.

The punishment we get for being disabled is extra duty, restriction, and worst of all we are forced to sleep on the ground on only one blanket. We dont know what to do or who to see because you know this army has us tied down.

I am writing in behalf of myself and 60 other men like me. The medical officer refuses to give us an examination. The commanding officer of our Reg. is Col. Butler. Please give this information to the N.A.A.C.P.

Yours

A Negro Soldier

Free Negroes or Still Slaves?

Mr. Carl Murphy, President
Afro-American Newspapers
628 North Eutaw Street   Camp Hood, Texas
Baltimore, Maryland   November 24, 1943

Sir:

We as soldiers here in Camp Hood, Texas, are really being treated worse
than these German prisoners here. We in the camp stockade are being beaten
every day until we can't stand up; drilled all hours of the night. One soldier
had a bad case of appendicitis and instead of giving this man medical care he
was worked harder and beaten until his appendix burst. Then he was sent to
the hospital for operation. Are we still in America or are we over in Japan or
Germany? Are we free Negroes, or still slaves.

A copy of this has been sent to the War Dept. Asking for an investigation.
Thank you in advance.

Pvt. John Rivers,
Camp Hood, Texas.

Bullet in Spine, Broken Ribs, and Broken Left Foot

New Orleans, La.
December 5, 1943

Dear Mrs. Bethune:

I am 42 years old have been in the army nearly 13 month Havent been able to train or do any amount of Duty since I been in here Due to my physcal condition I have a Bullet in my spine Brokens Ribs also my left foot have been broken I am unable to perform military Duty I am married The Father of 6 children one son in the U.S. Navy one son in Law in the U.S. army I am now in the Hospital with this same Foot Badly Broken I am Willing To Do anything I can Do To Help win Victory but as it seem to me I am out here ruining The Morale of the younger soldiers My pleas for Discharge always gets a Deaf Ear although I first lie and sit around Doing Nothing I was inducted at Camp Blanding Fla Nov. 29th 1942 My home is in Jacksonville Fla I have 2 small childrens and a Wife there at 1573 paseo st, I am almost Helpless Will you please use your influence to help me get my Discharge My physical conditions plus my age Handicaps me Very much Thank you Very Much.

Pvt Richmond Walker (ASN), 34533413
Jefferson Branch N.O.S.A.
Co. F 6th Bn. Prt   ASFUTE.
New Orleans La

Asprin Tablets and Castor Oil

Pfc Benjamin J. Lowry
Post Detachment
Camp Davis, N. C.
3/8/44

Dear Mr. Gibson:

I am writting in regards to the poor medical treatment we are receiving here at this camp.

Recently a number of us were sent from various camps where we were listed as casualties to this camp. The majority of us were recommended for discharge but was shipped before they were enacted upon.

Here we were assigned to jobs that we find extreamly difficult due to our physical condition. We asked to be given some jobs that wouldn't agrivate our injuries but was repeatedly refused. Due to the assigned duties we were affected physically and was obligated to go on sick call. Although our ailments are different, most of us were given asprin tablets and castor oil and other remedies which couldn't possibly give us ease. Today we were forbidden to go on sick call at all. We get no consideration what so ever as to our physical ailments. When ever we go to the various departments at the hospital, we are rushed through without proper examinations, given the old brush off and told not to return because they can't do anything for us. Yet they won't discharge us nor will they let our Battery Commander know of our conditions so that he would know what we could or couldn't do. We are told that the discharges are frozen in the forth Service Command but that evidently applies only to Colored, since we see the whites being discharged almost daily.

I have been here one month and some days. My feet pains me severly also my legs and back. I am forced to stand all day on my feet shoveling sand and ashes, I've asked to given a job which wouldn't require my standing but have been refused. At the present time my feet have become so painful that it is pure agony to stand on them. The arch supporters and appliances doesn't help at all.

Frankly I am no good to the army in my present condition. I am a mortician by profession and since the army can't use me, I feel that they should discharge me and allow me to return to my business. They can't cure my condition and readily admitts it yet they refuse to release me. Enclosed a letter from my former Company commander to my present officials here. I've shown it to the C. O. also the doctors yet they refuse to consider it.

I would appreciate an investigation and I voice the sentiments of the men in the same condition as I. Thanking you in advance for any effort in our interest.

Respectfully

Pfc Benjamin J. Lowry

Lost Sight and Bleeding Mouth

PFC Roy W. Thompson
Dibble Gen Hospital
Menlo Park Calif
April 30, 1944

Dear Editor Vann

I am a patient in one of the army hospital, I would like you to know how I am treated, after arriving back in the States from the South west Pacific, I have been cussed at and dog, everything has been done to me except killed. I have been a very sick patient and these Southern Doctors, havent giving me any kind of treatment. But they want me to do detail or else be Court Martial. Now do you think thats fair. I have served 16 months Overseas, I have tried to do but my health wont allow me to work I lost the sight out of one eye and have bleeding at the mouth all this come from vomiting. There are lots of colored boys here treated the same way. But they are from the south and afraid to talk. I would like to know what the Negro soldier are fighting for, I have served three years in the American Army to help restore so call democracy. So please put this issue in the Courier. I would appreciate it very much.

Is there any way possible that you could send this to the NAACP and from there to War Department. I have lots of riend that are called (N) and are put in Wards that are segragated, Some are beating by MP who will probably die on account of no medical treatment. If there is any way you can help me I would appreciate it to the highness

From a Soldier Friend
Thompson

Bars at All Windows

Mr. Truman K. Gibson, Jr.   May 5, 1944
Civilian Aide to the Secretary   Station Hospital
of War   Ward F-4
Washington, D. C.   Fort Leonard Wood, Mo.

Dear Sir:

This is to inform you that I a patient at this hospital suffering with a factured right arm from two years ago. For about six months I have had no use of my right hand. This all happen to me in Fort Belvoi Va. I went to doctors there time after time and they each told me there was nothing that could be done for my arm. I was sent here to Fort Leonard Wood, Mo. I also went to doctors here time after time. On the 24th of April 1944 I was enter to this hospital and since I have been here it seem to me that I am a prisoner of some kind. On the 28th of April I was taken before a board of doctors to look at my arm and hand. I don't know what they decided to do about it. But the same day I was told I was to be sent to a Genral Hospital where I do not know. The ward that I am in has bars at all the windows infact the ward is like a jail, but doors or open, but in order to go any place I have to get a pass from a Officer who are always nurses and it seem to be a great job for me to get one. It seem to me that I am place here a some kind of a prisoner, there is nothing being done about my arm and hand. The doctors comes around every morning and only ask how I feel and say good morning which I see in no way of helping my arm and hand. So I have come to the place that I know I am not being treated right. So I would like to know if there is any way that you could help me or if you know of anyone who can help me. Sir I would be more than greatful to you if you can.

Yours Truly

Pvt. DeLeon J. Wood
13064031
Station Hospital War F-4
Fort Leonard Wood, Mo.

We the Colar Soldier

The Pittsburgh Courier
To The Ediste   May 8, 1944

Dear Sir

We the Colar Soldier who just return from over-sea would like to asked some question of a few things about this place the Woodrow Wilson General Hospital.

1. How We are treated here
We cant even walk down the hall unlet we are called names

2. We cant not ride the bus unless we have a fight. You see some of us has spend from 18 to 34 months over-sea some of us are wounded and some are sick and we relized this is the south but we could be treated like men and not dogs.

3. Even When go over asked them for some Consaderation we cant get it. So please give us some avanch if you please or we will take it in hand.

Yours Truly

S/sgt B. E. Dixon

Tired of Suffering!

Co. B. B. K. 10
Fort Harrison
Indianapolis, Indiana
May 28, 1944

Editor: The Courier:

I just can't help writing you this letter. I am a sick disabled man in the
Army. They brought me here this way. I am ruptured and have heart attacks.
I am suffering terribly and if I don't get out of here alive very soon I'll end it
all by killing myself. I am tired of suffering. I'd rather be dead than suffer this
way. I am not just saying that I am ruptured they have it on their record that
I am ruptured on one side and that I have a heart mumier. I am ruptured on
both sides and have heart attacks terribly. We Negro men in the Army has no
chance. Since I've been here I've seen many cripple Negroes. They bring
them in here disabled. There are no disabled white men brought into this camp
just colored men. I cannot walk without my truss and they still keep me. The
ruptures works on my bladder. I get up 3 times or more nightly or I wet my
bed in my sleep. The Courier has done many good things please look into this
matter. Please—I don't want to die by degrees I would rather die at once. I
beg you please.

Sincerely yours,

Y. Z. Perry

P.S. They keep our men in the army disabled until they die I know; it has
happen here last week.

No More Sick Call

To: Mr. Truman K. Gibson, Jr.   3381st Q M Trk Company
Civilian Aide to the   A.P.O. 980 c/o Postmaster
Secretary of War.   Seattle, Washington
Washington, D. C.   June 5, 1944

I T/5 Albert S. Wilkerson (A.S.N. 32356143) a member of the 3381st
Q.M. Trk. Company. Due to my physical disability, I am disable to perform the
different duties are required of me to do in the U. S. Army. I have been
suffering for a long period of time and is still suffering. I have been in the
hospital four (4) time. The doctors says they can't find my complaint and order
me to stop going on sick call. He also said I am nothing but a Gold-brick and
that it is nothing wrong with me. He told my Company Commander to put me
back on duty and he said if I refuse to work to give me a court martial. To
keep from being given a court martial, I am doing regular duty. And I am
unable to do duty.

I have been ill for a period of little over a year and have been constantly
going on sick calls about the same length of time. The doctors says they
cannot do any more for me. But refuse to give me a discharge and I am still
suffering from the same illness. Therefore, I am mailing my problem to you.
To see if you can be of help to me.

My wife have been writing letters to the War department in Washington,
D.C. But she was unable to obtain any result.

If it isen't any more that they can do for me, I would like to obtain a
discharge and be sent back home. Where I can go to doctors and have
something done for myself. I cannot mail this letter direct to you. Therefore,
my wife Callie V. Wilkerson mail it for me.

Yours very truly,

T/5 Albert S. Wilkerson

11

Jim Crow Goes Abroad

> We are writing you enlisting your aid concerning segregation of Negro troops in India and we would like you to take an appeal to NAACP.
>
> First off on the ship a lecture was given by Dr. Paul D. Lindbergh and he asked the Negro troops not to mention racial prejudice in the States. And right on the ship we weren't allowed to drink from the cool water fountains.
>
> Then the first thing we encountered in India is segregation. American, British, Indian, Chinese and Negro troops, all attend the same show and Negroes are piled in a huddle right in the rear.
>
> Negro Troops in India

What to do with black soldiers was as much of a dilemma overseas as it was for the Army in the States. In general, however, patterns of segregation and racial discrimination American-style prevailed there just as they did at home in America. Black soldiers were usually relegated to labor and supply units, forced to live and be entertained in segregated and inferior facilities, and subjected to the slurs and racist propaganda of white American troops. They also suffered from the racial indignation of local European communities.

For instance, in 1942, whites in Matadi, Belgian Congo, objected to the stationing of black quartermaster troops in their community. In fact, the exiled Belgian government attempted to force the U.S. government to recognize an agreement between the two countries that would have excluded black soldiers from being stationed in the country. Of course, the War Department denied any knowledge of the alleged agreement. Nevertheless, the attitude of the whites in Matadi was indicative of many white communities stateside. Protest in Matadi was so loud that Captain James V. Harding, who commanded the black truck company, asked the War Department to reassign the company. In a glaring statement, Harding reported:

Racial restrictions are extreme, and no consideration is given our Colored troops above that of the Native Negro by the local white population. . . . There are no place where our troops may go to be served food, or drink, in contrast to the freedom which is enjoyed by our white troops. . . . The Native villages are 'off limits' to all American troops due to sanitary conditions and safety precautions, and this effectively precludes possibility of correcting the situation. . . . Our men are accorded the same pass privileges as White troops in the area, but exhibit no desire to avail themselves of such privileges as they state that a general outward and bold exhibition on the part of the populace showing Colored soldiers' presence and services are not wanted makes their status very obvious. . . . The condition of the Native population is exciting considerable comment among our men who are rapidly becoming to feel that things they are fighting for are [a] fallacy.[1]

Black soldiers, indeed, had long thought that their participation in the war effort was a great illusion. Such was the case of Private John R. Wright who was stationed in Munich, Germany. In a letter to the editor of the black *Pittsburgh Courier*, Wright penned this: "Most of us did not want to come in this army [because of racial discrimination] in the first place, and Mr. Eastland [a Mississippi Senator] says we, the Negro Soldier, has made America loose prestege in Europe, but it's just the other way around. There have been many times that Jim Crow and prejudice have made me very very shame to say that I was an American. And even here in Germany, the people are not as bad as we were told. The majority of the people here admire a colored man so it seem to me. I served in North Africa, Italy, France, and now Dutchland. . . . I can not understand why the people of America will let the Bilbo's [a Mississippi senator] and others preach such hatred against the Negro citizens."[2]

Similar complaints came from elsewhere overseas. As far east as India black troops reported that the soldiers were "getting plenty fed up of being troddled on when they are giving their lives for America." They also complained that "when a complaint is taken to an officer the only answer we receive is, 'I'll see about it tomorrow.' "[3]

Although the experiences of black troops in India were representative of American racial patterns, race relations in the British Isles became the most frustrating dilemma for the War Department. It was generally considered—by British public opinion and by American travelers and journalists—that most British people accepted black soldiers as American soldiers without regard to race and color; however, "the problem lay in the importation of American racial patterns to Britain by American white troops, resulting in clashes, ideological and physical, between American soldiers."⁴Thus black troops felt that "instead of leaving our problems of this sort at home the [white] Americans have tried to instill their ways and actions over here and try to make the English do things like they have done and become terribly indignant when they all don't do things like they would see them done."⁵

Black soldiers also believed that "in England a few of the narrow minded possibly Southern White American soldiers have already, poisoned the mind of a few of the British people toward us. States that we were 'bears without tails,' 'wild, sex crazy maniacs,' etc."⁶

Often it was reported that the British people were dumfounded and "increasingly resentful of the intrusion of American racial mores upon their customs." Because of this some British authorities insisted that the root of the racial problems in their country lay with the failure of the U.S. armed forces to properly indoctrinate white American troops to the fact that black soldiers "in Britain could not be treated as they were in the States." A number of racial clashes occurred there because "Americans transported their values as well as their troops overseas," and chose to "adopt . . . the American pattern of enforcing racial segregation."⁷

Response to the controversial issue of whether black troops would be used in combat zones overseas also mirrored the Army's discriminatory racial policies. As early as 1943, the newly created Advisory Committee on Negro Troop Policies recommended to Secretary of War Henry L. Stimson that "Negro combat troops be dispatched to an active theater of operations at an early date. In the opinion of the committee, such action would be the most effective means of reducing tension among Negro troops."⁸

Rather than act on the committee's recommendation, Secretary Stimson chose to accept a recommendation from his staff and announced on January 28, 1944, that, in spite of the Army's urgent need for more seasoned combat troops, the black Second Cavalry Division would be converted into various service units. This action was taken, though this was not made public, to release white soldiers for combat and more technical duties, and because black soldiers were more acceptable as service than as combat units to American commanders overseas. Also, Stimson's staff had suggested that the War Department "quit catering to the Negroes' desire for a proportionate share of combat units. Put them where they will best serve the war effort."[9]

Although the War Department felt the vast majority of black soldiers would be more useful in service units, the conversion policy was an affront to black soldiers as well as to black and white national leaders. Interestingly, Secretary Stimson was aware of the impending black protest. He had written in his diary a day earlier:

> The Staff had just recommended the transformation of the Second Cavalry Division which is our only remaining cavalry division into a service corps and that aroused melancholy feelings in the minds of McCloy and myself and others in my civilian staff because it means the wiping out of the two famous old colored regiments, the Ninth and Tenth Cavalry. These gentlemen came today and laid out the whole situation before me and it appeared that there was nothing else to be done; our manpower is so short and the emergency requirements are so immediate that we had to take a division which has trained as this one has and put it to use. It was to go to France to take part there and while not a combatant division it will be in vigorous use and vigorous peril. The talk led to a discussion of what we should do with our colored inductees. I told them I had come to the conclusion that we must face the situation more seriously and courageously. We have got to use the colored race to help us in this fight and we have got to officer it with white men in my opinion and although it injures their sensibilities, it is better to do that than to have them massacred under incompetent colored officers.[10]

The irony of Stimson's rationale was that the Second Cavalry had trained for combat duty since the War Department's announcement in 1940 that black troops would be utilized in combat. Moreover, some of the officers had fought and won battle medals in World War I. Hence, the decision to convert this diversion to service units left many black and white Americans angry. New York Congressman Hamilton Fish (white), for example, asked Stimson to submit to his office the plans for utilizing black troops in combat. Stimson submitted a detailed letter instead in which he explained that prior to 1942 the Second Cavalry was a defensive corps, but after that date not only it but some white defensive units were being converted into service units because the possibility of an enemy attack in the United States no longer existed. Then, too, he claimed that several units of the Second Cavalry had not mastered the techniques of modern weaponry due to their inferior educational status. Never once did Stimson address the question of why the most experienced and most useful black combat units were being relegated to service and supply units when manpower shortages of ground forces were urgent, and when no black units to date had been committed to overseas combat duty, despite the War Department's 1940 promise to do so.[11]

Judge William H. Hastie (former black civilian aide to Secretary of War Henry L. Stimson) went further than Congressman Fish. But rather than attack Stimson publicly, he privately accused him and the War Department staff of deliberately devising plans to keep black soldiers out of combat. Hastie maintained that of the five infantry regiments, the two cavalry regiments, the five field artillery regiments, and the five anti-aircraft artillery units mobilized in 1941 for combat duty not a single outfit had been used in overseas combat. Moreover, he called Stimson's attention to the fact that the Ninth and Tenth Cavalry were created by law for combat duty; yet, they were being converted into a service corps. Hastie emphasized that the defensive unit and poor educational qualification explanation to Congressman Fish confirmed the beliefs of many black and white citizens that the War Department never intended to use black soldiers in overseas combat. Finally, he challenged Stimson to repudiate the following statement:

> The truth of the matter is that these original Negro combat units have been the problem children of the Army for more than two years, not because they were incompetent, but because no one wanted them. Nurtured on the myth that Negro troops cannot be relied upon in combat and fearing to add a 'racial problem' to other headaches in the theatre of war, field commanders and the Operations Branch of the War Department turned thumbs down on the utilization of the great majority of the Negro combat units. Anti-Aircraft Artillery was in a special category. Such a unit could be given a separate and more or less permanent defensive station in the theatre of operations. It need not be integrated with other combat forces. So the utilization of Negro Anti-Aircraft units in the theatre of operations was adopted as a device best calculated to confound the critics of any policy

as to Negro combat troops without basically changing that
policy. It is respectfully submitted that it is time and past
time that the matter of utilization of Negro combat units
pass out of the hands of those who deal with this matter as a
distasteful search for compromise born of political necessity,
and into the hands of those who have the will and the understanding to exploit the great combat potential of the Negro
soldier as a valuable asset in the winning of the war.[12]

Stimson's reply to Hastie was essentially what he had written to Congressman Fish except that he introduced the matter of the Army General
Classification Tests as the major reason preventing the usage of black
soldiers overseas in combat zones. Hastie, however, never knew that the
classification tests were, according to Stimson's diary, deliberately manip-
ulated to minimize the number of blacks in the armed services.[13]

The black press, other black leaders, and national black protest groups
publicly ridiculed Stimson for his decision to convert the Second Cavalry
into service units. They believed the conversion policy was racially moti-
vated. It was ironical to them that the War Department could justify
converting trained combat troops to service and supply units when its
field commanders were calling for more combat personnel. Roy Wilkins
noted particularly the inconsistency in Stimson's thinking. He was anxious to know how the army could be satisfied with the Second Cavalry as
a defensive unit to protect the borders of the United States when it could
not master the techniques of modern weaponry to fight in the combat
zones of Europe.[14]

Black soldiers themselves also questioned the wisdom of the War Department's decision. Those of the Second Cavalry who wanted to participate in combat reportedly commented on this issure and believed that the
breakup of the cavalry was a deliberate attempt of the War Department
to claim in the future that black troops did not measure up and thus
failed to do their part in combat. Their attitude was echoed in such representative statements as: "Someone had to be a stevedore, longshoreman,
etc. It was a simple matter—give it to the colored man. After the war is
over demands couldn't be so great, didn't his white brother (?) die on the
front line, while he was comparatively safe in the rear echelon; that's
right, isn't it?" And, "The reason why I prefer combat is because we all
are suppose to be American citizens and there aren't any of us Negro
people fighting in this war. Since we are citizens we should be granted the

privilege that the rest are getting because we are just as good as the next man. Under the condition it will better our status after the war."[15]

Whether the status of black soldiers improved after the war due to their limited combat duty is a matter of conjecture. But as a matter of policy and practice, the overseas experiences of black troops undoubtedly became another one of their "unenviable plights."

NOTES

1. Quoted in Ulysses Lee, *U.S. Army in World War II: Special Studies: The Employment of Negro Troops*. (Washington, D.C.: United States Printing Office, 1966), 437–438.

2. Letter, John R. Wright to the *Pittsburgh Courier*, November 16, 1943, Civilian Aide to the Secretary of War Subject File, 1940–1947, National Archives Record Group 107 (hereafter cited as NARG).

3. Letter, Negro Troops in India to the Editor of the Afro-American Newspapers, December 10, 1944, Civilian Aide to the Secretary of War Subject File, 1940–1947, NARG 107.

4. Lee, *The Employment of Negro Troops*, 440–441; Neil A. Wynn, *The Afro-American And The Second World War* (New York: Holmes and Meier Publishers, 1976), 32–33.

5. Quoted in Samuel A. Stouffer and Others, *The American Soldier: Adjustment During Army Life*, Volume I (New Jersey: Princeton University Press, 1949), 544.

6. *Ibid.*

7. Lee, *The Employment of Negro Troops*, 441; Wynn, *The Afro-American and the Second World War*, 34; Stouffer and Others, *The American Soldier*, 544–545.

8. Bernard C. Nalty and Morris J. MacGregor, editors, *Blacks in the Military: Essential Documents* (Delaware: Scholarly Resources Inc., 1981), 123.

9. Lee, *The Employment of Negro Troops*, 415, 413–423.

10. Henry L. Stimson Diary, January 27, 1944, Yale University Library, New Haven, Connecticut.

11. Letters, Hamilton Fish to Stimson, February 1, 1944; Stimson to Fish, February 19, 1944, Civilian Aide to the Secretary of War Subject File, 1940–1947, NARG 107.

12. Letter, Hastie to Stimson, February 29, 1944, William H. Hastie Papers, Howard University Law School Library, Washington, D.C.

13. Letter, Stimson to Hastie, March 31, 1944, Civilian Aide to the Secretary of War Subject File, 1940–1947, NARG 107; Stimson Diary, May 12, 1942. For a discussion of the Army General Classification Tests, see Phillip McGuire, "Black Civilian Aides and the Problems of Racism and Segregation in the United States Armed Forces, 1940–1950" (unpublished Ph.D. dissertation, Howard University, 1975), 45–48.

14. "Many Negro Combat Units Being Broken Up," *Pittsburgh Courier*, October 30, 1943; "Fish Protests Breaking Up of Negro Cavalry," *The Chicago Defender*, April 2, 1944; "Secretary of War Attacks Record of Race Combat Units," *Pittsburgh Courier*, March 4, 1944; Letter, Wilkins to Stimson, March

2, 1944; Letter, Adelaide C. Hill, executive secretary of the Englewood Urban League, Inc., to Stimson, March 15, 1944; Letter, T. D. McNeal, St. Louis Unit Director of the March-on-Washington Movement, to Stimson, March 9, 1944; Letter, Colonel Harrison Gerhardt to MacNeal, March 13, 1944, all in Civilian Aide to the Secretary of War Subject File, 1940–1947, NARG 107.

15. Stouffer and Others, *The American Soldier*, 527–535.

But It's Just the other Way Around

Pvt. John R. Wright
3252 nd. Q.M.
Ser. Co. A.P.O. 403 c/o P.M.
N.Y. N.Y.
Munich Germany
The Pittsburgh Courier   November 16, 1943

Dear Mr. Editor:

I have just finished reading your paper, the July 7th edition and I enjoyed it
very much as usual. I have eighty five points myself, and I had hoped to be
home by now but, for some reason or the other, we all still over here. My
outfit has been here in Europe three years to the date yesterday. Most of these
guys have 103 points. I have been over here 28 months, but here is one
fellow that has 144 points and he has been over here three years. We all think
that we have not been treated fair by this point system here. Isn't any kind of
break for service troops. Most of us did not want to come in this army in the
first place, and Mr. Eastland says we, the Negro soldier, has made America
loose prestege in Europe, but it's just the other way around. There have been
many times that Jim Crow and prejudice have made me very very shame to
say that I was an American. And even here in Germany, the people are not as
bad as we were told. The majority of the people here admire a colored man so
it seems to me. I served in North Africa, Italy, France, and now Dutchland. I
have worked very hard for our country. I can not understand why the people
of America will let the Bilbo's and others preach such hatred against the Negro
citizens.

Yours Truly,

John R. Wright

This 'Morale' Stuff Is All 'Bunk'

Pfc. Prescott J. Sunday, 28th
Charlie Co. (Dacon) CWS, APO#928
C/O Postmaster, San Francisco
California, Base # A4
The Pittsburgh Courier 8/25/44

Dear Sir:

I would like to know whether or not, you would inquire from the War Dept., whether or not any provisions are being made to provide any relief for this Unit, in the near future.

The Unit has been over seas 30 mos, some portion of this outfit has been here at Milne Bay, almost 2 years, they are constantly sending troops off the Island, but very few colored, one boat left here with 2400 men, out of them, only 4 colored. There is something I want to get straight, may be you use it to a successful conclusion, in our behalf, this "morale" stuff is all the "bunk," no body, white or colored can remain near these Islands, without feeling rather depressed, miserable and also, they don't want to end up, and get locked up in the Guard House, for they fear the unit might be returned either to the States, or the mainland of Australia, so they hang on, hoping against hope, that the "impossible," at this time will happen. The Officers knowing that the men feel this way about the whole thing take advantage of this great display of principle in the men, and also the fellows don't want to create no great "stink," for fear they'll hunt the record of these colored Officers, in making promotion, but unless "they" try to cooperate with the Company in trying to get some men of the older men away from here home, I fear greatly, in the near future, if these guys don't see some changes being made for the betterment of the Unit, they may resort to violence to gain personal gratification, now they tell us through some old phoney letter that is supposed to be issued by MacArthur, regarding men returning to the "states," no "troops," will be relieve until they have proper relief here to "take over," before they can be shipped home, find out, from the War Dept when are they going to see that some body is sent here specially designated from Wash, to be our relief, otherwise, We'll be here till "Duration Day, please look into this matter, hoping to hear from you in the near future.

I am,

Respectfully Yours
Prescott J. Sunday

Segregation in India

CO. B, 1st Bn. 5182 M. (TK)
APO 467,
c/o Postmaster, New York, N.Y.
Dec. 10, 1944

The Afro-American Newspapers

Dear Editor:

We are writing you enlisting your aid concerning segregation of Negro troops in India and we would like you to take an appeal to the NAACP.

First off on the ship a lecture was given by Dr. Paul D. Lindbergh and he asked the Negro troops not to mention racial prejudice in the States. And right on the ship we weren't allowed to drink from the cool water fountains.

Then the first thing we encountered in India is segregation. American, British, Indian, Chinese and Negro troops, all attend the same show and the Negroes are piled in a huddle right in the rear.

The boys are getting plenty fed up of being troddled on when they are giving their lives for America. And when a complaint is taken to an officer the only answer we receive is, "I'll see about it tomorrow."

And we would greatly appreciate you giving this letter to the NAACP and let them see if they can do anything concerning it. We would also like for this to get into some Negro paper.

Yours with thanks,

Negro Troops in India.

This Is Not 'Bilbo' Country

3478 QM Trucking Co.

Mr. Walter White   c/o A.P.O. 541

N. A. A. C. P.   New York, New York

New York, New York   26/2/46

My Dear Sir:

I am a soldier station in Salsbury (Austria) with the unit written above we've
only been here a short time, we were formally in Vienna and was transferred
to this damn place. Now my complaint is this a couple of month ago I read an
article in the army news paper stars and stripes that the army had a sum total
of $15,000,000 dollar solley for the purpose of entertainment of soldiers in
the E.T.O. now why is it colored soldiers recieves very little benefit from these
funds. When this unit was in Vienna we had a fairly nice club but since
leaving there we have nothing more than a barn what we are suppose to call a
club. I'm in a trucking unit an is capable of knowing that the clubs used by
(whites) are triple times as good as those of colored soldiers all through Austria
an germany. I can name you numerous of clubs such as the (owol) in Vienna,
ling, wells, salsburb, an even in germany because we transport material practically everywhere you can mention. What I wish you all to do if possible to
help the negro soldier overseas is try in help us get better places to go for
intertainment than we now have (a barn) ocated in an alley. There are a few
friends of mine who sit down nightly an discuss the maters providing we're not
on a long distance trip. Its really an honest to goodness shame to look at our
club an those of white. When some of the fellows an I start a discussion of
this, one will say that the soldiers involved of a (division) that is why they have
larger an better places an also they're on musicians that is a (lie) I know that
this restaurant they have is strictly for headquarters compay an I'm certain
that each individual unit has its on club just as we have this (honky tonk den)
the white soldiers outnumber the colored soldiers five to one because there is
only two full units an a negro band here, if so many soldiers can have clubs an
restaurants why can't two units have one club each large an beautiful enough
so that the decent girls of the town won't be ashamed to be seen in. That is
why these (crackers) don't want us to have any better club is because of the
better an more decent class of girls here want attent. Before the war ended an
redeployment started there were a great deal of negro soldiers over here but
now there's not so many I think every colored unit should have negro officers

so that if there's any injustices done the soldier or soldiers wont think that its done because of prejudices not that our officers are so prejudice I think thats for the better. Since being overseas I've read numberous of cases where the N.A.A.C.P. helped individual soldiers or whole units I wish you would do it again.

Here recently I happen to meet a girl who had a high social standing an her people are nice an have everything a rich family could ask for I could go to their home an do as I pleased (but) I could not get her to go to this barn with me to dance an enjoy herself. She asked why is it we don't have a better place than this there was nothing I could say but tell a damn lie. This letter is not for me or any of the present group of men because we expect to be going home soon its for the fellows who will replace us. The army use to orientate soldiers about the different people of Europe before coming over they may have stopped this but I an other soldiers who have been over for sometime notice that they or shy an approach of the people thats because of the (new crackers) also coming over here they should be told to act like they've been over here all they're lives an that they or one of the natives of the country they're in. Some of them lets these new (crackers) scare them up they are not in (Bilbo) country when over here. I'm hoping you take an interest in the situation.

Sincerely yours,

Fifteen GIs overseas

P.S. It is my hopes that you all investigate these incidents among the soldiers personally because these higher commanders dont actually no ask the soldiers personally negro soldiers are few now. I an a few others would like to see colored officers in this unit soon an a band of our own at least three or four times a week at the club hoping you all can get us a better an larger one. If the officers know I written this letter to you everything in their power to hurt me.

Pvt. Eddie Thomas 37411835

Conclusion

WHEN WORLD WAR II ended in 1945, a legacy of discrimination and racial segregation plagued the military, black soldiers, and the black community. The soldiers' letters support this contention, although some are probably exaggerated or misleading. Changes put into effect while the war was in progress establish the legitimacy of the soldiers' complaints and the protests of the black community. Thus, a *prima facie* case can be made that the military's policy of segregation, which resulted in racial discrimination, was maintained throughout the war. However, important shifts in policies affecting blacks and the changing status of black Americans in the larger society suggested the beginning of an end to an old order of restrictive outlooks and actions toward black soldiers in the armed services.

Although black soldiers and the black community had not achieved their single most objective—integration of the armed forces—the Army Air Force, for example, began training black pilots in 1941, and in 1942 the Navy began enlisting blacks other than for messman duty.[1]

Other significant changes affecting black soldiers also occurred: an increasing number were attending officer candidate schools; the War Department banned the use of racial epithets by commanding officers; a film on black contributions to the war effort was made and distributed throughout the country; more blacks were enrolled in and graduated from the Army's special training schools on an integrated basis, although they were returned to segregated army units in the regular army; black schools participated in the Air Force Enlistment Program; more black medical personnel were commissioned, with the establishment of two black medical facilities at Fort Huachuca, Arizona, and Tuskegee Air Base; the Army and Navy, in conjunction with the Red Cross, agreed to accept blood donations from blacks; the Army Air Forces allowed blacks to fly combat missions over North Africa; and in 1944 fatigued black and

243

white soldiers returning from Europe were assigned to the same redistribution centers.[2]

With the aim of eliminating racial prejudices in all camps, the army
also published and distributed magazines such as *Army Talk*, and made
available to black and white soldiers alike pamphlets on race relations.
Moreover, notables such as boxing champion Joe Lewis and black band-
leader Noble Sissle appeared at Army camps in an effort to raise the level
of morale among black troops.[3]

The military was not alone in relaxing major restrictions and racial
attitudes toward black soldiers. Race relations in the larger society had
also changed. The Second World War had created a new social and political climate in which black Americans could forge ahead in their determination to eliminate discrimination and racial segregation. The ballot
gave them new political power, and black migration from the South provided new economic and educational opportunities. Such was the racial
climate that encouraged black pressure organizations, notably the
NAACP, black leaders, and the black press to work even more vigorously
to obtain racial equality for blacks in the armed forces.

Other segments of the society also provided new opportunities for black
Americans. Blacks took full advantage of the persuasive powers of liberal
politicians, major civil rights decisions in the federal courts, and the
liberal civil rights policies of President Harry S. Truman. These forces
aided blacks, and helped to produce new attitudes in the War Department. The new Secretary of War Robert P. Patterson took special note,
and in 1945 directed a three-member board under Lieutenant Alvin C.
Gillem, Jr., to prepare a comprehensive policy on black manpower in the
postwar period.[4]

In March 1946, this board of officers issued its report, known as the
Gillem Board Report. The Board concluded that black manpower was
poorly utilized in World War II. Among its more positive findings, the
report recommended that manpower be utilized more efficiently in the
postwar Army because of an advancement in black education, skills,
crafts, and economic attainment; that remedial steps be taken to eliminate
deficiencies of black soldiers in future wars; that more black officers and
enlisted personnel be added to the Army to provide cadres and leaders for
future national emergencies; that female components be added to the

military as black manpower increased; that preference be given to black combat units as the military expanded its base of black personnel; that the War Department and major commands create standing committees of military officers to devote full-time efforts to solving problems that black troops were experiencing in the military; that all forms of segregation and racial discrimination against black officers be eliminated.[5]

These and other positive recommendations of the Gillem Report failed to address adequately the question of integration. It recommended, for example, that segregated educational, recreational, and messing facilities be maintained where blacks were stationed; that the postwar black units be stationed near communities where their presence would not be offensive; that black manpower should make up only 10 percent of the regular army; and that small black units should be integrated into larger composite white divisions.[6]

Experimenting with small integrated units represented progress toward eliminating racial discrimination and segregation, but the report did not recommend the abolition of segregation within the armed forces of the United States. Yet, it was significant because its thrust had the effect of gradually destroying the War Department's position that segregation was necessary in order to maintain military efficiency.[7]

Former civilian aide Truman K. Gibson, Jr., considered the Gillem Report "a watershed in race relations in the Army." In *Strength for the Fight: A History of Black Americans in the Military*, Bernard C. Nalty claimed that "Gibson took heart from the fact that the War Department seemed willing to modify its old policy instead of defending it as military necessity, for he was certain that any softening of segregation would reveal its folly and lead inevitably, though perhaps slowly, to its elimination."[8]

When the War Department released the Gillem Report publicly, black leaders and the black press rejected the new policy because it failed to recommend an end to segregation. Roy Wilkins of the NAACP and Lester Granger (successor to Eugene Jones as executive secretary of the National Urban League) branded the report a jim crow document. The *Chicago Defender* stated: "The Negro's position is that, if conscription is maintained, it must be strictly along democratic lines with no Jim Crowism or segregation in any forms." The *Philadelphia Tribune* asserted that the

Gillem Report was "by no means integration and will not answer legitimate complaints of Negro officers and enlisted men who served in the last war." The *New York Age* maintained that "the policy is still a little foggy and falls far short of its advanced advertising that it would abolish segregation in the Army." And the black Publishers' Association reported in July that the recommendation that called for mixed units had not been implemented among the residual forces in Europe.[9]

Some members of the Publishers' Association, however, supported the Gillem Report. For example, the *Norfolk Journal and Guide* stated: "It appears that the War Department has definitely turned the corner in policy." The *Baltimore Afro-American* declared: "We believe that the Army is headed in the right direction and recommended that its sister services also get in step." And the *New York Amsterdam News* found the Gillem Report "still some distance from the elimination of a jim crow army; but it represents advance and progress. As such, we say hurray and good deal."[10]

The new black civilian aide to the secretary of war, Colonel Marcus H. Ray, also endorsed the Gillem Report but stated, following a tour of European forces, in a December report to Secretary of War Robert P. Patterson that the recommendation to integrate the structure and function of small army units had not taken place. Colonel Ray further maintained that "to accept the racial prejudices of the German people as a reason for non-utilization of the American soldiers who happen to be non-white is to negate the very ideas we have made part of our re-education program in Germany."[11]

Although Colonel Ray questioned the army's failure to implement the European phase of the Gillem Report, he and Assistant Civilian Aide James C. Evans supported other recommendations of the new policy. For example, they approved of the one-to-ten ratio for intermingling black troops with large white divisions, the plan to deny re-enlistment to all soldiers who failed to meet the Army's minimum standards, and the policy of freezing black volunteer enlistment in order to ensure the 10 percent black quota, which represented no change from the 1940 policy.[12] To ensure that black strength did not rise above the 10 percent quota, Colonel Ray sent a proposal to Secretary of War Patterson that if carried out would have honorably discharged all soldiers (blacks) in the regular army who did not meet minimum army standards.[13]

There was other evidence that Colonel Ray supported the quota concept. In a federal suit to enjoin the U.S. Army and the Selective Service
System from banning black volunteer enlistment, Colonel Ray proposed a
compromise to NAACP attorneys Charles H. Houston and Joseph C.
Waddy that would have permitted black I-A registrants to volunteer only
for the Army Ground Forces. Houston and Waddy rejected Ray's compromise, and rather than go through a court trial and perhaps face the
possibility of having to explain and justify a racial quota in peacetime, the
War Department amended the Gillem recommendation and directed the
Selective Service to accept additional blacks in the Ground Forces as well
as in the Army Air Forces but on an unassigned basis.[14]

This new directive caused more black protest. Black leaders berated
the policy because it did not answer such basic questions as: What did
unassigned mean? What would the new volunteers do? Did unassigned
mean assignment to labor and supply units? Because they viewed him as
an adjuster of racial discrimination and segregation rather than as a voice
of black protest, black leaders could not rely on new Civilian Aide James
C. Evans, who replaced Colonel Marcus H. Ray in October 1947, for
answers to their questions. Instead they criticized him for his gradual
approach to solving racial problems in the armed services. Their view of
him was probably justified because Evans said himself that "neither the
War Department nor Walter White and his group were ever able to pin me
down." In fact, he told White, Roy Wilkins, Thurgood Marshall, A.
Philip Randolph, and Lester Granger, "You go your way and I'll go mine.
We'll see who gets there quickest." "I was," stated Evans, "not about to
dictate their policy to the War Department."[15]

While Evans was perceived as an effective civilian aide by War Department officials, black leaders continually questioned his effectiveness as a
spokesperson for unfettered military integration.[16]

Moreover, though this was unknown to black leaders, Evans approved
of a memo sent to Secretary of the Army Kenneth Royall in which Director
of Personnel Major General Willard S. Paul defined the Army's position
on "unassigned" black volunteers. In the 1947 memo, General Paul said,
"My observations have led me to the conclusion that a more usable Negro
soldier can be developed under a system of rigid training with carefully
controlled conditions which insure, insofar as possible, the development

of pride in self and organization. The eliminations must be accomplished before the *misfits* are assigned to units for duty."[17]

This memo was important because Secretary Royall would prove to be the last major military official to oppose the integration of the armed services, and he would use the contents of such memos and special reports to buttress his position.[18]

In spite of the support Secretary Royall received from Civilian Aide Evans, conservatives, and diehard political, military, and white civilian leaders, the issue of armed forces integration gained momentum during the latter half of 1947 and early 1948. Several significant developments accounted for this unprecedented upsurge: A. Philip Randolph's National Committee Against Jimcrow In Military Service and Training threatened civil disobedience if segregation in the armed services was not ended; discussions of the claim that mixed units had good fighting records during the war began to surface in Congress and at the White House; reports of the success of the Navy's policy of integrating its training and fighting forces were prepared for Secretary of Defense James V. Forrestal;[19] Chief of Staff Omar N. Bradley publicly criticized segregation in the armed services; the Armed Forces Radio Service began to broadcast programs fostering racial equality; civilian resolutions sent to the White House demanded integration, and meetings between President Truman and black leaders were held; the black press demanded an immediate end to segregation and racial discrimination in all branches of the armed services; and Secretary Forrestal convened a conference of black and white military and civilian leaders to discuss and propose ideas for integrating all branches of the armed services.[20]

National and state politicians were also active in the drive to integrate the armed forces. For instance, President Truman made resounding civil rights speeches to regular and special sessions of Congress, and spoke at the 39th Annual Meeting of the National Association for the Advancement of Colored People, where he promised to end segregation. His Committee on Civil Rights and the Advisory Commission on Universal Military Training recommended the integration of the armed forces in their 1947 and 1948 reports. Influential black and white congressmen such as Senators Henry Cabot Lodge, Jr., Robert A. Taft, and William Langer, Speaker of the House Joseph Martin, and Congressmen Adam C. Powell,

Jr., Vito Marcantonio, William Dawson, and Jacob Javits introduced antidiscrimination amendments to the 1948 draft bill. The governors of Minnesota, New York, and New Jersey urged President Truman to use his executive authority to end segregation so that they could begin non-discriminatory programs in their National Guard units. And, with respect to the armed forces, both Republican and Democratic National Platform Committees adopted antidiscrimination planks in 1948.[21]

These developments spurred the black community to push even harder for integration. For example, A. Philip Randolph and Reverend Grant Reynolds (Harlem civic leader) organized the Committee Against Jim Crow in Military and Training. On March 22, 1948, they and several other prominent black leaders met with President Truman to solicit his support for the antidiscrimination amendments to the proposed draft bill. Randolph in particular wanted the President to know that "Negroes are in no mood to shoulder guns for democracy abroad, while they are denied democracy here at home." He then told Truman that he would counsel civil disobedience if Truman did not end segregation in the armed services.[22]

At a New York meeting on March 27, the NAACP and several other black organizations also called for the immediate end to segregation in the armed forces. By this time, however, presidential politics had become a major topic of discussion among the conferences. Subsequently, they passed resolutions and released a public statement declaring black support in exchange for the elimination of segregation and racial discrimination in the armed services.[23]

Meanwhile, on March 30, A. Philip Randolph and Grant Reynolds appeared before the Senate Armed Services Committee. There, they repeated their threats to encourage young blacks to boycott the draft unless segregation and racial discrimination were ended.[24]

The black community, however, was divided on this issue. At the hearing former civilian aide Truman K. Gibson, Jr., and Grant Reynolds almost clashed physically. Gibson was so angry that he threatened to knock Reynolds' teeth out. However, the main reason for Gibson's behavior probably stemmed from an earlier incident when Gibson was at the War Department. Reynolds had written him to protest discrimination against black soldiers in a local bar near Fort Huachuca, Arizona, in which Gibson's father had business interests. Moreover, Reynolds and Randolph had publicly called Gibson a "Negro Judas Iscariot" and accused him of being a mouthpiece for the War Department because Gibson had publicly reported in 1945 that troops in the all-black 92nd Division were "melting away" in combat.[25]

Gibson's contempt for Reynolds and Randolph prompted him to say in an April conversation with his friend White House Assistant on Minority Affairs Philleo Nash, "Randolph and Reynolds did not represent the opinion of the majority of American Negroes when they told the President that Negroes would not fight unless the Army's racial policy was changed."[26]

Contrary to Gibson's views, black leaders such as Walter White, Lester Granger, and Congressman Adam C. Powell, Jr., supported Randolph and Reynolds for voicing black grievances but cautioned the black community against the idea of civil disobedience. The black press also backed them, but it, too, opposed civil disobedience.[27]

In the meantime, Secretary of Defense James V. Forrestal finalized plans for a "National Defense Conference on Negro Affairs." On April 26, 1948, sixteen prominent blacks met with defense officials and voiced strong opposition to the racial policies of the armed services. They insisted on immediate integration rather than supporting the gradual approach encouraged by Secretary Forrestal. Interestingly, conference member Truman K. Gibson, Jr., had written in a letter to Philleo Nash on April 15 that "the Forrestal Conference is dangerous because of the opportunity it will afford to call for some oversimplified solution like the issuance of an Executive Order abolishing segregation in the Army. The President should be on the offensive in this area."[28]

By the middle of 1948, President Truman had joined the forces for integration. Secretary of the Army Royall, his successors, and the advocates of segregation continued, however, to maintain that integration would impair military efficiency and damage the moral of American troops, but the forces of integration were too strong to be overlooked. Secretary of Defense Forrestal, Secretary of the Navy John L. Sullivan, Secretary of the Air Force W. Stuart Symington, black and white political and civic leaders, powerful civil rights organizations, presidential politics, and the black press put increasing pressure on the White House. On

July 26, 1948, President Truman acted. He issued Executive Order 9981, which called for "equality of treatment and opportunity for all persons in the armed services, without regard to race, color, religion, or national origin." The order also established the President's Commitee on Equality of Treatment and Opportunity in the Armed Services. The committee was authorized to examine race relations in the armed services and to determine how best to implement the new policy. Known as the Fahy Committee after its liberal white chairman Charles Fahy, in 1950 the committee, after working with all branches of the military, issued its report which recommended an end to segregation in the armed services.[29]

Although segments of the military were slow, especially the army, to comply with the new policy, significant changes took place when the U.S. entered the Korean Conflict. For example, the U.S. Army and Air Force abolished racial quotas; black soldiers were used as replacements in white combat units; eyewitness accounts of mixed units in combat resulted in recommendations to integrate the American forces; white officers who had experience with racially mixed combat units suggested integration as the most effective way to utilize black troops; and Korean commanders such as General Matthew B. Ridgway asked the Pentagon for permission to integrate all units under their command. Moreover, the army itself had commissioned Johns Hopkins University to study the effects of both segregation and integration on its forces. Known as "Project Clear," the study concluded that "racially segregated units limited overall Army effectiveness." It also determined that integration in the Army "was feasible and that a quota on black participation was unnecessary." Furthermore, liberal white politicians such as Senators Hubert H. Humphreys of Minnesota and Herbert H. Lehman of New York called for an immediate end to segregated armed services. And black leaders and the black press continued their protest for an integrated military."[30]

By 1954 integration in the armed services was a reality. The Pentagon accepted this fact and would use its authority to see that it was effectively implemented throughout the services. Major General Anthony C. McAuliffe said it best when he summed up why the armed forces integrated: "I should say that integration of the Negro in the Armed Forces has worked very well and that we are getting greater usefulness from the available manpower than we ever did under segregation. It was merely a matter of getting the best out of the military personnel that was available."[31]

But to black Americans, military integration meant *Taps* for an old order of restrictive outlooks and actions toward black soldiers. To them, as Sergeant First Class John Lawrence stated, "The young Negro in uniform feels big in it. It shows he's an American and that he's as good as anyone else." Or, as Deputy Assistant Secretary of Defense for Civil Rights and Industrial Relations Jack Moskowits put it in 1966: "That uniform gives prestige and status to a guy who's been 100 year on the back burner."[32]

Some vestiges of military segregation and racial discrimination continued into the 1960s. For example, some army facilities on and off military posts were still closed to black soldiers; black promotions continued to be disproportionately low; off-post discrimination hindered blacks educationally and impeded their economic growth; the military justice system continued to be disproportionately hard on black troops; low black morale continued on some military posts; the National Guard continued to segregate and practice racial discrimination; and black soldiers often found it difficult to obtain decent housing in surrounding communities. In 1963 Captain Sylvain Wailes, who had been transferred to Fort Bragg, recalled: "When I was at Fort Belvoir, Virginia, there was no decent place to live unless you went into Washington. Housing is segregated around Fayetteville. I stay on the base for athletics and movies, sometimes go to Raleigh, an hour's drive, for a stage play."[33]

The military, after dragging its feet during the Eisenhower administration, began to address the remaining racial problems of black servicemen in 1961 when President John F. Kennedy entered the White House. Kennedy appointed the President's Committee on Equal Opportunity in the Armed Forces. Known as the Gesell Committee after its chairman Gerhard H. Gesell, the Committee issued its initial report on June 13, 1963. They praised the military for "significant progress in eliminating discrimination among those serving in defense of the nation" but concluded that "much remains to be done, especially in eliminating practices that cause inconvenience and embarrassment to servicemen and their families in communities adjoining military bases."[34]

Reacting to the Gesell Committee Report and other internal investigations, Secretary of Defense Robert S. McNamara issued a far-reaching directive. He said that "every military commander has the responsibility to oppose discriminatory practices affecting his men and their dependents and to foster equal opportunity for them, not only in areas under his immediate control but also in nearby communities where they may live or gather in off-duty hours."[35]

According to Nalty, James C. Evans was significant in his role as civilian aide and as advisor on racial matters, and "the Defense Department's machinery for ensuring equal treatment and opportunity became complete when . . . in the summer of 1963 [he] joined the new office of the Deputy Assistant Secretary of Defense for Civil Rights."[36]

In 1964, the Gesell Committee issued its final report. The report focused on segregation and racial discrimination against black soldiers overseas and concluded that base commanders should make vigorous attempts to prevent segregation and racial discrimination against black servicemen in public accommodations and nearby communities. Moreover, the committee emphasized, "it is particularly urgent to do this where the discrimination reflects attitudes of some of our own military personnel and is not generally practiced by nationals of the host country involved."[37]

Although the military made rapid progress toward eliminating the remaining areas of segregation and racial discrimination against black soldiers, the Vietnam War delayed this process.

Meanwhile, changing conditions for black Americans in the larger society kept pace with changes for black soldiers in the military. Since the 1950s black Americans had made significant progress in redressing their grievances. The social and political climate that allowed them to do so was facilitated largely by the 1954 Brown Decision, in which the U.S. Supreme Court overturned the 1896 "separate but equal" doctrine and declared that separate facilities were inherently unequal and that racial segregation violated the Fourteenth Amendment to the U.S. Constitution. This decision destroyed the legal basis for institutional racism and racial segregation in America. It also laid the basis for the Civil Rights Movement of the 1960s and 1970s, which revolutionized black/white relations in the United States.

The major civil rights issues of the 60s and 70s were the struggles by blacks, aided by white Americans, to vote, to obtain decent housing and equal educational opportunities, and to secure themselves economically in decision-making job positions.

The efforts of black Americans proved beneficial. President Kennedy banned, by executive order, racial and religious discrimination in federally aided housing, Congress passed the far-reaching and comprehensive Civil Rights Act of 1964 and the Voting Rights Act of 1965. The U.S. Supreme Court handed down decisions enforcing the civil rights of blacks. Some public schools and universities opened doors to blacks for the first time, and public accommodations were integrated. In 1967 Thurgood Marshall was the first black to be named to the U.S. Supreme Court; Robert C. Weaver, as Secretary of Housing and Urban Development, was the first black appointed to a Cabinet post; Carl B. Stokes of Cleveland, Ohio, was the first black elected mayor of a major American city; Leontyne Price opened the Metropolitan Opera in 1966; in 1963 Sidney Poitier was the first black male to win an Oscar for best actor; Reverend Doctor Martin Luther King, Jr., won the Nobel Peace Prize in 1964 for civil rights leadership; Patricia Harris and other blacks were appointed U.S. ambassadors; and fifteen black representatives and one senator were serving in Congress.

These were but a few of the gains made by stateside black Americans during the era of the Vietnam War. When it ended in 1973, black soldiers, too, had distinguished themselves with honor in America's "first truly integrated war."[38] Perhaps the most fitting tribute to black America, both in and out of uniform, was President Jimmy Carter's 1976 appointment of Clifford A. Alexander to the post of Secretary of the Army.

During the years following the war, some old problems of segregation and racial discrimination remained in the armed services. However, since the 1970s the Department of Defense has instituted human/race relations education programs, established affirmative action programs, and created equal opportunity programs in off-base housing. All segments of the military are required to make progress reports on recruiting, assignment, evaluation, training, promotion, discipline, separation, recognition, utilization of skills, and discrimination complaints.[39]

By the 1980s, integration of the armed forces was an accomplished fact. Civil rights issues were no longer of major concern to the military or to black America, for blacks had achieved much to be proud of: twenty-five general officers were on active duty in the Army, five in the Navy and Marine Corps, twelve in the Air Force, and four in the Army and Air National Guard. Moreover, twenty-four black civilians held executive and senior executive positions in the Department of Defense.

By 1990 the number who held general officer rank had risen to seventy-seven: fifty in the Army, eight in the Navy and Marine Corps, thirteen in the Air Force, and six in the Army and Air National Guard. But the most glaring recognition of an integrated armed forces was President George Bush's 1989 appointment of General Colin L. Powell as the first African-American chairman of the Joint Chiefs of Staff.

The latest overall statistical data available from the Department of Defense on African-American officers on active duty as of 1990 reflected equally respectable numbers in the United States armed forces. Out of 294,000 active duty officers in the armed services, 20,923 were African-Americans, which comprised 7.1 percent of the total number of officers. For a total breakdown of the numbers of African-American as well as other minority officers within each branch of the armed forces, see table 1. For the racial distribution of the selective reserve officers as of 1991, see table 2.

When the decade of the 1990s began, the "color line" was not a significant factor in the military experiences of black soldiers. African-Americans in and out of uniform during World War II, and to some extent during the Korean Conflict, waged a campaign against a discriminatory and segregated armed forces. Those who leveled charges of racism concerning Vietnam raised questions about the disproportionately high number of black casualties and alleged that the military used African-Americans more prevalently in frontline combat engagements. During the 1991 Persian Gulf War African-Americans again raised questions about the prospect of large numbers of black troops being overly represented as casualties of war. Fortunately, the war was atypical and short-lived, thus quelling the probability of a major discussion among African-Americans over the issue of military racism and the probable disproportionate number of black troops who would be called to serve in frontline combat situations.

The armed forces in the 1990s nevertheless continues to play an important role in providing career opportunities and upward social mobility for

Table 1. Distribution of Active Duty Officers

	Number	Percentage
Total number of Officers	294,000	100%
White	257,941	87.8
Black	20,923	7.1
Other minority	15,136	5.1
Total minority Officers	36,059	12.2

U.S. Active Officers by Service			
	White	African-American	Other Minority
Army	83.8%	11%	5.2%
Navy	90.6	4.1	5.3
Marine Corps	90.3	5.1	4.6
Air Force	89.4	5.6	5

Note: Data as of 1990.
Source: Department of Defense.

Table 2. Distribution of Selective Reserve Officers

	Number	Percentage
Total number of Reserve Officers	178,714	100%
White	155,739	87.2
Black	11,643	6.5
Other minority	11,332	6.3
Total minority Reserve Officers	22,975	12.8

U.S. Active Officers by Service			
	White	African-American	Other Minority
Army National Guard	91.3%	6.3%	2.4%
Army Reserve	84.3	10.4	5.3
Naval Reserve	91.2	3.1	5.7
Marine Corps Reserve	94.0	4.2	1.8
Air National Guard	94.5	3.5	2.0
Air Force Reserve	93.6	4.2	2.2
Coast Guard Reserve	95.8	2.2	2.0

Note: Data as of 1991.
Source: Report of the Reserve Forces Policy Board, Department of Defense.

young African-American men and women. The end of the Cold War, however, and the ongoing drastic reduction in military personnel no doubt will produce voices from the black community pointing out that African-American service men and women are sure to become the first significant group to suffer the consequences of the much vaunted "new world order."

NOTES

1. For detailed discussions of blacks in the U.S. Navy and Army Air Forces during World War II see Dennis D. Nelson, *The Integration of the Negro into the U.S. Navy* (New York: Farrar, Straus & Young, 1951); Alan M. Osur, *Blacks in the Army Air Forces during World War II* (Washington, D.C.: United States Printing Office, 1977); Frederick S. Harrod, "Integration of the Navy (1941–1978)," *United States Naval Institute Proceedings*, CV (October 1979), 41–47; Phillip McGuire, "Black Civilian Aides and the Problems of Racism and Segregation in the United States Armed Forces, 1940–1950" (unpublished Ph.D. dissertation, Howard University, 1975), 119–127.

2. Phillip McGuire, "Black Civilian Aides," 101–119.

3. Ibid.

4. General Gillem stated in the Gillem Report: "In accordance with verbal instructions from the Secretary of War, a board of three general officers met on 1 October 1945 and subsequent dates to conduct a broad investigation into utilization of Negro manpower in the military establishment," November 17, 1945, Military Personnel Division, General Staff, National Archives Record Group (hereafter cited as NARG), 165.

5. "Report of Board of Officers on Utilization of Negro Manpower in the Post-War Army," Alvin C. Gillem, Jr., to George Marshall, March 4, 1966, Military Personnel Division, General Staff, NARG 165; Bernard C. Nalty and Morris J. MacGregor, *Blacks in the Military; Essential Documents* (Delaware: Scholarly Resources Inc., 1981), 207–244.

6. Ibid.

7. Ibid.

8. Bernard C. Nalty, *Strength for the Fight: A History of Black Americans in the Military* (New York: Free Press, 1986), 215.

9. "Raps Gillem Report; Still Jim Crow Army, Roy Wilkins and Granger Decide," *The Pittsburgh Courier*, April 26, 1946; Editorial, *Chicago Defender*, March 9, 1946; "New Army Policy Fails to Abolish Segregation," *The Philadelphia Tribune*, March 16, 1946; Editorial, *The New York Age*, March 9, 1946; Report, "The Negro Newspapers Publishers' Association on Troops and Conditions in Europe," to Robert P. Patterson, July 18, 1946, Army General Staff, NARG 407; "General McNarney Ignores Gillem Report, Isolates GI's," *Pittsburgh Courier*, October 26, 1946; "More on the Gillem Report," *Pittsburgh Courier*, May 4, 1946.

10. Editorial, *Norfolk Journal and Guide*, March 9, 1946; Editorial, *The Baltimore Afro-American*, March 9, 1946; Editorial, *The New York Amsterdam News*, March 9, 1946.

11. Nalty and MacGregor, *Blacks In The Military*, 217.

12. "Army Adopts 1–10 Ratio For Negroes," *Pittsburgh Courier*, May 11, 1946; Letter, Marcus H. Ray to Charles R. Lawrence, Jr., Social Science Institute of Fisk University, November 6, 1946, Civilian Aide to the Secretary of War Sub-

ject File, 1940–1947, NARG 107; Nalty and MacGregor, *Blacks in the Military*, 224–226.

13. "Ray Proposes Plan to Discharge Men in Army below Standards," *Norfolk Journal and Guide*, August 10, 1946.

14. War Dep't Tries Compromise To Halt Test on Race Quota," *Pittsburgh Courier*, October 5, 1946; "A $64 Question: Army Drops Induction?" *Pittsburgh Courier*, October 19, 1946; James C. Evans, private interview with author, 3533 Warder Street, N.W., Washington, D.C., November 30, 1974.

15. James C. Evans, private interview with author, October 6, 1974.

16. Ibid.

17. Memorandum, Thru Civilian Aide—Mr. Evans, General Willard S. Paul to Secretary of the Army Kenneth Royall, December 2, 1947, Military Personnel Division, General Staff, NARG 165.

18. For detailed discussions of Secretary Royall's position on integration see Richard M. Dalfiume, *Desegregation of the U.S. Armed Forces; Fighting on Two Fronts 1939–1953* (Missouri: University of Missouri Press, 1969), 158–219.

19. In 1947 the military establishment was reorganized under the Department of Defense with James V. Forrestal as its first secretary. Forrestal supported a gradual approach to integration.

20. "Calls UMT Bill Public Enemy No. 1," *The Washington Afro-American*, December 27, 1947; "Randolph Urges Army Advisers To Denounce Jim Crow Policy," *Chicago Defender*, November 22, 1947; "Drive Seeks To Ban Segregation in Bill for Universal Training," *New York Post*, December 2, 1947; "Harlem Leader Hits Jim Crow U.M.T. Plans," *New York Post*, December 2, 1947; "General Bradley Lashes Bias in Armed Services," *The Pittsburgh Courier*, January 24, 1948; Letter, Walter White to James V. Forrestal, February 17, 1948; Letter, Lester Granger to Marx Leva, May 14, 1948; Report, Lieutenant Dennis D. Nelson, United States Naval Reserve, to Marx Leva, May 24, 1948, all in Secretary and Assistant Secretary of Defense Files, NARG 330; "Threats of Treason Resented," *Norfolk Journal and Guide*, April 10, 1948; "Hurl New Blow at Army Bias; Randolph Opens Up," *The Pittsburgh Courier*, July 3, 1948; Letter, Grant Reynolds, National Chairman of the Committee against Jim Crow in Military Service and Training and New York City Alderman, and A. Philip Randolph, National Treasurer, to President Harry S. Truman, July 15, 1948; "Resolutions Adopted by 39th Annual Conference of the NAACP, June 26, 1948, both in Secretary and Assistant Secretary of the Army Files, NARG 335.

21. "Draft Bill Faces New Hurdles As Civil Rights Riders Loom," *The New York Times*, May 27, 1948; "Taft Pledges Jim Crow End for Military," *The New York Amsterdam News*, January 3, 1948; "UMT Has Not Been Bias-Proof—Negro Segregation Apparently Slated," *New York Post*, January 16, 1948; "Martin Says He Will Fight Jim Crowism in UMT Measure," *New York Post*, February 5, 1948; "GOP Leaders Condemn Bias in Army Training," *The Pittsburgh Courier*, February 14, 1948; "Call South's War Our Civil Rights Pressure Battle," *Pittsburgh Courier*, July 17, 1948; *Congressional Record*, 80th Congress, 2nd Session (1948), 3714, 4543, 8390–8394, 8691–8694; "Truman's Speech on Civil Rights," June 29, 1947, Harry S. Truman Papers, Harry S. Truman

Library, Independence, Missouri; Letter, Luther W. Youngdahl Governor of
Minnesota, to James V. Forrestal, March 6, 1948; Memorandum Marx Leva,
special assistant to the Secretary of Defense, to James V. Forrestal, March 8,
1948; Newspaper Clipping, "Attention Minnesota Democrats," April 16, 1948;
Letter, Henry C. Lodge, Jr., to James V. Forrestal, April 19, 1948; Letter,
Hubert H. Humphrey, Mayor of St. Paul, to James V. Forrestal, April 26,
1948; Telegram, Youngdahl to President Truman, July 19, 1948, all in Secre-
tary and Assistant Secretary of Defense Files, NARG 330; *Public Papers of the
Presidents of the United States, Harry S. Truman 1945–1953* (Washington,
D.C.: United States Government Printing Office), 311–315; The President's
Committee on Civil Rights, *To Secure These Rights* (Washington, D.C.: United
States Government Printing Office, 1947), 41–43; 82–87. For detailed discus-
sions of President Truman and Civil Rights during this period see William C.
Berman, *The Politics of Civil Rights in the Truman Administration* (Ohio: Ohio
State University Press, 1970); Donald R. McCoy and Richard T. Ruetten,
Quest and Response; Minority Rights and the Truman Administration (Lawrence:
University of Kansas Press, 1973).

22. Quoted in Berman, *The Politics of Civil Rights in the Truman Administration*,
    97–98.

23. "Declaration of Negro Votes," Box 376, National Association for the Advance-
    ment of Colored People Papers (hereafter cited as NAACP Papers), Manuscript
    Division, Library of Congress, Washington, D.C.

24. United States Senate, Armed Services Committee, *Hearings on Universal Mili-
    tary Training* (Washington, D.C.: United States Government Printing Office,
    1948), 644–689; Berman, *The Politics of Civil Rights in Truman Administra-
    tion*, 98–99; Dalfiume, *Desegregation of the U.S. Armed Forces; Fighting on
    Two Fronts 1939–1953*, 164–169; Nalty and MacGregor, *Blacks in the Mili-
    tary*, 237–239.

25. United States Senate, Armed Services Committee, *Hearings on Universal Mili-
    tary Training*, 644–689; "Civil Disobedience Movement Urged; Gibson and
    Reynolds Nearly Swap Blows," *The Pittsburgh Courier*, April 3, 1948; James
    C. Evans, private interview with author, August 6, 1974.

26. Letter, David K. Niles, special assistant to President Truman on minority af-
    fairs, to Matthew J. Connelly, President Truman's secretary, April 5, 1948,
    Truman Papers. Gibson's conversation with Nash was reported in the April
    letter from Niles to Connelly.

27. *Pittsburgh Courier*, April 10, 1948; Judge William H. Hastie, private interview
    with author, U.S. Court of Appeals, Washington, D.C., March 8, 1974; Ber-
    man, *The Politics of Civil Rights in the Truman Administration*, 99–100.

28. Letter, Truman K. Gibson, Jr., to Philleo Nash, April 15, 1948, Truman Pa-
    pers; Nalty and MacGregor, *Blacks in the Military*, 241–242. Blacks attending
    the National Defense Conference On Negro Affairs included: Sadie T.M.
    Alexander, John W. Davis, Truman K. Gibson, Jr., J. W. Gregg, Charles H.
    Houston, John H. Johnson, Mordecai Johnson, P. B. Young, Ira F. Lewis,
    Benjamin E. Mays, Loren Miller, Hobson E. Reynolds, Channing H. Tobias,
    George L. P. Weaver, Roy Wilkins, and Lester B. Granger.

29. Joint Army and Air Force Bulletin No. 32, *Executive Order 9981* (Washington,

D.C.: Department of the Army and the Air Force, August 2, 1948), 2–3;
Letter, Bayard Rustin, Secretary of the Campaign To Resist Military Segrega-
tion, to James V. Forrestal, August 20, 1948; Press Release, "Negro Leaders
Submit Report and Recommendations On Segregation," September 8, 1948;
Memorandum, James V. Forrestal to Secretaries of Army, Navy, and Air Force,
October 21, 1948, all in Secretary and Assistant of Defense Files, NARG 330;
Memorandum, Representative Lyndon B. Johnson to Kenneth Royall, March
22, 1948; "General Eisenhower's Testimony on the Race Issue in the Army,"
April 5, 1948; Memorandum, Brigadier General John J. O'Hare, Chief of the
Personnel Management Group, to Kenneth Royall, March 9, 1948; "Depar-
tment of the Army Statement Regarding Utilization of Negro Manpower," July
21, 1948; Letter, Major William H. Ramsey to General Omar Bradley, July 30,
1948; Memorandum, Kenneth Royall to James Forrestal, November 18, 1948;
Memorandum, W. Stuart Symington to James V. Forrestal, December 17,
1948; "Truman Orders End of Bias in Forces and Federal Jobs; Addresses
Congress Today," *The New York Times*, July 27, 1948; "Army Segregation To
Go, Says Truman," *The New York Times*, July 30, 1948; "Secretary Royall
Insists Present Pattern Will Not Now Be Modified," *Norfolk Journal and Guide*,
May 1, 1948; "Jim Crow Has No Place in U.S. Army," *The Pittsburgh Courier*,
January 10, 1948; "Truman Executive Order 9981," *Pittsburgh Courier*, July
31, 1948; "The Order Mr. Truman Did Not Issue," *Pittsburgh Courier*, August
7, 1948; "Senator Allen J. Ellender On Executive Order 9981," *The Baltimore
Sun*, July 27, 1948; "Truman's Army Program Is Repugnant," *The Montgomery
Advertiser*, July 29, 1948; "President Truman Is Grandstanding," *The
Shreveport Times*, August 1, 1948; "Proposed Policy for the National Military
Establishment Office of the Secretary of Defense," March 17, 1949; Memoran-
dum, Lieutenant General Edward H. Brooks, Director of Personnel and Admin-
istration, to Deputy Chief of Staff For Administration, March 30, 1949, Army
General Staff, NARG 407; "Meeting of the President and the Four Service
Secretaries with the President's Committee on Equality of Treatment and
Opportunity in the Armed Services," January 13, 1949; Memorandum, Gordon
Gray, Secretary of the Army to Louis Johnson, September 30, 1949; both in
Secretary and Assistant Secretary of Defense Files, NARG 330; Letter, Louis
Johnson to Senator Vinson, July 7, 1949; Memorandum, Charles Fahy to
President Truman, December 14, 1949, all in Secretary and Assistant of the
Army Files, NARG 335; Memorandum, Gordon Gray to Louis Johnson, May
26, 1949, Military Personnel Division, General Staff, NARG 165; *Congres-
sional Record*, 81st Congress, 1st Session (1949), 6135; "Johnson Approves Air
Force Plan To Distribute Negroes among Units," *The New York Times*, May 12,
1949; Jacob Javits, "Address Delivered on Floor of House Thursday," *Pitts-
burgh Courier*, January 12, 1950; Letter, Jacob Javits to Louis Johnson,
January 24, 1950, Civilian Aide to the Secretary of War Subject File, 1940–
1947, NARG 107; Memorandum, "Discontinuance of Racial Enlistment
Quotas," March 10, 1950; "Policy On Integration Program," March 31, 1950;
"Data Pertaining to the Comments of the Navy and Air Force," April 5, 1950;
Letter, Roy Wilkins to Frank Pace, Jr., July 21, 1950; Letter, Pace to Wilkins,
August 8, 1950, all in Military Personnel Division, General Staff, NARG 165;
Congressional Board, 81st Congress, 2nd Session (1950), 9078, 12852,
13183–13184; "Senate Strikes Out Segregation Plan in Its Bill on Draft," *The
New York Times*, June 22, 1950; The Presidents' Committee on Equality of

Treatment and Opportunity in the Armed Services, *Freedom To Serve* (Washington, D.C.: United States Government Printing Office, 1950). For detailed discussions of the Fahy Committee see Dalfiume, *Desegregation of the U.S. Armed Forces; Fighting on Two Fronts 1939–1953*, 175–200; Nalty and MacGregor, *Blacks In The Military*, 243–294.

30. "White GI's Join All Negro Unit," *The Pittsburgh Courier*, September 9, 1950; "Racial Gains Speed by War, Army Says," *The New York Times*, March 19, 1951; "Bias Rules Army Courts Says Lawyer," *Norfolk Journal and Guide*, March 3, 1951; "Officials Maintain Strict Segregation of Soldiers," *Norfolk Journal and Guide*, July 28, 1951; "Says Allies Not Blind to U.S. Racial Hypocrisy," *The Pittsburgh Courier*, February 3, 1951; "Military Integration Progress," *Pittsburgh Courier*, March 31, 1951; "Torpedoes Army Bias in Pending House Bill," *Pittsburgh Courier*, April 21, 1951; "Camp McCoy Race Policy Vilest in U.S.," *Pittsburgh Courier*, June 9, 1951; "Negro GI Wins Medal of Honor," *Pittsburgh Courier*, June 23, 1951; "Courier Articles Influenced Army," *Pittsburgh Courier*, August 4, 1951; "Army Sees End of Segregation," *Pittsburgh Courier*, March 15, 1952; "Truman Speaking," *The New York Times*, June 14, 1952; "Army Sets Deadline for Segregation End," *The New York Times*, October 13, 1953. For detailed discussions of integration efforts during the Korean Conflict see Dalfiume, *Desegregation of the U.S. Armed Forces: Fighting On Two Fronts 1939–1953*, 201–219; Nalty and MacGregor, *Blacks In The Military*, 295–323.

31. Quoted in Richard Stillman, "Negroes in the Armed Forces," *Phylon; A Review of Race and Culture*, XXX (Summer 1969), 142.

32. Ibid.

33. Quoted in Stillman, "Negroes in the Armed Forces," 150; Nalty and MacGregor, *Blacks In The Military*, 327–343; Dalfiume, *Desegregation of the U.S. Armed Forces; Fighting on Two Fronts 1939–1953*, 220–222.

34. Nalty and MacGregor, *Blacks in the Military*, 327–330. The Gesell Committee included: Gerhard A. Gesell, Nathaniel S. Colley, Abe Fortas, Louis J. Hector, Benjamin Muse, John H. Sengstacke, and Whitney M. Young, Jr.

35. Nalty and MacGregor, *Blacks in the Military*, 336; Dalfiume, *Desegregation of the U.S. Armed Forces: Fighting on Two Fronts, 1939–1953*, 222.

36. Nalty, *Strength for the Fight*, 290.

37. Nalty and MacGregor, *Blacks in the Military*, 331–332.

38. Department of Defense, *Black Americans in Defense of Our Nation* (Washington, D.C.: Office of Deputy Assistant Secretary of Defense for Equal Opportunity, 1981), 38–64; Whitney M. Young, Jr., "When the Negroes in Vietnam Come Home," *Harper's Magazine*, CXXLIV (June 1967), 63–69.

39. For detailed discussions of segregation and racial discrimination, and the equal opportunity programs established in the military after the Vietnam War see Nalty and MacGregor, *Blacks in the Military*, 332–352; Department of Defense, *Black Americans in Defense of Our Nation*, 64–74.

Recommended Books

I USED A WIDE RANGE of primary and secondary sources in preparing this book. However, instead of listing all the works consulted, I shall cite a selected number of important and generally available sources. Those available in paperback editions are marked with an asterisk.

For general discussions of integration and changes in military policy relating to blacks, see A. Russell Buchanan, *Black Americans in World War II** (Santa Barbara, California: ABC-Clio Press, 1977); Richard M. Dalfiume, *Desegregation of the U.S. Armed Forces: Fighting on Two Fronts, 1939–1953* (Columbia, Missouri: University of Missouri Press, 1969); Lee Nichols, *Breakthrough on the Color Front* (New York: Random House, 1954); and Richard J. Stillman, *Integration of the Negro in the U.S. Armed Forces* (New York: Frederick A. Praeger, 1968). Dennis D. Nelson's *The Integration of the Negro into the United States Navy* (New York: Farrar, Straus and Young, 1951) is an excellent account of policy changes in the Navy. For a good summary of black integration in the Army Air Corps, see Alan M. Osur, *Blacks in the Army Air Forces during World War II** (Washington, D.C.: U.S. Government Printing Office, 1977). And the most recent and best summary of official documents regarding blacks and military integration is Bernard C. Nalty and Morris J. MacGregor, editors, *Blacks in the Military: Essential Documents* (Wilmington, Delaware: Scholarly Resources Inc., 1981).

Index

NOTE: The index is arranged alphabetically, word by word. All characters or groups of characters separated by spaces, dashes, hyphens, diagonal slashes or periods are treated as separate words. Acronyms not separated by spaces or punctuation are treated as if each letter is a complete word. Numerals identifying military divisions are alphabetized according to their word equivalents in all cases. Personal names beginning with capital Mc, M' and Mac are all listed under Mac as though the full form were used, and St. is alphabetized as if spelled out.

Names of persons, places, military forts and divisions are listed as they were cited in the text with two exceptions: numbers under ten identifying military divisions are expressed by their word equivalents, and proper names have been listed in their fullest form where known.